THE
SOCIAL
ROOTS
OF RISK

HIGH RELIABILITY AND CRISIS MANAGEMENT
SERIES EDITORS Karlene H. Roberts and Ian I. Mitroff

SERIES TITLES

Learning From the Global Financial Crisis: Creatively, Reliably, and Sustainably
Edited by Paul Shrivastava and Matt Statler
2012

Swans, Swine, and Swindlers: Coping with the Growing Threat of Mega-Crises and Mega-Messes
By Can M. Alpaslan and Ian I. Mitroff
2011

Dirty Rotten Strategies: How We Trick Ourselves and Others into Solving the Wrong Problems Precisely
By Ian I. Mitroff and Abraham Silvers
2010

High Reliability Management: Operating on the Edge
By Emery Roe and Paul R. Schulman
2008

THE SOCIAL ROOTS OF RISK

PRODUCING DISASTERS, PROMOTING RESILIENCE

Kathleen Tierney

STANFORD BUSINESS BOOKS

An Imprint of Stanford University Press

Stanford, California

Stanford University Press
Stanford, California

Special discounts for bulk quantities of Stanford Business Books
are available to corporations, professional associations, and other
organizations. For details and discount information, contact the
special sales department of Stanford University Press.
Tel: (650) 736-1782, Fax: (650) 736-1784

Printed in the United States of America on acid-free,
archival-quality paper

Library of Congress Cataloging-in-Publication Data

Tierney, Kathleen J., author.
The social roots of risk : producing disasters,
promoting resilience / Kathleen Tierney.
pages cm—(High reliability and crisis management)
Includes bibliographical references and index.
ISBN 978-0-8047-7263-1 (cloth : alk. paper)—
ISBN 978-0-8047-9139-7 (pbk. : alk. paper)
1. Risk—Social aspects. 2. Disasters—Social aspects.
3. Risk management—Social aspects. 4. Emergency management—
Social aspects. I. Title. II. Series: High reliability and crisis management.
HM1101.T54 2014

302'.12—DC 3   2014010892

ISBN 978-0-8047-9140-3 (electronic)

Typeset by Classic Typography in 10.75/15 Sabon MT Pro

To the new generation:
Violet and Rita K.
Lulu, Tommy, and Gus
Bea and Roland
Rowan
Ava
Michael and Emily

Contents

Acknowledgments

THE IDEAS IN THIS BOOK have been germinating for quite some time with the help of many individuals and institutions along the way, but I will focus on acknowledging more recent sources of support and inspiration.

My work has benefited consistently from support from the National Science Foundation (NSF), most recently from grants 0826983 (SES), 07293994 (AGS), 1034861 (CMMI), and 1030670 (CMMI). Other support from NSF and NSF-funded research programs has made it possible for me to concentrate on studying the societal dimensions of hazards and disasters over the long term and in different contexts. My various NSF projects have involved collaborations with gifted researchers within and outside of the discipline of sociology, including collaborators from computer science, various engineering disciplines, economics, geography, and so on. For seventeen years, beginning in 1990, I received research grants from the NSF-sponsored Multidisciplinary Center for Earthquake Engineering Research (MCEER, formerly the National Center for Earthquake Engineering Research), a research and educational consortium headquartered at the State University of New York at Buffalo. MCEER grants supported much of my research on businesses and disasters, and my forays into the analysis of resilience were begun under MCEER's aegis.

NSF provides core funding for the Natural Hazards Center at the Institute of Behavioral Science, University of Colorado Boulder, which I currently direct. Other current funders of the center include the Federal Emergency Management Agency, the National Oceanic and Atmospheric Administration, the U.S. Geological Survey, and the U.S. Army Corps of Engineers.

I owe NSF a debt of thanks for providing direct and indirect support for my work on disasters outside the United States and with international collaborators. Under the sponsorship of the Earthquake Engineering Research Institute's "Learning from Earthquakes" program, which was funded by NSF, I traveled to Iran after the 2003 Bam earthquake and to Japan after the 2011 Tohoku earthquake. Additionally, through NSF's partnership with the Japan Society for the Promotion of Science, I received grants for travel to Japan on two other occasions, and NSF support also enabled me to take part in a series of workshops on urban hazards and in collaborative research projects with Japanese colleagues.

Few outside a small circle of academics and practitioners recognize the important role NSF has played over the years in the development of the field of social science disaster research. Early U.S. studies of disasters were funded largely by military and civil-defense-related agencies, but starting in the mid-1970s NSF assumed a preeminent role in supporting that research and building the knowledge base. Counterintuitively, the Engineering Directorate has been home to NSF's most extensive social scientific programs on disasters. For more than two decades, the disaster research portfolio at NSF was managed primarily by the late William Anderson, who went on to hold important disaster-related positions at the World Bank and the National Academy of Sciences. The position of "disaster guru" is now held by Dennis Wenger, who works regularly with Robert O'Connor and other program managers in the Social, Behavioral, and Economic Sciences Directorate and other arms of NSF to fund studies that continually improve our understanding of disasters and risk. In the intellectual history of the field, Bill, Dennis, and Bob loom large, and I am delighted to acknowledge them as mentors and as friends.

From 2005 to 2009, my research was also supported by the National Consortium for the Study of Terrorism and Responses to Terrorism, known as START. This consortium, which is headquartered at the University of Maryland and directed by criminologist Gary LaFree, is one of twelve academic "centers of excellence" supported by the Science and Technology Directorate of the U.S. Department of Homeland Security. My role within START was to coordinate and collaborate with a group of amazing researchers whose projects focused on preparedness for terrorist events, the societal impacts of terrorism, and the conceptualization and measurement of societal and community resilience.

Thanks are also due to the Community and Regional Resilience Institute (CARRI), headquartered at Oak Ridge National Laboratory, and to CARRI leaders Warren Edwards and Tom Wilbanks. Among other projects, CARRI supported the convening of a workshop on resilience in 2009, which brought together seventy participants and which was hosted by the Natural Hazards Center. Needless to say, none of the agencies that provided support for my work are responsible for the ideas that appear here.

The discussions in these pages reveal intellectual debts to research colleagues whom I am also proud to call friends. Sociologists Robert Bolin, Carter Butts, Lee Clarke, Emmanuel David, Elaine Enarson, the late William Freudenburg, Shirley Laska, Walter Peacock, Lori Peek, and the incomparable Charles Perrow have influenced my ideas about risk and resilience in important ways, as have political scientists Daniel Aldrich and Louise Comfort, community psychologist Fran Norris, geographer Susan Cutter, and medical anthropologist Monica Schoch-Spana. The assistant director of the Natural Hazards Center, Liesel Ritchie, who is my research partner and close friend, helped me in ways that extend far beyond her admirable scholarship. Thank you, Liesel, for all you have done and continue to do on a daily basis. You are an inspiration, and nobody could wish for a better friend and colleague. Karlene Roberts and her high-reliability-organization (HRO) collaborators at Berkeley and other institutions have also been inspiring and supportive, both through the activities of the Center for Catastrophic Risk Management at Berkeley and through HRO workshops that were recently held in Washington, D.C., and at Vanderbilt University.

Teachers always learn a great deal from their students and postdocs, and in this respect I too have been fortunate. At the University of Delaware, it was a special privilege to work with James Kendra and Tricia Wachtendorf, particularly on our research on the terrorist attacks of September 11, 2001, in New York City. At the University of Colorado and the Natural Hazards Center, I have had the opportunity to work with a really smart and creative group of students, including Jeannette Sutton, Erica Kuligowski, Christine Bevc, Brandi Gilbert, and Ali Jordan, all of whom have done or are doing important work on disaster resilience. I express my appreciation to Nnenia Campbell and Wee-Kiat Lim for helping me during the final drafting process, and also to Barbara Ryan, who pitched in to offer assistance at the eleventh hour. Special thanks to research assistant Courtney Farnham for her help in preparing the references, and especially to graduate student assistant Jamie Vickery, who put them into final form. Jamie and Nnenia provided invaluable assistance during the last stage of this book's production, for which I am immensely grateful.

My friends Valerie Hans (Cornell University) and Ruth Horowitz (New York University) provided much-appreciated comments and criticisms when the book was in outline form.

Shirley Laska and Richard Krajeski reviewed the draft manuscript of the book and offered important suggestions for revisions. I thank them both for taking the time to provide comments, particularly on discussions related to social vulnerability, social capital, and the need for transformative change in the ways in which we conceptualize risk and manage it.

Special thanks to my editor, Margo Beth Fleming (she was Crouppen when I started this project and became Fleming partway through). Patient, unflappable, supportive, and wise, Margo steered me through some rocky periods and always lifted my spirits, whether we were talking by phone about my writing challenges or sharing meals and shoe-shopping excursions in San Francisco and Washington, D.C. Margo, your support for this project extended far beyond your editorial duties and meant more than I can say. I hope the completion of this project doesn't mean that our lunches together have come to an end.

I could not have finished this book without the help and support of my colleagues at the Natural Hazards Center: senior researcher RoseMarie Perez Foster; research associates Leah James and Courtney Welton-Mitchell; office manager Diane Smith and staffer Anne Watts; editors Jolie Breeden and Dan Whipple; librarian Wanda Headley and our library assistants; and former project manager Ezekiel Peters. You are the best colleagues anyone could wish for, and I am grateful for the many ways you supported me during this project.

My husband Peter Park has been a loving companion and valuable critic, and also my biggest cheerleader, throughout the long process of writing this book. Peter, you give me strength. I cherish every one of our many years together. My son Justin Horner and daughter-in-law Amy

Lemley are a constant loving presence in my life, and I thank them for supporting and inspiring me. This book is dedicated to my granddaughters, my step-grandchildren, and my grandnieces and grandnephew. May they inherit a safer and more resilient world.

THE
SOCIAL
ROOTS
OF RISK

CHAPTER I

Risking More, Losing More

Thinking About Risk and Resilience

DISASTERS, RISK, AND RESILIENCE

The first decade of the twenty-first century was marked by disasters of epic proportions, both in the United States and around the world. The terrorist attacks of September 11, 2001, left over two thousand dead and ushered in a new age of terror. In late 2004, the Great Sumatra-Andaman Earthquake and the tsunamis that followed killed approximately 230,000 people in fifteen nations. Hurricane Katrina struck the Gulf Coast in August 2005, washed away coastal communities, and drowned the city of New Orleans, killing at least 1,800 and displacing hundreds of thousands of people. In May 2008, tens of thousands died in a major earthquake in China's Sichuan province. A crisis in the global financial system, which began slowly and almost invisibly gained momentum, came close to causing a total meltdown of the world financial system in the fall of 2008. Complete collapse was averted, but the United States and other nations around the world were plunged into a deep and prolonged recession. In January 2010, a 7.0-magnitude earthquake struck Haiti. The death toll in that catastrophe is in dispute but could number as many as 300,000. More people lost their lives in Haiti than in any disaster that had ever occurred in the Western Hemisphere. Relative to the size of Haiti's population, the death toll made the earthquake the deadliest disaster to strike any nation in modern times. Just weeks later, a massive 8.0 earthquake struck off the coast of Chile; it was among the largest temblors ever recorded. In April 2010, a volcanic eruption in Iceland resulted in widespread flooding in that nation and spewed ash into the atmosphere, shutting down air travel to and from numerous airports in Europe, including its two largest, London Heathrow and Frankfurt, for days. That same month, on April 20, an explosion on the British Petroleum-operated *Deepwater Horizon* oil platform and drilling operation caused the largest oil spill in U.S. history, far surpassing the 11-million-gallon *Exxon Valdez* spill of 1989. The environmental, economic, and human consequences from that event were catastrophic for a region that was still in the process of recovering from Katrina.

As the first decade of the twenty-first century closed, the bad news kept rolling in. The summer of 2010 saw massive wildfires in Russia that blanketed Moscow in an ashen haze and threatened facilities storing nuclear material. Pakistan saw the worst flooding in its history that same summer as the rain-swollen Indus River inundated one fourth of the nation's land and affected over twenty million people. In 2010 and 2011, a series of earthquakes devastated the central business district and numerous residential areas in Christchurch, New Zealand. Then in March 2011 came the most costly natural disaster of modern times: the Richter magnitude 9.0 earthquake in Japan and the deadly tsunami it spawned, which was followed by a nuclear power plant emergency that rivaled Chernobyl in its severity. This trifold horror was the best-documented disaster in history. People around the world were stunned by images of the almost unbelievable destruction caused by the earthquake and tsunami—images that were soon replaced by those of damage, explosions, and frantic efforts to avert total catastrophe at the troubled Fukushima Daiichi power plant. Many asked how such a series of events could so devastate a nation that is considered a model for earthquake hazard mitigation and preparedness.

In 2012, Superstorm Sandy battered New Jersey and New York City, washing away parts of coastal downs, inundating large sections of New York City's underground infrastructure, destroying or damaging hundreds of thousands of homes and businesses, and causing life-threatening power failures. Sandy was the second-most costly hurricane in U.S. history, after Katrina, and its destructiveness served as a wakeup call for those who either don't believe that climate change is real or think that its impacts will be felt far in the future or somewhere else.

While disaster losses continued to escalate, scientists around the world increasingly endeavored to understand the extent to which heat waves, wildfires, floods, and other extreme events could be attributed to a changing climate and to discern what the future might hold with respect to climate-related extreme events. Sea-level rise began to affect communities in Alaska and elsewhere across the world, and the term "environmental refugees" gained currency as a way to describe people and communities moving in retreat from the impacts of climate change.

At the same time, the public and the media struggled to make sense of what they were seeing and experiencing. As the first years of the new century wore on, people in the United States who had been stunned and traumatized by the 9/11 attacks became less concerned about the potential for a terrorist attack and more concerned about burgeoning losses from disasters like Katrina and Sandy and the ongoing fallout from the financial crisis and the BP oil spill. Decisions about the usefulness of purchasing insurance for hazards like floods, hurricanes, and earthquakes became more problematic, and insurers and reinsurers worried about their exposure to catastrophic events. At the same time, disaster experts continued to advocate for insurance premiums that would reflect the risk of building or buying in a particular location. New flood risk maps released by the Federal Emergency Management Agency caused widespread public dismay and no small measure of outrage, as property owners who previously believed they had some idea of the risk they faced from flooding were told that they were more, or sometimes less, at risk than they thought.

Like the Three Mile Island nuclear disaster of 1979 and the Exxon oil spill of 1989, the *Deepwater Horizon* catastrophe and the Fukushima nuclear disaster led direct victims and the general public alike to again question the faith they place in the ability of corporations and the governmental institutions that oversee them to manage risky technologies. Throughout this ceaseless parade of misfortune, people were always happy to contribute aid to disaster victims, both in the United States and around the world, but compassion fatigue became increasingly common as media attention skidded from one disaster to the next.

The first years of the new millennium left little doubt that whatever else economically well-off and technologically advanced nations like the United States have achieved, they have not discovered the antidote for disaster. More lives are lost as a result of disasters in less developed nations than in developed ones, but economic losses tend to be much greater, and on the increase, in developed countries; and as the earthquake that struck Kobe, Japan, in 1995 and the 2011 triple disaster demonstrated, disasters in prosperous nations can also exact large death tolls when the right—or rather, wrong—conditions are present. Poverty often leads to high disaster vulnerability, but vulnerability does not always translate into larger impacts. Not only does wealth have perils of its own, like exposure to disruptions in global air travel and the cyber infrastructure and to nuclear accidents, but the lack of wealth can motivate poor people to develop mutual aid and support systems that help them cope and recover well when disaster strikes. The idea that high incomes automatically provide protection from danger, like most oversimplifications, is undercut by evidence of disasters that affect the rich as well as the poor. Similarly, as discussed later in this volume, even though the poor often suffer disproportionately when disasters strike, the notion that poor people are invariably helpless in the face of disaster is another simplifying trope that is invalidated by empirical findings.

The experiences of the new millennium's first few years raise many questions. What accounts for escalating disaster losses, and why do they seem so out of control? With so much available scientific knowledge regarding hazards and risks, why do we seem to be unable to anticipate and prevent future disasters? Why was the nation blindsided by the financial meltdown that occurred in 2008? Worse yet, why didn't trusted financial experts like former Federal Reserve chief Alan Greenspan see the meltdown coming and warn us? Why did the *Deepwater Horizon* disaster resemble the *Exxon Valdez* spill so closely, with BP standing in for Exxon Shipping, first offering reassurances about its ability to fix a massive oil gusher a mile under the Gulf of Mexico, and then promising to make whole the victims of its risky drilling strategy, even as it became increasingly clear that those statements were falsehoods? Was nothing learned in the twenty-one years that separate those two catastrophic spills?

This book offers a framework in which to view questions like these. The general answer is that disasters of all types occur as a consequence of common sets of social activities and processes that are well understood on the basis of both social science theory and empirical data. Put simply, the organizing idea for this book is that disasters and their impacts are socially produced, and that the forces driving the production of disaster are embedded in the social order itself. As the case studies and research findings discussed throughout the book will show, this is equally true whether the culprit in question is a hurricane, flood, earthquake, or a bursting speculative bubble. The origins of disaster lie not in nature, and not in technology, but rather in the ordinary everyday workings of society itself.

The idea that disasters are socially produced represents a departure from current and historical ways in which disasters have been characterized. Looking at disasters as social productions requires a shift in thinking, away from the notion that the forces of nature—or in the case of financial catastrophes, human nature—produce disasters and toward a fuller understanding of the role that social, political, economic, and cultural factors play in making events disastrous. A key contribution of this book is to connect events that the general public, the media, and many risk scholars consider unique events and to show that despite their surface differences, such occurrences can be traced back to similar causal factors.

This book also focuses on the concept of disaster resilience and the ways in which risk and resilience are related. While risk and disaster scholarship have historically focused on disasters and their negative consequences, studies have only recently focused explicitly on preexisting, planned, and naturally emerging activities that make societies and communities better able to cope, adapt, and sustain themselves when disasters occur, and also to develop ways of recovering following such events. Like risk, resilience also arises from the social order as an inherent property of social organization, as a consequence of intentional actions aimed at lessening the impacts of disaster, or as a spontaneous outpouring of collective innovation when disastrous events occur.

Because the roots of both risk and resilience exist within the social order itself, societies, communities, and organizations have the power to reduce risk and become more resilient. This theme appears throughout the volume. Catastrophic disasters like Hurricane Katrina, the Haiti earthquake, and the BP oil spill and economic disasters like the financial meltdown of 2008 and its aftermath were not inevitable. A key element in preventing future catastrophes is to better understand the social forces that produce them, and then to take action to address those forces and strengthen our capacity for resilience in the face of future threats. Floods, hurricanes, and earthquakes will inevitably occur because of natural processes that are outside our control, but flood, hurricane, and earthquake disasters can be greatly reduced through a broad range of risk reduction and resilience-enhancing activities. The boom-and-bust cycles that are characteristic of global capitalism can be made less extreme, and measures can be instituted that cushion the negative effects of economic downturns. An argument anchoring many of the book's discussions is that we already know a great deal of what we need to know in order to reduce the pain, suffering, and other losses associated with disasters, but that applying that knowledge is difficult because of institutional inertia and especially because of the benefits those in power obtain through activities that increase risk.

UNDERSTANDING RISK AND RESILIENCE

Risk and resilience are the twin topics that guide the discussions in the chapters that follow. Risk represents the potential for loss—a potential that is actualized in the presence of "triggers" that are either external or internal to social systems. Such triggers can include natural occurrences (such as tornadoes and heavy rainfall, leading to floods), accidents involving technology, and crises in societal sectors such as financial institutions.

The book also focuses on resilience, a term that has become something of a buzzword in research and policy circles, but that understood appropriately, points to ways in which risks and losses can be reduced. The concept of resilience refers to the ability of social entities (for example, individuals, households, firms, communities, economies) to absorb the impacts of external and internal system shocks without losing the ability to function, and failing that, to cope, adapt, and recover from those shocks. Like risk, resilience arises from the social order. It is no accident that some families, communities, and societies are more resistant to and better able to cope with disastrous events than are others. Disaster resilience in its many forms is rooted in a range of social structural, economic, and cultural preconditions. Moreover, I argue that the same general social arrangements and attributes that enable social entities to be resilient in the face of many other types of crises operate in similar ways in disasters. Risks and subsequent losses can be contained if individuals, groups, and other entities undertake actions that make them less "brittle" and failure-prone, and more robust, flexible, and adaptable. In a certain sense, then, resilience is the obverse of risk; risk-inducing processes set the stage for more frequent and (in particular) more catastrophic failures and losses, while resilience-inducing processes counter that tendency.

Considering risk and resilience in tandem is important. While risks can be reduced—and must be, unless we are willing to tolerate ever-ballooning losses—no society can eliminate risk. Increasing resilience can both contain risk, making disastrous events less likely, and help those who are at risk better cope with crisis when it happens.

The theoretical and conceptual frameworks introduced here are based on a range of sources. Prior research on the sociology of disasters and the social production of risk is one such source. Research on organizational performance, adaptation, and risk-reduction strategies is another. Discussions of the financial collapse draw upon materials ranging from recent publications to news reports and analyses.

The discussions of societal resilience are based on scholarship in a number of fields, including ecology, psychology, engineering, and sociology. Here again, the emphasis is on identifying and analyzing the social and institutional sources of resilience. Like a number of other scholars, I characterize resilience as consisting, on the one hand, of inherent and preexisting qualities and attributes that enable at-risk entities to absorb stresses caused by external shocks, and on the other, of adaptive or post-event activities and processes that enhance coping capacity. As with risk, my perspective on resilience is shaped by my prior research experience, which includes work on resilience conceptualization, predisaster capacity building, and resilient postdisaster responses.

The book is divided approximately equally between discussions of its two primary concepts. This chapter sets the stage for later discussions by arguing that because both risk and resilience have their origins in the social order itself, communities, societies, and organizations have the ability to reduce their risks and increase their resilience; however, powerful social forces stand in the way of such improvements. The second chapter focuses on the concept of risk and on some of the ways it has been studied in the past. While scholars have done a good job of shedding light on some aspects of risk, such as the factors that influence how people perceive risk, their laboratory experiments have not done as well in illuminating how risk-related decisions are made in the real world. More significant from my point of view, they have almost always ignored even more important questions, such as how risks are generated in the first place. I take up that question in Chapter 3, describing in general the societal sources of risk, including culture and institutional and organizational practices that contribute to the buildup of risk. The ideas are unsettling, because they show that risk is a normal consequence of everyday practices employed by societies and communities as they go about their business. I then delve more deeply into the social production of risk. Chapter 4 provides a perspective on cultural assumptions and cognitive styles that help to produce risk, such as the value placed on continual growth and wealth accumulation, faith in technology's ability to protect us from risk, routine aspects of organizational cultures that suppress knowledge concerning the riskiness of places and practices, and other cognitive blinders that create an inability to envision what can happen when things go disastrously wrong, as they did in the financial crash of 2008. Chapter 5 discusses institutional and organizational arrangements and practices that increase risk or cause organizations and institutions to overlook it. One such practice is the offloading of risk, which occurs when social actors create risks that are passed on to others. Another is the failure to learn and change behaviors in response to crises and near failures. We like to think that the risks that arise from our dealings with nature and technology do so in a manner that is unintended. However, discussions of disasters in this chapter and elsewhere in the book show how the potential for catastrophic failures is often well understood beforehand, but is ignored or downplayed. In Chapter 6, the final chapter in the section on risk, I discuss broader trends in the social production of risk, such as globalization, urbanization, and lax controls on land use.

Many of my discussions on risk-producing processes, as well as the examples I provide, draw upon principles from the field of political economy, which, broadly speaking, emphasizes the links that exist among politics, the exercise of political power by elites, and economic activities, as mediated by formal institutions and informal cultural practices. This intellectual influence can be seen in my emphasis on the politics of the local growth machine as a driver of risk production; on various forms of rent seeking, such as regulatory capture and the use of political influence to increase land values and profits while also increasing risk; and on the dark side of globalization, which too often culminates in the expansion of disaster vulnerability. Using a political economy lens shows us that risk is quite often a byproduct of the pursuit of profit, enabled by too-pliable institutions that unknowingly or knowingly allow risk to expand.

Chapter 7 focuses on the concept of resilience and discusses two types of resilience: inherent and adaptive. In addition to already existing in particular types of social arrangements, resilience is commonly enhanced through planned activities (for example, appropriate land-use management), as well as through spontaneous or emergent actions that develop during crises. The chapter concludes with discussions on inherent resilience. Chapter 8 focuses on adaptive resilience, which is activated when disasters occur. Adaptive resilience is manifested in many ways; examples include the spontaneous mobilization of people and resources during disasters, improvisation, and collective sensemaking. Along with Chapter 7, this chapter discusses how to assess and enhance the capacity for postdisaster adaptation. Both chapters emphasize the role of social capital in cushioning the effects of disasters, encouraging successful postdisaster coping, and speeding recovery.

The concluding chapter revisits the argument made in this one that both risk and resilience are socially produced—pointing out again that since this is the case, societies, communities, institutions, and organizations can reduce risk and achieve higher levels of resilience. However, because risk and vulnerability are outcomes of the exercise of political and economic power in their various forms, confronting risk also means confronting power. For this reason, risk- and resilience-related efforts must go far beyond current approaches.

Throughout I offer examples of the ways risk is produced and allowed to grow, as well as examples of resilience-enhancing activities. Cases focus on risk management successes and failures, and discussions deal with disasters that have occurred and disasters that are waiting to happen, such as a catastrophic earthquake in Northern California and perhaps even in the New Madrid Fault Zone in the Central United States. Here again, the point is that a lot is already known about risk buildup and how to slow it; however, because current political and economic arrangements keep that knowledge from being applied, risk and vulnerability will continue to expand.

CHAPTER 2

Looking Back

The Evolution of How We Talk About Risk

INTRODUCTION

This book focuses on potential and actual losses arising from various kinds of extreme events and how those losses can be averted or reduced. Since the study of disasters is related to the study of risk more generally, a good way to begin approaching disaster-related challenges is through an examination of how risk has been conceptualized and explored over time. In this chapter, I discuss some key foci in the study of risk, including studies on risk perception and the social construction of risk. Even though a lot has been learned through numerous studies on the perception of risk, much of that work tells us little about risk-related social behavior. More important, most existing scholarship on risk has failed to address questions such as how risks originate in the first place and how and why they are allowed to proliferate.

RISK, HAZARD, AND VULNERABILITY

There is a large body of scholarship surrounding the concept of risk that we do not need to explore in detail here. However, even if its meaning seems clear, defining risk and identifying its dimensions are important for ensuing discussions. Risk is commonly conceptualized as the answer to three questions: What can go wrong? How likely is it? And what are the consequences? The study and analysis of risk are thus concerned both with the likely frequency of things that can go wrong and with their expected impacts; even when an event is assessed as relatively unlikely, major investments may be made in preventing such an event if its consequences are judged to be unacceptably severe.

Throughout I use the term *risk* to refer to "a situation or event in which something of human value (including humans themselves) has been put at stake and where the outcome is uncertain" (Jaeger et al. 2001: 17). This definition implies several things. First, risks exist independently of our ability to observe and assess them. However, as I discuss later, ideas concerning risk, including those developed through putatively scientific risk assessments, are socially constructed, and actions are taken (or not) based on those social constructions. Second, the idea that something of value is "at stake" means that there exists some potential for harm, damage, or loss in any risky situation or event, even if there is also the potential for gain or benefit. Many activities that bring us joy and excitement, like skiing, mountain climbing, and skydiving, are also accompanied by some degree of risk. Finally, the very notion of risk implies uncertainty. We do not speak of the risk of death, for example, because we are all going to die. Rather, we speak of the risk of death from cancer or from a particular type of cancer, or the risk of death for persons in a particular age group. Notice also that the concept of risk implies a focus on possibilities and probabilities that lie in the future, not on certainties or on events that have already occurred.

This book deals primarily with the risks that are related to extreme events, but the scope of the concept is of course much broader. The term applies to a wide array of potential harms, such as the daily risk of being a victim of a crime and the health risks associated with smoking, diet, and lifestyle choices. Because the focus here is on the potential for disaster, it is necessary to introduce two other risk-related terms that crop up regularly when disasters are discussed: hazard and vulnerability. In scholarly parlance, the term *hazard* refers to the agent or means through which harms and losses might be realized. We thus refer to earthquake, hurricane, and tornado hazards, and also to chemical, nuclear, and other environmental hazards. The concept of *vulnerability* refers more specifically to what is at risk—that is, to things of value that are exposed to hazards. It is common to conceptualize disaster vulnerability both in terms of *space and place* and in terms of the characteristics of different *exposures* that represent the potential for damage, harm, and loss. Vulnerability is partly geographic; in the United States, for example, so far as can be determined, Florida is not vulnerable to earthquake hazards, but much of California is. New Orleans and Miami are vulnerable to hurricane hazards, but Bismarck, North Dakota, is not. Flood vulnerability is not equally distributed geographically, nor is the potential for harm caused by accidents at nuclear power plants or by heat waves.

In addition to being related to hazards that are characteristic of specific geographic locations, vulnerability arises from properties or characteristics of systems and subsystems that are of importance to people and societies: ecosystems, infrastructure systems and the built environment in general, and social systems. The enormous harm and loss that were experienced when Hurricane Katrina struck New Orleans did not arise from the city's geographic location alone. Instead, they were the consequence of a distinctive set of vulnerabilities. Long before the hurricane came ashore, New Orleans was in the process of losing many environmental and ecosystem assets, such as the vast wetlands of the Mississippi River Delta, that provided protection against hurricane-related storm surges and winds. Levees and other flood protection works that had suffered from decades of neglect also proved inadequate as a line of defense against Katrina. Social vulnerability was also high in New Orleans; many in the city's largely African American population lacked the resources to evacuate and otherwise protect themselves, and as a consequence they were directly exposed to the hurricane's ravages. The devastating effects of Katrina's landfall thus arose out of a combination of place-based vulnerability and ecosystem, built environment, and social vulnerability—vulnerabilities that were well understood by the disaster research community and by journalists who focused on environmental issues in the Gulf region before Katrina struck (*Times-Picayune* 2002; Laska 2004).

A key point here is that although the magnitude of the physical event caused by a particular hazard is not unimportant in determining the consequences of the event, the various forms of vulnerability are perhaps more important. The earthquake experiences of two societies illustrate this point. The Northridge earthquake struck the Los Angeles metropolitan region on January 17, 1994, and the Great Hanshin-Awaji earthquake struck the Kobe metropolitan region exactly one year later, on January 17, 1995, at almost exactly the same time of day. The two earthquakes were not of the same magnitude; Northridge was a 6.7 moment-magnitude event, while the Kobe earthquake was measured at 6.8. The ground motions caused by the earthquakes were also different; the Kobe area experienced stronger ground shaking than the Los Angeles area. However, these differences alone do not account for the large disparities in the death and destruction that occurred in the two earthquakes. Both regions of impact had about the same population—around three million people—when the earthquakes occurred, but while the Northridge earthquake resulted in the deaths of thirty-three people, the Kobe event killed more than five thousand. Thousands were left homeless after the Northridge earthquake, but those numbers were in no way comparable to the dislocation of nearly 500,000 people that resulted from the Kobe disaster. These differences in deaths and displacement were partly the result of differences in the two earthquakes' size and strength, but they were mainly the result of differences in the vulnerability of the built environment and infrastructure systems in the two events. Houses, commercial structures, highways, bridges, and other facilities were less resistant to earthquake forces in the Kobe region, and thus more likely to be destroyed or severely damaged, than they were in the Los Angeles region. A very substantial number of those killed in the Kobe earthquake died in the collapse of traditional wooden houses. Many of those who died were elderly persons, who tended to live on the ground floor of their homes. In contrast, while there was a great deal of residential damage following the Northridge event, most structures survived the earthquake, and relatively few people died outright in building collapses. Fires broke out after both earthquakes, but the fires burned out of control in a large section of the city of Kobe owing mainly to residential and commercial density and the types of construction materials used. In other words, the driver of loss and harm in these events was differential vulnerability.

The 2010 Haiti earthquake represents the intersection of a large-magnitude physical event and high vulnerability. The 7.0 earthquake occurred not far from the capital, Port-au-Prince, which was home to approximately one third of the country's population of an estimated nine million. Except for a few well-designed, well-built structures, most buildings and other elements in the built infrastructure, such as the highways and the nation's major port, lacked even the most basic resistance to earthquake forces. Because so many structures collapsed immediately or were very severely damaged, the death toll was extremely high and residential dislocation was extensive. At the same time, the vast major-ity of Haiti's population was already highly vulnerable, as evidenced by high rates of poverty, unemployment, disease, and malnutrition prior to the earthquake. For those who survived, these forms of vulnerability persisted after the earthquake, further complicating recovery efforts and exposing the population to additional risks.

The likelihood of negative outcomes resulting from particular events is influenced in substantial ways not just by hazards and not just by loca-tion, but importantly by the vulnerabilities that characterize what is at stake, whether the things that are at risk are human lives, human physi-cal and psychological well-being, structures and places that have sym-bolic importance, economic stocks and flows, or other things of value. On the one hand, when potentially harmful events occur, losses can be contained if vulnerability is low. On the other, when the same kinds of events occur under conditions in which vulnerability is high, losses may result that are disproportional to the severity of the physical event itself.

As used here, the study of disaster risk is inseparable from the study of hazard exposure and vulnerability. As I discuss in the following chap-ters, part of the story of how risks are produced can be told through understanding the factors that increase the size and scale of exposures and that produce both physical and social vulnerability. However, a great deal of risk scholarship ignores these dimensions of risk, focusing instead on cognitive, psychological, and social psychological processes that are involved in how people think about risk. I turn next to a brief overview of this work, which despite its importance, leaves the produc-tion of risk itself unexamined.

TRENDS AND THEMES IN RISK RESEARCH

Many of our current risk-related concerns are rooted in a growing recog-nition on the part of the public and key institutions that despite massive scientific and technological progress, the advances achieved by modern industrialized societies come with a cost. The late 1950s in Japan saw the discovery of Minamata disease, which occurred as a result of mercury poisoning caused by chemical wastewater. The same disease was later discovered in the mid-1960s in another part of Japan. In 1961, the drug thalidomide was taken off the market after it was found to cause serious birth defects. Rachel Carson's *Silent Spring*, published in 1962, highlighted the impact of toxic pesticides on the environment and helped inspire the environmental movement. Subsequent concerns about environmental threats led to the establishment of the Environmental Protection Agency in 1970.

Nuclear weapons were originally developed in an atmosphere of total secrecy, and the same was initially the case for nuclear power, as both the government and industry viewed public opinion regarding nuclear power as essentially irrelevant (Rosa and Freudenburg 1993). However, concerns about the safety of nuclear reactors began to emerge in the early 1970s, and later public attention also began to focus on potential risks associated with nuclear waste—concern that peaked in debates over the long-term storage of waste at sites such as Yucca Mountain, Nevada (Dunlap, Kraft, and Rosa, 1993).

In 1976, an accident at a chemical plant in Seveso, Italy, led to widespread dioxin contamination that killed thousands of animals and caused a host of health problems in exposed populations. In 1978, residents of the Love Canal neighborhood in Niagara Falls, New York, began to connect the numerous health problems they were experiencing to the presence of large amounts of toxic chemicals in the soil and groundwater near their homes. The environmental disaster at Love Canal led directly to the passage in 1980 of the Comprehensive Environmental Response, Compensation, and Liability Act (CERCLA), known as Superfund. Then, in 1979, the partial core meltdown at the Three Mile Island nuclear plant caused a surge in public worry about the safety of nuclear power. Four years later, the federal government bought out the entire town of Times Beach, Missouri, and subsequently relocated approximately two thousand of the town's residents. Like Seveso, Times Beach had been contaminated by dioxin.

The occurrence of major disasters such as the 1900 Galveston hurricane, the 1906 San Francisco earthquake, the Mississippi River floods of 1927, the 1964 Alaska earthquake, the 1971 San Fernando earthquake, hurricanes Betsy, Camille, and Agnes, and other large-scale events also stimulated research on disaster risk in the basic sciences, social sciences, and engineering disciplines. Scientists sought to understand and model the earth and atmospheric processes associated with hazards and disasters. Engineers tried to understand how to design and build systems that could stand up to those processes. Scientific and engineering research gave rise to many of the methods that are currently used in analyzing hazards, vulnerability, and risk, such as probabilistic risk analysis and loss estimation modeling.

In the face of this growing concern, some social scientists began to focus on how people perceive different risks and on the factors that influence risk perception. Early research was dominated by cognitive psychology and the emerging field of decision science, but later researchers began to explore the cultural dimensions of risk perception and the notion that ideas about risk are socially constructed.

RISK AS PERCEPTION

As members of the public became more aware of and involved in debates over environmental and technological hazards, they often clashed with government, industry, and scientists over the magnitude of the risk posed by such hazards and what to do about reducing potential impacts of adverse events. Early on in that process, public views on risks began to be characterized as extreme and irrational, largely because public assessments seemed overblown when compared with assessments made by experts—assessments that at the time were thought to constitute more accurate characterizations of "real risk."

This gap between public and expert positions on various risks, and the policy implications of those differences, provided much of the initial impetus for pioneering research on risk perception. As the authors of an article entitled "Why Study Risk Perception?" put it in 1981:

The daily discovery of new hazards and the widespread publicity given them is causing more and more individuals to see themselves as the victims, rather than as the beneficiaries, of technologies. These fears and the opposition to technology that they cause have puzzled industry promoters and policy-makers, who believe that the public's pursuit of a "zero risk" society threatens the nation's political and economic stability. (Slovic, Fischhoff, and Lichtenstein 1981: 83)

Research on the factors that shape the perception of risk was thus seen as a necessary step in understanding (and managing) the public's reactions to both existing and emerging risks. Risk perception researchers were interested in studying a range of topics, including what factors shape risk perceptions, how individuals and groups arrive at decisions concerning acceptable risks, and the relationship between public perceptions and public policies for the management of risky technologies. The study of risk perception passed through a series of stages. At first, researchers' concerns centered on trying to explain why the general public held beliefs about the magnitude of many risks that were so drastically out of line with those of scientists. Early studies yielded a raft of findings, many of which related in one way or another to pioneering research by Nobel laureate Daniel Kahneman and his colleague Amos Tversky on the cognitive shortcuts that people employ in making judgments under conditions of uncertainty, which often involve risks of various kinds. Influential work by these authors (Tversky and Kahneman 1974; Kahneman, Slovic, and Tversky 1982) dealt with errors in judgment that people commonly make because they misunderstand prior and posterior probabilities, the laws of chance, sampling, and statistical theory in general. These researchers are credited with the development of the "cognitive heuristics" approach to understanding risk perception. The logic underlying this approach is that rather than engaging in extensive calculations, people tend to respond initially to probabilities in intuitive ways, using heuristics that often yield inaccurate results. Research by Tversky and Kahneman and others on three such heuristics—availability, anchoring, and representativeness—has had a lasting effect on the study of risk perception.

Availability refers to the ease with which a person can retrieve an occurrence from her memory, which is related in turn to factors such as the recency of similar occurrences, the drama associated with particular events, and the ability to imagine or visualize an event. This cognitive heuristic explains why, following exposure to media reports on a fatal air crash, people might believe that airline travel is very risky, or why they might downplay the risks associated with climate change, an unfamiliar hazard whose effects are difficult for most people to grasp.

Anchoring refers to the tendency for people to establish an "anchor" or "starting point" in thinking about phenomena such as risk-related probabilities on the basis of information they receive, and even information they generate on their own. For example, if asked whether the likelihood of a magnitude 6.7 or larger earthquake in greater Los Angeles is greater or less than 60 percent in the next thirty years, an individual would first offer a probability that is somewhere close to 60 percent, the "anchor" that was suggested, and then adjust estimates from there.[1]

Representativeness operates when an individual focusing on a person, situation, or some other phenomenon of interest "knows" things about that object of concern based on its resemblance to other objects or experiences that are seen as similar. Two problems here are that in many cases the assumption of similarity is incorrect, or the experiential basis for making risk projections is too small. On the latter point, for example, both hurricanes and seismic activity go through cycles that recur on a multidecadal basis. Southern Florida happened to be in a quiescent cycle in hurricanes and landfalls in the two decades prior to Hurricane Andrew. Those decades also happened to coincide with a period of very intensive coastal development in that part of Florida. Similarly, urban areas in California underwent extensive development beginning in the midtwentieth century, but the only major earthquake to strike an urban area between 1950 and 1980 was the 1971 San Fernando earthquake in Southern California. In the 1980s, more typical patterns of seismicity began to return, and then two highly damaging earthquakes—the 1989 Loma Prieta earthquake in the San Francisco Bay Area and the Northridge earthquake in greater Los Angeles—occurred less than five years apart. In both Florida and California, people who had experienced the low periods in hurricane and earthquake activity could have been lulled into believing those low periods were representative, when they were not.

Over time, other heuristics—or cognitive biases, as they are often called—were discovered, and some were applied extensively in the study of risk perception. For example, *optimistic bias* refers to a person's tendency to recognize risks but to think that others are more at risk (Chandler et al. 1999). *Myopia* refers to a bias toward thinking in short-term timescales as opposed to longer-term ones, which results in the downplaying

of disaster risk. With respect to flood hazards and disasters, the availability heuristic could help explain why people have more of a tendency
to purchase flood insurance after floods (Browne and Hoyt 2000), while
myopia might explain why they tend to cancel that insurance after a few
years if flooding does not occur (Michel-Kerjan and Kunreuther 2011).
Myopia has also been offered as an explanation for why people are loath
to invest dollars today in disaster loss-reduction measures that may have
significant payoff in future disasters.

This cognitive perspective on risk perception was subsequently supplemented by research that focused to a greater extent on how the perceived
properties of different risks affect risk judgments. An early influence on
this line of research was work by Chauncey Starr, a physicist, veteran of
the Manhattan Project, and nuclear power advocate who first made the
case that risks assumed voluntarily are judged by people to be significantly
more acceptable than those that are involuntarily imposed (Starr 1969).
Soon more research was being conducted within what would come to be
known as the psychometric perspective on risk research. Among the best-
known early researchers in this arena were Paul Slovic, Baruch Fischhoff,
and Sarah Lichtenstein, who were affiliated with the Oregon Research
Institute and later with Decision Research in Eugene, Oregon, which was
founded in 1976. Their article "Rating the Risks," which appeared in the
journal *Environment* in 1979, addressed the question of why the risk-
related views of "laypersons" differ so much from those of experts. Their
research showed that perceptions and judgments about risk acceptability
are in part a reflection of attributes people associate with different risks,
such as whether risks are seen as voluntarily assumed or involuntarily
imposed; known and familiar or unknown; controllable or uncontrollable;
whether effects are immediate or delayed; and whether effects are seen as
catastrophic or less severe. The authors noted that attention to these kinds
of attributes helps explain why people's perceptions of the risks associated with nuclear power differ so much from those of experts; exposure
to nuclear hazards is seen by people as an involuntary risk that is unfamiliar and uncontrollable, with delayed and potentially catastrophic effects.

It is impossible to overstate the influence of research on heuristics and
publications in the "Rating the Risks" tradition on subsequent work in

the areas of risk perception. Cognitive biases such as myopia and availability are widely invoked to explain all sorts of behavior. For example,
the authors of an article published after the 2010 *Deepwater Horizon*
oil spill, entitled "Overcoming Myopia," argued that the spill revealed
the extent to which BP is "myopic with respect to risk" (Kunreuther and
Michel-Kerjan 2010). The decline in airline travel following the terrorist attacks of September 11, 2001, was attributed to the fact that people
viewed the possibility of dying in another attack using planes as a dread
and involuntary risk, even though that possibility was miniscule. Much
was subsequently made of the flawed nature of those judgments, since
driving is more dangerous than flying, and research was published pur-
porting to show that excess lives were lost in traffic accidents as a result
of people's desire to drive rather than fly.

While still concerned with the perceived properties of different risks,
risk perception researchers moved next to considering the ways in which
individuals' social attributes and roles influence judgments regarding risk
severity and acceptability. This research development marked the first
time researchers seriously considered the social-structural factors that
influence risk perceptions, as opposed to psychological ones. Gender
and race are two commonly studied factors. Women tend to view a wide
range of risks as more severe than men view them, and nonwhites are
more concerned about risks than whites. Within these general patterns,
studies have found that white men find risks significantly less problematic than do both white women and minority men and women. However,
explanations for this "white male effect" appear to hinge not on gender
or race per se but rather on the fact that a particular subgroup of white
males is simply less concerned about risks than many other people. That
group includes white men who are well educated, with high incomes, and
who are politically conservative—in short, men who are beneficiaries of
the status quo (Flynn, Slovic, and Mertz 1994; Slovic 1999).

RISK AS FEELINGS

Early research on risk perception, particularly studies comparing laypersons and experts, was tinged with the notion that laypersons react to
risks in an emotional manner that verges on irrationality, whereas experts

are objective and rational and thus better able to calculate "real risks." Gradually, however, researchers began to recognize that all risk perceptions are influenced by emotion, that the influence of emotion on cognition is inescapable, and interestingly, that affect is an important component of rational thinking. This "risk as feelings" framework has several variants, all of which are related to the idea that judgment and decision making under uncertainty involve a "dual processing" of risk-related information. On the one hand, individuals use logical and analytical reasoning when assessing risks. On the other, however, more experientially based and intuitive information processing also takes place in which emotions play a key role. According to this view, the emotional or affective component of decision making does not bias or distort risk perception; rather, it is an integral element of that process. (For good discussions, see Loewenstein et al. 2001; Slovic et al. 2004, 2005.)

Feelings toward objects in the environment have always influenced decision making; such feelings have contributed significantly to the evolutionary advantages of being human. Indeed, some "risk as feelings" researchers fault other forms of risk perception research for its consequentialist bias—that is, its assumption that people make decisions about risks through weighing the consequences of alternative courses of action (Loewenstein et al. 2001). Instead, other researchers stress that risk judgments are driven by anticipatory emotions such as fear and dread, which are based at least in part on past experience.[2] One important insight from this line of research is that feelings precede and directly influence judgments about risk in a process that Slovic and colleagues (2004) term the "affect heuristic." Affect-based assessments are also rapid assessments, and individuals may in many cases be unaware of the affective bases of their judgments.

This newer approach to the study of risk perception has received various kinds of theoretical and empirical support. Damasio's somatic marker theory, for example, argues that images serve as the basis for thought and that over time these images become imbued with, or marked by, positive and negative affect. In making decisions, we imagine outcomes that are linked to these markers and the feelings they reflect (Damasio 1996). Somatic markers are at work, for example, when we have a "gut feeling" about how some activity or decision will turn out. This carryover from earlier negative experiences and subsequent affective responses would partly explain, for example, research findings regarding the perception of dread risks. It would also provide a rationale for how the availability heuristic operates, in that events that are dramatic and vivid, and thus "available," also tend to evoke strong emotions. It might even help explain women's tendency toward risk aversiveness, because women and men experience emotions differently, women generally feeling emotions more intensely (see Loewenstein et al. 2001 for more extensive discussions).

LIMITATIONS OF THE PSYCHOMETRIC APPROACH

I do not claim to be familiar with findings from the thousands (perhaps tens of thousands) of publications on judgments under uncertainty, cognitive biases, and risk. Entire careers are spent contributing to and critiquing this voluminous literature. However, one does not have to be an expert on the psychometric literature to raise questions about the validity and usefulness of the psychometric framework. First are the pitfalls of trying to generalize to the real world findings developed primarily from laboratory experiments and surveys. Subjects in the vast majority of psychometric studies are presented with carefully manipulated stimuli (for example, statistical reasoning problems, vignettes, words or phrases denoting different risks) and then asked to answer questions about them, typically in a highly structured way. They are also asked to answer those questions *as individuals*, which is of course appropriate because the research is centered on individual perception and cognition. However, even though numerous studies of this kind have been undertaken, including extensive replication studies, there remains a need to address questions of ecological validity, or the extent to which findings from these studies can be generalized beyond the settings in which they were conducted to the real world.

In the case of risks and hazards, it is clear that people in the real world are not confronted with risk-related situations that resemble those the subjects in psychometric studies encounter. In everyday life, individuals are typically exposed to a variety of types of information about risks, ranging from whatever scientific information they manage to find, to facts gleaned from the media and the internet, to the opinions and views of those with whom they interact. Answers to questions about probabilities and risks are not answered once and for all as they are in lab studies; instead, they are answered provisionally and revised on the basis of additional information. And people in the real world do not form judgments about risk in a vacuum but rather respond to a range of social and environmental influences that both enable and constrain their judgments.

The study of judgments under uncertainty, and by extension risk perception, is just that: the study of judgments and perceptions. Psychometric research focuses largely on risk-related attitudes and beliefs. However, for decades researchers in psychology, social psychology, and sociology have explored questions about the relationship between attitudes and subsequent behaviors. Do attitudes and beliefs predict behavior? If so, how strongly, and under what circumstances? Or on the other hand, do we form attitudes after we behave in certain ways? If we do harbor certain attitudes, to what extent are we free to act on them? How strongly do we hold different attitudes? How salient are many of our attitudes to circumstances we encounter in real life? Forests have been turned into paper in an effort to answer these kinds of questions, but the complexity of the connections among attitudes, beliefs, and behavior is obscured in much of the discourse surrounding risk perception and risk-related behaviors.

Looking at these issues another way, psychometric research finds considerable evidence for the operation of heuristics and biases at the level of individual cognition. For example, individuals are said to be myopic in that they have difficulty envisioning risk-related impacts that will occur far out in the future. But what does it mean to say that BP, a multinational corporation, is myopic about risk? Don't we run into serious methodological difficulties when we apply concepts developed at the individual level to collective actors? Note also that when psychometric concepts are applied to real-world examples, this is typically done in a post hoc fashion; when the decisions and behaviors of individuals and organizations are analyzed, heuristics, risk attributes, and other constructs employed in psychometric research are invoked as explanations, often in the absence of clear evidence. Using cognitive heuristics to explain perceptions and behavior has itself become a kind of heuristic—a cognitive shortcut used by analysts to avoid delving deeper into the complex foundations of risk decision making.

BRINGING SOCIETY BACK IN:

THE SOCIAL AMPLIFICATION OF RISK

Another way of analyzing the origins and characteristics of risk-related perceptions and behavior was pioneered in the late 1980s by Roger Kasperson of Clark University and a group of collaborators that included Paul Slovic. The objective of the Kasperson group was to examine broadly, and in social and historical context, how risk and risk events interact with psychological, social, institutional, and cultural processes in ways that amplify or attenuate risk perceptions and concerns, and thereby shape risk behavior, influence institutional processes, and affect risk consequences (Pidgeon, Kasperson, and Slovic 2003: 2). In developing what came to be known as the "social amplification of risk framework" (SARF), Kasperson and his colleagues sought to take into account not just individuals' internal cognitive processes but also a broader range of social influences that shape risk perceptions and behaviors. Early formulations of the SARF employed mechanistic communications imagery to explain the formation of individual and collective ideas about risk and subsequent institutional and policy responses. Risks (which were assumed to be real and objectively measureable), as well as risk-triggered events, were characterized as generating "signals" that could be strengthened or weakened as they circulated through information sources and channels and through individual and social "stations," leading to subsequent individual, social, and institutional behaviors and policy responses. The media were seen as critical influences on the process, especially because of their potential for increasing the perceived severity of some risks, for instance those associated with nuclear power. Owing to processes of social amplification and attenuation, public views on threats and potential disasters could thus differ markedly from their actual likelihood and effects.

One advantage of the SARF is that it seeks to integrate findings from earlier research within the psychometric paradigm with broader considerations concerning the role of cultural beliefs and practices, social networks and social influence, and the actions of government agencies and media organizations in shaping how different types of risks are characterized and risk-management strategies developed. The SARF supplements the psychometric paradigm by explicitly taking into account how information about risks is shaped by institutions such as the media, by public trust in risk information, and by the activities of organizations that stand to gain or lose according to how risks are framed. The SARF takes for granted that risk-related information is never a reflection of "objective risk" but always reaches audiences through institutional and organizational filters. It also takes into account downstream or second-order impacts of risk amplification, such as the effects of the stigma of risk attribution on communities and community residents.

RISK AS SOCIAL CONSTRUCTION

Another perspective, the idea that risk is socially constructed, contradicts the realist notions of risk that undergirded earlier studies. Whereas the psychometric paradigm is rooted in cognitive and decision science and the SARF was developed by geographers and psychologists, social constructionist views on risk originated in sociological theories concerned with the social construction of reality, as originally put forth by symbolic interactionists and by Berger and Luckmann in their highly influential book *The Social Construction of Reality* (1966). The key insight of social constructionism is that both perceptions and social activity are based not on our direct apprehension of "objective reality" (in our case, risk) but rather on systems of meaning that are provided by culture, developed through social interaction, and produced through claims-making activities that advance particular views of the world. The "reality" of social life thus consists of myriad social constructions that are taken for granted by members of particular cultures and subcultures. Following this logic, all aspects of social life, including those that are viewed as immutable and acted on accordingly, are social creations that show variation both across societies and over time. These include such seemingly biologically based conditions as sex and sexuality, illness, childhood, and old age. Social activities and institutions are organized around such meanings, which receive reinforcement from culture.

Viewing social life through a constructionist lens provides insights on such questions as why the psychiatric community once argued that it had evidence that homosexuality was a mental disorder but has now reversed its position; why symptoms associated with schizophrenia were at one time constructed as resulting from demonic possession, were later viewed in Western psychiatry as caused by inadequate and "cold" mothering, and are now seen as produced at least in part by genes and brain chemistry; and why post-traumatic stress disorder (PTSD), a psychiatric diagnosis that did not exist until it was developed to address the emotional and behavioral problems of Vietnam-era veterans, is now widely viewed as a potential effect of disasters.

The social constructionist framework is applicable to the entire spectrum of "risk objects" (Hilgartner 1992), spanning properties such as the incidence and severity of risks as well as their causes and consequences. For example, Western ideas about the origins of so-called natural disasters have recently shifted from the notion that disasters are acts of nature to the idea that human activity and negligence are equally if not more to blame for such events and their impacts, which is the position articulated in this volume. Social constructions involving the causes of disaster losses continue to evolve. As an illustration, as of this writing, seven Italian scientists and public officials have been convicted of manslaughter for failing to inform residents of L'Aquila, Italy, of the potential dangers posed by a series of small earthquakes that were followed by a major damaging earthquake in 2009, which killed nearly three hundred people. The conviction rested on the argument that the scientists misinterpreted scientific findings on the relationship between smaller "earthquake swarms" and larger quakes, that their public risk communications were overly influenced by political leaders, and that therefore they were responsible for the 2009 earthquake's deaths and injuries. In this case, what once would have been seen as mortality resulting from a naturally occurring event was framed by the court as the consequence of human negligence. With the increasing attribution of many weather-related disasters to climate change, events once constructed as natural are increasingly being seen as anthropogenic.

Many social constructionist analyses focus on processes involved in constructing social problems, such as child abuse, violence against women, crime, and mental illness. Such studies show, for example, that while behaviors such as child beating and woman beating have existed since the dawn of human society, these behaviors have been constructed as social problems only recently and mainly in the United States and a number of other Western societies. The construction of social problems is typically the result of the activities of organized groups that press claims regarding the severity of the putative problem and the need to act. Similarly, the solutions advanced to deal with problems that society identifies are also based on the socially constructed causes of social problems (for classic examples, see Platt 1969; Spector and Kitsuse 1973; Mauss 1975; Pfohl, 1977; V. Rose 1977).

Consistent with the literature on the social construction of social problems, the identification of and concerns about risks can be viewed as outcomes of narratives produced by established institutions and social movements. For example, sociologist Robert Stallings (1995) documented the ways in which organized groups of scientists and engineers advanced claims in an effort to construct earthquakes as a social problem meriting a governmental policy response. Claims making centered on a variety of concerns, such as the threat earthquakes pose to life safety, but also on the potential negative macroeconomic effects of major earthquakes and their possible impacts on national defense. The claims-making efforts of what Stallings called the "earthquake establishment" resulted in, among other things, the passage of the National Earthquake Hazards Reduction Act in 1977 and the development of the National Earthquake Hazards Reduction Program (NEHRP), a federal initiative that supports both loss-reduction programs and basic and applied research on earthquakes. No comparable programs exist for floods, wind hazards, or heat waves despite the fact that these perils are more common and deadly and generate higher losses than earthquakes (for more detailed discussions, see Tierney 2007).

The earthquake establishment is an example of an elite-driven social movement that developed around a specific risk. Other risk-related movements, such as the local citizen advocacy groups that emerged to call attention to the health threats posed by toxic contamination at Love Canal and numerous "citizen science" groups concerned with technological hazards, are more community based (Brown, Morello-Frosch, and Zavestoski 2011). Social movement activity can be especially important for bringing to light hazards and risks, in part because these threats are produced by the decisions and actions of established political and economic actors. Their interests are already well institutionalized, so challenges to those interests must often take extrainstitutional forms, such as movements and protest activities.

Saying that risk is socially constructed does not obviate the fact that risks actually do exist in the physical world or the idea that risks are socially produced (Rosa and Clarke 2012). Rather, a social constructionist stance argues that while risks are obdurate facts, societal and group perceptions of and responses to various risks, including ideas about reducing them, are shaped by socially and culturally derived knowledge and understandings. Like other social constructions, risk-relevant social constructs have their roots in a variety of sources, including scientific knowledge, mass media, folklore and popular culture, and positions advocated by interest groups and opinion leaders. Subsequent chapters go into more detail on how social and cultural constructs can amplify or downplay threats. I also highlight the role of constructs in justifying activities that cause risks to proliferate.

The foregoing discussions have provided examples of trends in the study of risk perception, a topic that has attracted the attention of scholars to the virtual exclusion of the equally and perhaps more important subject of how risk is produced. Public perceptions have been scrutinized, in part because such studies were of interest to developers of technologies like nuclear power and also because initial social science research on risk was carried out by psychologists, who were professionally disposed toward analyzing attitudes and beliefs. Developing an understanding of perceptions was also seen as an important element in risk communication, an activity that grew in importance in tandem with public concerns regarding technological hazards. At the same time, studies of perception have been criticized for sidestepping fundamental questions concerning the societal origins of risk. Writing about the SARF, for example, sociologist William Freudenburg observed that

so long as we focus merely on the ways in which societal *perceptions* of risk are amplified . . . we are missing a significant fraction of the insight that I know to have been possessed by those who first put forth this framework: There are also important ways in which social processes prove to amplify and/or attenuate *risks themselves*. Particularly important are the societal institutions that are entrusted with the management of risks. (2003: 107)

We will take a closer look at those social processes in the chapters that follow.

CHAPTER 3

A Different Perspective

The Social Production of Risk

EXPLAINING PERCEPTIONS, BUT IGNORING RISK

In retrospect, it seems puzzling that researchers have devoted so much time to studying how individuals and groups perceive risk and so little time to exploring where risks come from in the first place. Much of the research of the past thirty years proceeded on the assumption that risks simply exist "out there" and that they can be analyzed, assessed, and subsequently managed, but it did not delve into the origins of risks themselves. It would seem more reasonable to examine how different risks come into being in order to determine what can be done to eliminate or avoid them, than to take their existence as given and try to manage them.

Risk-related scholarship has largely assumed that risk is a natural consequence of human interactions with nature and technology or, in a slightly different variant, that risks are an inevitable by-product of the pursuit of benefits that are important to societies and communities, such as greater industrial productivity and improved human health. These ideas make intuitive sense. Cities originally developed along rivers to take advantage of shipping opportunities, for example, which also resulted in exposing residents to the risk of flooding. New chemicals brought advantages such as higher agricultural yields, while their production exposed workers to chemical hazards. People are attracted to environmental amenities such as coastlines and river basins, which in many cases can leave them vulnerable to natural hazards. This "risk as a by-product" way of thinking seems very straightforward, but it leaves open important questions about risk, such as why flood risks and chemical hazards are so much more severe in some communities and countries than in others. Why was the earthquake risk in Haiti so large that when a large earthquake did strike, it took the lives of so many people and did damage equivalent to the nation's entire gross domestic product for the previous year? What made Haiti so vulnerable? Elsewhere, in a wealthy, advanced industrial society with established risk and emergency management institutions, why did so many people die in Hurricane Katrina? Why did the worst industrial accident in history occur in Bhopal, India, and not somewhere else? Where do such high levels of risk and loss come from? And how is it that some groups obtain benefits from risky activities without being directly exposed to risk, while others who are put at risk do not receive a comparable share of those benefits? Such questions have been largely ignored by risk perception researchers and risk analysts and managers. I first introduce social science perspectives that focus not on the perception of risk but rather on risk creation, and then go on to present a framework for explaining how risk develops and grows.

FORAYS INTO RISKY TERRITORY: THE SOCIAL ORIGINS OF RISK

Risk Society?

Ulrich Beck, a German sociologist, is perhaps the best-known social theorist to attempt to explain how risk is produced at the societal level. Beck's book *Risk Society: Towards a New Modernity* generated a great deal of interest when it was originally published in 1986 in German and then in English translation in 1992. Since then, the idea that present-day society is a risk society has given rise to a virtual scholarly industry. Along with collaborators that include Anthony Giddens and Scott Lash, Beck has succeeded in moving the notion of the risk society into everyday social and political discourse and in the process has become one of Europe's most widely revered theoreticians and social analysts. Beck's original arguments were compelling, but it also didn't hurt that the Chernobyl nuclear disaster occurred the same year *Risk Society* was published, making his arguments seem prescient.

Although much of Beck's writing is maddeningly impenetrable, the core argument that explains the emergence of the risk society is relatively straightforward. According to his formulation, the risk society in which we now live is the culmination of a long-term process of stage-like social change. Western societies and their institutions have passed through a traditional or premodern stage that was followed by early modernity, a transition that was marked by the rise of industrial society.

During roughly the second half of the twentieth century, a transition to late modernity took place. In contrast with the social structures around which early modern society was organized, such as bureaucracies and social classes, late modern society is organized around information and communication and is characterized by the rise of individualized selves that are disembedded from the social structures that characterized early modernity. Under these conditions, individuals are challenged to create new biographies and identities and also to reflect on the social order and their positions within it.

This transition also gave rise to the risk society, a new and distinctive societal form. Whereas in premodern and modern societies human beings faced hazards and dangers arising from natural forces, in late modern society they face new kinds of risks to which they are exposed as a consequence of human decision making. The risk society has come about as a consequence of the dynamics of late modernity, including the development of technologies such as nuclear power. Pollution, hazardous chemicals and wastes, and the threat of nuclear war are also examples of risks produced by late modern society. Owing to the rise of the global economy, the risks of late modernity are also global, and their effects are potentially catastrophic, uncertain, and ultimately unknowable. As Beck puts it,

new kinds of industrialized, decision-produced incalculabilities and threats are spreading within the globalization of high-risk industries. . . . [A]long with the growing capacity of technical options . . . grows the incalculability of their consequences. (1992b: 22)

The risks that have emerged as a consequence of late modern social institutions are distinctive in other ways, including their wide spatial distribution and ability to affect both current and succeeding generations. Many risks are beyond the control of societies and their institutions, in part because those who create risks are able to avoid responsibility and in part because new risks extend beyond the boundaries of nation-states.

In *Risk Society* Beck acknowledged that disparities exist in risk exposure, both within societies and among regions and nations worldwide, but at the same time he also stressed the leveling effect of the risk society, arguing, for example, that "poverty is hierarchic, smog is democratic" (36), and that risks "boomerang" back onto those who produce them, so that "perpetrator and victim sooner or later become identical" (38). His thinking in this respect has evolved over time, however, and later work (Beck 1998, 2008) placed more emphasis (although not consistently) on the inequitable distribution of loss and harm, especially within the global system.

Beck's most important general contribution to the study of risk is his contention that risk originates from within the structure of society itself and specifically from human decision making. His work also contains a strong critique of techno-scientific approaches to risk assessment, and of the dysfunctional aspects of the close ties that exist between scientists and the entities that produce environmental and other risks.

Critiques of the Risk Society

At the same time, Beck's risk society thesis has generated a good deal of criticism. Robert Dingwall (1999) has argued that *Risk Society* was influenced more by German cultural and intellectual traditions than by a careful analysis of risks over time and across societal contexts. In his view, risk society theory cannot be generally applicable because it is rooted in one scholar's delimited perspective, derived from one society's historical experience. Deborah Lupton (1999) has pointed out, among other things, that Beck's writings reveal an ontological confusion about risk, in that he sometimes adopts a realist approach to risk while at other times he comes across as a social constructionist. Sociological theorist Jeffrey Alexander (1996) has strongly criticized Beck, Giddens, and Lash (1994) for their claims regarding reflexive modernization. Anthony Elliot (2002) has faulted Beck along various lines, for example for ignoring important dimensions of how risk is perceived, but more important, for assuming that risk is a central feature of contemporary social life and that it is increasing—a position Elliot calls "excessivist" (2002: 312).

For purposes of this discussion, two criticisms of the risk society thesis seem most relevant. The first has to do with the question of whether, as Beck claims, the risks societies face today are so large that they are qualitatively different from those that existed in the premodern and modern eras. Like Elliot, Bryan Turner challenges this assumption, asking instead,

[W]ere the epidemics of syphilis and bubonic plague in earlier periods any different from the modern environmental illnesses to which Beck draws our attention? That is, do Beck's criteria of risk, such as their impersonal and unobservable nature, really stand up to historical scrutiny? The devastating plagues of earlier centuries were certainly global, democratic and general . . . [and] with the spread of capitalist colonialism, it is clearly the case that in previous centuries many aboriginal peoples such as those of North America and Australia were engulfed by environmental, medical and political catastrophes that wiped out entire populations. (1994: 180–181)

The Black Death killed an estimated 30 percent of the population of Europe. In the twentieth century, the waves of influenza that spread worldwide in 1918 and 1919 killed between 50 and 100 million people (Barry 2005), or up to 6 percent of the world's population at the time. The last century also saw the emergence of the scourge of AIDS. In 2008, an estimated 33 million people worldwide were infected with HIV, and 67 percent of those cases were concentrated in Africa, where numbers were expected to rise. Clearly the potential for catastrophe on a worldwide scale existed both prior to and independent of the technologies of late modern society.

Beck didn't just underestimate nontechnological risks like epidemics. He also appears to have been so preoccupied with the perils associated with the technologies he viewed as risky that he overlooked two of the world's most significant human-induced threats, climate change and financial risk, as well as risks associated with terrorism. It is especially significant that Beck took so long to ponder the perils of climate change, which scientists have been writing about for decades. He corrects these omissions to some degree in *World at Risk* (2008) and other recent work, and he also folds terrorism into the risk society framework, but clearly he is outside his comfort zone in attempting to grapple with these kinds of risks. For example, in his commentaries on climate change in works such as *World at Risk*, he still seems unable to decide whether poorer and more environmentally vulnerable societies and groups will suffer disproportionately as a result of climate change—which they almost certainly will—or whether everyone is equally at risk.

A second area of concern relates to Beck's idea that the environmental risks that are characteristic of late modernity are unique in terms of their societal origins. Beck's theory views technological hazards as arising out of social processes that are distinct from those of other types of hazards, such as putatively "natural" ones. In various writings (e.g., Beck 1992a, 1992b, 1999), Beck is explicit in arguing that the risks that appear in late modernity are different from the natural disasters that occurred during preindustrial times, because the more recent are the result of collective decision making within society, while earlier perils were qualitatively different in that they were attributed to an "other," which could be God, nature, fate, or some other force external to society.[1]

In addition to its confusion regarding the ontological nature of risk, Beck's approach is an example of risk gerrymandering: some perils (those appearing in late modernity) arise from decision making, while earlier ones did not. In contrast, the position taken here is that the consequences of all types of disasters, both historical and contemporary, arise from decision making by organizations, political groups, and other powerful actors. Decision making regarding nonindustrial risks predates late modernity by centuries, if not millennia. Lisbon was virtually destroyed in 1755 by an earthquake that was accompanied by a tsunami and widespread fires, which together killed as many as 100,000 people. In the aftermath of the quake, the Marquis de Pombal took charge of relief efforts, and during Lisbon's recovery, in order to avoid losses from future earthquakes, he instituted new earthquake-resistant urban design and building practices. This was a conscious decision made on the basis of observations of the earthquake's impact. Pombaline architecture is the physical embodiment of the idea that both vulnerability and safety are the consequence of decisions about the design of urban forms.

The Lisbon earthquake is also noteworthy because it engendered lively discussions among scholars such as Voltaire, Rousseau, and Kant concerning whether God or human beings were to blame for the devastation caused by disasters, and it also directly led to research in earthquake engineering (Dynes 2000). Clearly the connection between decisions and the risks associated with "natural" hazards was understood at that time, at least by the opinion leaders of the day.

The Lisbon earthquake occurred at a point in history when religious interpretations of disaster were being supplanted by the Enlightenment worldview. However, long before that time societies were making decisions to contain (and also to ignore) the potential losses and harms caused by "natural" events, again contradicting Beck's idea that they faced such perils fatalistically. For example, an engineering technique known as base isolation is currently considered a state-of-the-art approach to protecting structures against earthquakes. Yet as Booth and Key (2006) have documented, base isolation is not a new idea, or even a modern one. They note that the Roman scholar Pliny the Elder discussed a base-isolated building project in his magisterial *Natural History*, which was written around 77 C.E. Pliny observed that the builders of the Temple of Diana (Artemis) in Ephesus used a base isolation approach to avoid damage to the structure. The temple was located on a marshland, and according to Pliny, the builders placed a layer of charcoal and wool fleece between the soil and the foundation to protect the temple from seismically induced earth movement. Other ancient civil engineering works such as the pyramids, and the aqueducts, temples, bridges, and dams constructed during the time of the Roman Empire, show that premodern societies understood the importance of appropriate decision making in mitigating natural perils.

Beck's belief that environmental risks are the only ones that are dependent on decisions is curious when there is so much evidence to the contrary. In the twentieth century, China's decision to urbanize on a massive scale, along with other decisions that its leaders made regarding design and construction practices for that nation's numerous rapidly growing cities, were implicated in the deaths of 243,000 people in the 1976 Tangshan earthquake, and in the large death toll in the May 2008 earthquake in Sichuan. The Chinese government was of course knowledgeable about seismic design and construction techniques but in many cases did not employ or could not enforce them. Further, in the middle of the last century, during the Great Leap Forward, Mao and other Chinese leaders decided to collectivize agricultural production, and as a result tens of millions of people died of starvation. Those famine deaths were just as much the result of decisions as the potential deaths from nuclear accidents and nuclear war that preoccupy Beck.

More recently, an estimated 230,000 people died as a direct result of the 2004 Indian Ocean earthquake and tsunamis. This was not because it was impossible at the time to determine that a massive earthquake had occurred, or because technologies for monitoring the movement of tsunami waves did not exist, or because of a lack of knowledge regarding how to warn at-risk populations about impending threats. So many died because nations in the affected region had not developed or implemented systems for warning those at risk, or devised institutional arrangements that would render those systems effective. Not taking action is itself a decision, which in this case led to massive loss of life.

Closer to home, it has long been known that unreinforced masonry buildings become death traps when they are subject to earthquake shaking. In the 1970s and 1980s, Los Angeles landlords, led by Howard Jarvis, of Proposition 13 fame, decided to oppose vigorously a proposed city ordinance that would require property owners to retrofit old masonry buildings that would likely collapse during a strong earthquake. They fought against the measure because it would cost them money to upgrade their properties so that they would not kill people in a good-sized earthquake. Proponents of the ordinance were finally able to neutralize that politically influential group and obtain passage of the law after widespread building collapses during the 1985 Mexico City earthquake killed tens of thousands (Alesch and Petak 1986). Elsewhere, the level of hurricane resistance afforded by the levees surrounding New Orleans was well understood prior to Hurricane Katrina, yet for political and economic reasons no action was taken to ameliorate the risk, and even today new levee construction and repairs leave residents highly vulnerable to another significant hurricane event.

PIONEERING RESEARCH ON THE
SOCIAL PRODUCTION OF DISASTER

Risks of all types, not just those involving technology, flow in large measure from decision-making activities and the avoidance of decisions. Scholars whose careers have focused on the study of disasters understand this. For example, in *Disasters by Design* (1999), sociologist Dennis Mileti takes a position on risk that is quite different from Beck's and that is more empirically justifiable. As the title of the book suggests, Mileti argues that all risks and losses—whether associated with so-called natural perils or technological ones—are the result of decisions that communities, societies, organizations, and political actors make, or fail to make. Present-day disasters have, in other words, been "designed" through past decisions, just as future perils will be the consequence of decisions that are made (or avoided) in the present. The processes that generate risks of all types and that over time lead to risk buildup are part of the social fabric itself.

Mileti was not the first to point this out. In an edited volume entitled *Interpretations of Calamity* (1983), which contained chapters mainly written by geographers from Europe and Canada, Kenneth Hewitt faulted mainstream disaster researchers—and here he was referring primarily to the U.S. research community and the fields of sociology and geography—for creating what he called a "disaster archipelago" that frames disaster events as separate from and originating outside of human societies, what Beck might refer to as "nature" or "the other." The alternative position advanced in *Interpretations of Calamity* is that risks and disasters emerge from the everyday, regularized, ongoing features and processes taking place in the societies in which they occur and from the socially linked vulnerabilities and capabilities of their populations. Worldwide, physical events such as earthquakes and tropical cyclones set the stage for the occurrence of disasters, but disasters themselves are largely the consequence of societal factors, such as the socioeconomic and political conditions that exist in affected societies and communities; global processes that contribute to so-called underdevelopment; legacies of colonialism, which include exploitation of natural resources and the environment; and processes that marginalize societies and groups within societies (Susman, O'Keefe, and Wisner 1983).

A decade later, *At Risk: Natural Hazards, People's Vulnerability and Disasters* (Blaikie et al. 1994; republished as Wisner et al. 2004) advanced a more systematic theory on the social production of risk. The authors laid out their basic assumptions in the first chapter of the book:

The crucial point about understanding why disasters occur is that it is not only natural events that cause them. They are also the product of the social, political, and economic environment (as distinct from the natural environment) because of the way it structures the lives of different groups of people. (1994: 3)

According to the framework set forth in *At Risk*, natural occurrences such as volcanic eruptions, landslides, and the spread of disease agents constitute "triggers" for the emergence of disasters, but the forces that result in risk buildup and that ultimately cause disasters are social and historical. Those forces consist of *root causes*, such as attributes of political and economic systems; *dynamic pressures* that are generated by those root causes, which include rapid population growth, rapid urbanization, and economic dislocations caused by debt restructuring requirements that are imposed on some societies; and the *unsafe conditions* that arise through the operation of those forces, such as the growth of settlements in hazardous locations, unsafe development and construction practices, and population vulnerability that arises out of poverty and powerlessness. Risk builds up over time as a consequence of long-term and ongoing social, political, and economic processes that characterize societies and communities around the world. These are the processes that produce physical and social vulnerability—the potential for harm and loss—that is realized when a triggering event strikes.

The "pressure and release" framework laid out in *At Risk* was concerned with risks arising from natural forces such as wind, water, and earth movement, but a look at the empirical record shows that the framework applies equally well to other types of risks. The Bhopal disaster is the prototypical example of the way in which social factors such as poverty, migration in search of jobs, lack of land-use controls, the growth of informal settlements, and poorly regulated industrial production led to catastrophe (Shrivastava 1987). Other ballooning technological risks are more subtle. Hazardous wastes and now electronic wastes are being transferred from industrialized to poorer regions of the world in ever-increasing volumes. Among others, the United Nations has warned that the e-waste problem is expanding dramatically and will increase even more in the future. Much of the dumping that takes place is illegal, unregulated, and encouraged by corrupt institutions (United Nations Environment Programme 2009).

Discussing in detail the various factors that account for exposure to different hazards is not my purpose here. Rather, the intent is to provide examples of how risk and vulnerability are structured by factors that are fundamentally social in nature. The effects of hurricanes, earthquakes, heat waves, industrial accidents, and environmental toxins are not so much determined by nature and technology as by societal characteristics and broad historical processes that shape both the "hazardousness of place" and the social groups that are most exposed to various risks.

FORMS OF EXPLANATION IN THE SOCIAL PRODUCTION OF RISK

Arguing that vulnerability expands as a consequence of rapid urbanization or that globalization and poverty are factors in the social production of risk amounts to tracing risk exposure to very abstract and macro-level concepts. Macro-level explanations tell only part of the story and shed little light on the complex causal paths that influence risk. A more theoretically and empirically sound approach starts with the assumption that large-scale conditions and trends exert their influence through processes that take place at smaller-scale levels of analysis, such as regions and communities, organizations and institutions. Within the context of broad-scale social forces, people and property are exposed to risks at particular times and in particular places; local conditions matter. Global and societal-level conditions and trends are filtered through and altered by meso- and micro-level factors. This is true everywhere but is especially true in countries like the United States whose political systems are federalist, that is whose powers and authorities are distributed among national, state, and local governments. Nation-states are important actors in the social production of risk, but equally important processes take place at subnational levels. These are the levels at which national policies are implemented and enforced and at which other policies are developed and carried out—or not. They are the levels at which policies can be rendered effective, on the one hand, or watered down and ignored, on the other.

As discussed in the chapters that follow, it also matters whether national-level governments can actually have an effect on actions that are undertaken at intermediate and local levels, or whether, as is increasingly the case worldwide, national-level governments are so weak that they have no real power over activities that take place on the ground. Many risky conditions and subsequent disaster losses can be traced to the fact that weak, failing, and failed states are unable to regulate, or in some cases even to influence, localized practices in areas such as land use and construction standards, and that the number of such states is growing.

INSTITUTIONS AND ORGANIZATIONS

Sociologist Charles Perrow (1991) has argued that U.S. society can be thought of as a "society of organizations." This is literally true; individuals in modern industrial societies live their entire lives within organizations of different kinds, from the time they are born—usually in hospitals—through schooling and work life. They then may spend part of their retirement years being cared for by organizations like nursing homes and assisted living facilities, and when they die, they do so with the assistance of hospitals, hospices, and funeral homes. Throughout this entire process, individuals interact continually with organizations, which in turn shape their attitudes and behaviors.

For good or ill, our lives are also continually affected by the decisions and activities of organizations with which we seldom or never come into contact. Communities grow when new employers come to town, and they shrink when employers move offshore. Organizations make decisions that influence where and how we work, what we have the opportunity to see, hear, and read, and even how we develop and maintain our most important social relationships. It is thus logical that organizations are also implicated in the risks to which we are exposed.

A focus on organizations and their role in the social genesis of risk is important for several reasons. An obvious one is that organizations that deal with hazardous materials and technologies can be a direct source of risk. In addition to being perpetrators, organizations can also become victims of disaster, as happens, for example, when businesses and governmental entities are damaged and destroyed. Organizational entities of various kinds are also responsible for containing risks. Such organizations include bodies that enforce safety regulations, entities charged with combating terrorism, and emergency response agencies that have to deal with harmful events when they occur. Most risk assessment and management activities are undertaken by organizations, and organizations in the insurance, reinsurance, and catastrophic risk management sectors are involved in the development and implementation of risk-spreading strategies. The role of media organizations can also be significant in that both a lack of media attention and particular media frames can allow risks to grow, while some forms of media scrutiny can help attenuate risk. And of course many types of governmental entities at federal, state, and local levels affect risk levels through their willingness (or reluctance) to act in the face of threats.

Attention to the role of organizations in creating and managing risks is crucial for another reason. As we saw in Chapter 2, the psychometric paradigm places a great deal of emphasis on individual perceptions and judgments concerning risk, and that paradigm has had important impacts on discourses concerning risk. However, what this perspective lacks is an appreciation of the extent to which risk-related attitudes, beliefs, and behaviors are context-dependent and the extent to which organizations provide those contexts. One of the most robust findings in the social sciences centers on the ways in which organizations and groups can shape behavior irrespective of individual attitudes. Even small groups have this ability, as shown in the classic Asch experiments on conformity (Asch 1951). Other classic studies led to the development of concepts such as "groupthink" and the "risky shift" to account for such influences. As indicated earlier, individual surveys and laboratory experiments like those that explored the dimensions of risk perception are useful, but things change in the transition from the laboratory to the real world—a world in which attitudes, beliefs, and actions come under the influence of a wide range of forces, many of which are organizational.

Commonsense thinking in the United States about individual and social behavior tends to be psychologistic, perhaps because America is an individualistic society. It thus seems logical and intuitively sound to see various behaviors—including those that are associated with risk— as reflections of psychological predispositions. This is perhaps one reason why the financial meltdown of 2008 is often attributed to massive greed, whether the greedy people considered responsible are bankers, the American public, or both. But did greed suddenly appear on the human scene ten or twenty years ago, at the time of the tech and housing bubbles? Were America's Robber Barons less greedy than today's hedge fund managers? If explosions of greed are so recent, why has excessive greed been a theme in myth and literature for millennia? And haven't speculative bubbles come and gone throughout history? The point here is that it is inappropriate to attribute behavior to psychological factors without placing equal or greater emphasis on broader influences that are at play at group, organizational, institutional, and cultural levels, which encourage some types of behavior while suppressing others.

Explaining the expansion of risk that culminated in the financial catastrophe of 2008 requires a careful exploration not only of the attitudes and behavior of individuals but more importantly of the behavior of the groups, organizations, and institutions in which that behavior took place: Fannie and Freddie, groups of influential "quants," the rating agencies, AIG, the Federal Reserve, banks and hedge funds, subprime lenders, and the rest of the cast of characters. The meltdown was a disaster in which organizations were both perpetrators and victims and about which psychological concepts like greed explain little.

The severity of risks and whether they increase or decrease over time are in large measure a function of the behavior of the organizations and institutions most directly involved. Some businesses are lax when it comes to policing risk, while others are diligent, as their safety records show. With respect to attentiveness to risk, there is a difference between Massey Energy and other large coal companies, and between BP and other large oil companies. Regulatory agencies also vary in strictness and permissiveness, both across agencies and over time, and in other important ways, such as their perspectives on what strategies are most likely to influence the organizations they monitor to avoid and reduce risks. Some may elect (or be forced) to make adherence to risk reduction principles voluntary rather than mandatory, with predictable results: organizations that are already on the right track will embrace voluntary standards, while others will not. When organizational disregard for risk is accompanied by lax external controls on risky activities, disaster can result.

ORGANIZATIONAL ECOLOGIES AND RISK

It follows, then, that a focus on organizations is critical for understanding the social production of risk. But even more broadly, attention must be paid to institutions, clusters of organizations, and multiorganizational networks in the risk production process. In sociology, institutional theory stresses that all organizations are embedded in wider networks that influence organizational actions in much the same way that organizational and other social contexts influence individual actions. Network theories point in the same direction: organizational entities must interact with other entities in a network in order to function, and in the course of those interactions they are influenced by network partners (Dimaggio and Powell 1983; Scott 2001; Meyer 2008; Greenwood et al. 2008). A key insight from institutional and network scholarship involves the importance of institutions and networks in the development and transmission of norms of behavior—norms that can range from the informal to the legally binding. Organizations thus function within larger multiorganizational ecologies that both enable and constrain their activities. Such ecologies span a range of relational forms that include supply and logistics chains, public-private partnerships, joint ventures, and industry coalitions, and that also include competitive and adversarial or quasi-adversarial relationships.

Institutional ties and network structures and processes strongly influence individual organizations. For example, when Walmart, the world's largest retailer and the largest grocery chain in the United States, announced in 2011 that it was launching an initiative to supply healthier and more nutritious foods—for example, by lowering the sodium content of many of its products—and that it would do so at a reasonable cost to consumers, that action had an immediate effect on the behavior of other organizations that share ties with Walmart, including in particular its suppliers. With its massive market share in the United States, global reach, and vast array of network ties, Walmart is in a position to literally transform the retail sales sector. If successful, the healthy food initiative could have extraordinarily positive effects over time. Walmart is an extreme case, but it does a good job of illustrating the way in which influence can flow within organizational ecologies.

The Walmart case is an example of how one influential actor in a large multiorganizational network can mobilize network members to work toward a goal that most people would consider laudable. Under a burgeoning obesity epidemic, Americans need a healthier diet. At the same time, however, pernicious norms and practices, including those that produce risk, can also diffuse within networks, resulting in risk buildup. For example, if an organizational entity whose activities involve risky technologies is known to have increased profits by cutting corners and paying less attention to safety, other similar entities will follow suit. Multiorganizational ecologies include organizations that create and take on risks and entities that are charged with regulating the behavior of those organizations and with managing risks. If regulators signal in one way or another that risky organizational behavior will not be policed, or if the penalties for causing harm and loss are insufficiently severe, risks will continue to grow. The *Deepwater Horizon* explosion and spill was only the largest in a trail of U.S. accidents that were caused by BP. Sanctions applied after those other incidents were anything but strict, and they served as a signal to BP that it could continue with business as usual. Relationships between banking entities and their regulators also provide a key to understanding how the risks associated with the housing bubble grew to then-unimaginable proportions. The key point here is that risk increases and things go wrong not because individual organizations somehow decide on their own to become bad actors, but rather because the ecologies in which they function become enabling environments for riskier activities.

CULTURE, SOCIAL PSYCHOLOGY, AND RISK

Social-structural and organizational forces help to determine risk exposure, but cultural and social-psychological forces are also important. Societal values and ingrained practices, ideologies and worldviews, various forms of social cognition (as opposed to individual psychology), belief systems, collective memories, other types of social constructions, and ideas that become influential through forms of collective behavior such as fads and crazes all play a role in the social production of risk. In some cases, these influences can provide reinforcement, justification, and other types of support for the risky strategies social actors wish to pursue. In others, they can function as blinders that prevent social actors from even becoming aware that some of those strategies will lead to catastrophe.

In still other cases, cultural values and beliefs may be cynically manipulated by those whose motives stem from other sources, such as their own economic interests.

I am not arguing here for a kind of cultural determinism. Following Swidler (1986), I see culture as more of a "tool kit" that can be drawn upon as social actors go about making choices and putting together strategies for accomplishing their aims. Cultural elements do not "cause" behaviors so much as permit us to make meaning out of the behaviors we undertake. Note, however, that it is culture that makes those meanings available. Elements of culture such as shared beliefs, norms, and socially constructed realities provide part of the basis for the social order, and they keep social activity consistent and to a large degree predictable. At the same time, they also shape perceptions, channel behavior in particular directions, and place boundaries around what is considered acceptable conduct. As the substrate from which meanings grow, culture provides frameworks through which events in the past and present are understood, as well as frameworks through which to view the future.

In Chapter 2, I discussed research that focused on individual cognitive limitations and their effects on the perception of risk. However, information processing at the individual level is also shaped by other factors, such as frames and mental models, that are primarily cultural in origin. New information is assimilated into existing frames and interpreted by means of those frames. Concepts such as frames and mental models are often applied at the individual level, for example to explain individual perceptions or worldviews, but they also operate at group, organizational, and institutional levels. For example, researchers spend a great deal of time studying organizational cultures as a way of understanding the behavior of organizations and their personnel.

Culturally derived habits of thinking and collectively-taken-for-granted assumptions function in a variety of ways. They highlight certain explanations and interpretations of events and social activities while downplaying others; they signal which interpretations represent consensus views; and they encourage conformity with such views through the use of sanctions. As I discuss in the next chapter, socially constructed perspectives can make it difficult to talk or even think about certain risks, and values and norms can justify increasingly risky behavior. Culture includes pressure toward conformity; risks are allowed to build up when whistle-blowers and others who call attention to risky activities are marginalized.

In addition to being influenced by long-standing elements of culture, behavior can also be influenced by novel or emergent cultural elements, such as new norms and collective definitions (Turner and Killian 1987). Scholarship in the field of collective behavior provides insights into how these new influences operate. That research indicates that under certain conditions emergent definitions can be so persuasive and compelling that they become widely adopted in very uncritical ways. Collective behavior theory provides part of the explanation for how financial crazes and panics emerge and are maintained, for example (Smelser 1965; Mann, Nagel, and Dowling 1976; Visano 2012). The kinds of bandwagon effects that are characteristic of financial bubbles like the recent housing bubble involve the development of new collective beliefs and social constructions that supplant older ones. During such crazes, many people can come to believe that trees really do grow to the sky, and that those who claim otherwise are not worth listening to. When a craze takes hold, what were once considered rock-solid economic fundamentals are defined as no longer valid. Tulipomania, the South Sea bubble, and the Roaring Twenties are not merely historical curiosities; they are examples of collective behavior processes at work. The same is the case for the financial bubble that burst in 2008, ushering in the Great Recession. Important here is that when the collective behavior processes that fuel financial crazes become very compelling, upside thinking is defined as the only kind of thinking that is sensible, and risks are rendered invisible—until the craze runs its course. Terms such as "irrational exuberance" and the "madness of crowds" (Mackay 2008; first published in 1841) are often employed to explain financial crazes, but those who participate in crazes believe themselves to be acting quite rationally and sanely—a view that emergent belief systems reinforce. Financial panics, the obverse of bubbles, are also driven in part by emergent collective beliefs and the social pressure they exert. In the case of panics, the collective beliefs that emerge highlight risk, encouraging mass escape from markets.

Still, like individual psychological predispositions, cultural practices are played out and cultural tools are brought to bear within specific group, organizational, and institutional contexts. Explaining how risks are produced and allowed to grow requires a simultaneous emphasis on psychology and social psychology, culture, and social organization.

Chapters 4, 5, and 6 proceed in the following sequence. Chapter 4 focuses on cultural factors that are implicated in risk production, including values, ideologies, frames, and culturally engendered cognitive styles. In Chapter 5, I return to a more detailed discussion of the role of organizations and institutions in the social production of risk. Chapter 6 takes an even broader view, focusing on large-scale global trends that generate risk.

CHAPTER 4

Culture and the Production of Risk

INTRODUCTION

Up to this point, we have focused on how disciplines concerned with risk have been so preoccupied with the study of risk perceptions that they have neglected the most fundamental issue in the study of risk, which is how risks are produced. In this chapter and the two that follow, I develop a framework for understanding risk production, beginning first by considering the cultural and ideational factors that contribute to risk, and then moving on to institutional and organizational factors.

Scholars from various fields have analyzed the cultural dimensions of risk (Douglas and Wildavsky 1983; Krimsky and Golding 1992; Kahan and Slovic 2006; Slovic 2010). The vast majority of such works, however, do not focus on the role of culture in risk production. Rather, following the dominant pattern of the scholarship that I have discussed, they deal primarily with risk perceptions and with related questions concerning why some risks are amplified, becoming major focal points for concern, while others are seen as less important or ignored entirely. These are important topics, but they are quite different from those on which we focus here. Our goal is to shed light on the influence of culture and belief systems, both on risks themselves and on behaviors that cause risks to proliferate. Elements of culture such as worldviews, styles of thinking, and ways of framing the natural and social world can blind social actors to the growth of risk and enable activities which cause risks to balloon out of control.

The role of culture and ideas in the production of risk have their foundations in three theoretical perspectives. The first is *social constructionism*, an idea that was introduced earlier in connection with the ways in which people perceive risk. As we saw, risk itself, as well as ideas about different risks, are social constructions. People do not form beliefs or act on the basis of some objectively derived calculus regarding the probability of loss, or "real risk." The constructivist stance argues that even though obdurate facts of the natural world and the environment do exist—we cannot deny the forces of gravity or of earthquakes and tornadoes, for example—social behaviors and activities revolve around the meanings that are collectively assigned to the natural world and the environment, and it is these meanings that are the appropriate object for study because they constitute the basis for individual and social action.

Social constructions are important in several ways. They serve as the basis for structuring beliefs and behaviors around specific objects. To the extent they are embodied in culture, they stabilize those beliefs and behaviors over time and space. And in many cases they become significant components of individual identity and the sense of self.

Constructions of reality permeate everyday life in ways that are both explicit and subtle. Formal and informal norms communicate expectations for people in different statuses and at different stages in life, on the basis of social constructions. Categories related to crime and criminals influence individuals' life chances and set boundaries around what behaviors societies consider acceptable. At all stages of life and in all walks of life, people receive various kinds of signals concerning convention and deviance; examples are laws, traditions, the rules of etiquette, and occupation norms. Both high and low culture contain constructions about nature and the social world, which are embodied in discourses that in turn shape and frame public perceptions.

Well-established constructions are taken for granted in the everyday lives of members of society, and they constitute the reality from which social activities draw their meaning. In medieval Europe, for example, church teachings inveighed against the threats posed by witches, and ordinary people not only believed in the existence of witches but readily found witches in their midst. Church doctrine and "how to" manuals like the *Malleus Maleficarum* taught the faithful how to uncover witchcraft and identify witches, and institutions such as the Inquisition developed around and maintained witch-hunting practices. Because the property of witches was subject to confiscation, witch hunting was a self-sustaining activity, which contributed further to efforts to find and punish witches. The witch as a social construction retained its power over time and successfully crossed the Atlantic to the New World, as exemplified by the Salem witch trials in the American colonies, in which neighbors turned against neighbors in their efforts to root out witchcraft.

Contemporary Western societies have largely abandoned the idea of witchcraft, but the same is not true for other societies. For example, a 2010 Gallup poll found that approximately 55 percent of the inhabitants of sub-Saharan Africa believe in the existence of witches, although there is considerable variation across societies. Moreover, even though most people who have been socialized in Western societies do not give credence to the notion that witches constitute an active force for evil, societies and communities do occasionally drift into witch hunts of other sorts. The anticommunist "red scare" that was led by Senator Joseph McCarthy in the early 1950s relied upon the logic of the witch hunt, claiming that communists had successfully infiltrated key American institutions and were subverting them from within. During the 1980s and into the 1990s, a number of U.S. communities experienced a rash of accusations related to putative physical and sexual abuse of children in day-care facilities (Nathan and Snedeker 1995; de Young 2004). In this form of collective behavior known as moral panic, day-care proprietors were accused of all manner of vicious and heinous crimes toward their charges—accusations that resulted in deep community divisions and long and expensive criminal trials. Day-care center operators lost their businesses and their reputations, and in other witch hunts parents were imprisoned on the basis of false accusations of abuse made by their own children. Collective emotions ran high in these cases, driven by fears that were later found to have little or no empirical basis. And important for arguments that will be made later, regardless of the truth or accuracy of the claims that were made against individuals in these episodes, just like the evil deeds of putative witches these socially constructed evil acts became the reality around which individuals and groups focused their activities.

These are extreme examples, but the powerful construction of witches illustrates that socially constructed ideas can lead large numbers of people to suspend disbelief and abandon their critical thinking capabilities, often to the detriment of others. The social constructions that shape our everyday lives are typically more prosaic and invisible in their influence.

Due to their pervasiveness, we "know," without having to think too much, what we believe and how we feel about particular people and situations. We are able to see specific events as manifestations of larger trends and patterns. And for the most part, these taken-for-granted styles of thinking serve us well as we navigate through our everyday lives.

The analysis of *frames* and *framing* is a second theoretical and conceptual thread that is closely related to constructionism. Following sociologist Erving Goffman (1974), a frame is a conceptual lens or set of ideas that enables individuals and groups to interpret and make sense of the world. Frames can be thought of as social constructions on a mission: they help to organize perceptions, events, experiences, and situations in ways that render them meaningful. Among other functions, frames serve as time- and energy-saving devices that enable us to live in society without constantly having to assess each event and topic of concern as if it were entirely new and unfamiliar. As we encounter new information in our everyday lives, that information can be folded more or less neatly into already existing frames. In many respects, culture can be conceptualized as a large array of social constructions and frames that make it possible for members to understand one another and coordinate their everyday activities and for institutions to function. Of course, not all constructions and frames are consistent with one another, as indicated by the competing frames that characterize political campaigns and discourses, variations in public opinion, and "culture wars" that erupt on a regular basis. Indeed, societies and cultures can continue to function even when such inconsistencies are large. This is because culture makes available a range of alternative strategies for interpretation and action; as individuals, groups, and organizations arrange their activities, they have the ability to draw upon reservoirs of diverse, ready-made social constructions and conceptual frameworks (Swidler 1986).

Socially constructed realities and conceptual frames are of course not static. If that were the case, social life would lack novelty, and social change would be impossible. Cultures are capable of experiencing huge sea changes; the supplanting of the medieval religious worldview by the Enlightenment and the modern secular worldview was one such change. Major social revolutions, such as the Bolshevik and Maoist revolutions, were also accompanied by cultural shifts of seismic proportions. Most change is not so extreme, and some alterations in social constructions and worldviews are temporary, or only affect particular institutional sectors. Widely shared beliefs concerning the nature of the "New Economy" and the ability to control financial risk through financial engineering fall into this last-mentioned category.

Finally, our analyses draw upon the work of Pierre Bourdieu, especially the concepts of *field, habitus,* and *doxa* (1980, 1984; Wacquant 2004). Following Bourdieu, fields are social arenas characterized by collectively shared systems of belief, expectations, and practices. Fields include institutions such as educational and political systems, the economy, the arts, and other collections of social relationships that are maintained over time. The habitus constitutes the world as experienced by the individual operating within a given field, and the doxa is made up of the unconsciously accepted and taken-for-granted worldviews of individuals and other social actors as they carry out their activities, both within specific fields and in the larger society. Field, habitus, and doxa constitute an integrated whole through which social action is organized, making it possible for individuals to "know" implicitly what kinds of ideas and lines of action are appropriate within a given field and to organize action accordingly. These social forces also put limits around what it is possible to know, and even what is thinkable. Within specific fields, then, certain constructs and interpretations can literally become unthinkable. Risks are often sequestered in this manner; the problem is that what cannot be thought about cannot be managed.

So far I have been silent on the question of the *content* of social constructions, frames, and other taken-for-granted ideas. Explaining how that content is generated is a massive project in and of itself, but a good rule of thumb for unearthing sources of social constructs is that they often reflect the interests of dominant groups within society—the main interest being the maintenance of power and privilege. After all, social groups self-consciously pursue their own interests, and some groups are more able to solidify those interests and shape culture. To use a simplistic example, if everyone "knows" and accepts that anyone in American society can succeed and achieve wealth through hard work and perseverance, then those who possess wealth are to be admired for their efforts, and those who are poor are presumed to be that way because they lack ambition and drive. It is in the interest of the wealthy to promote such ideas—and wealthy people generally possess enough power and influence to do so. Wealth itself then becomes a symbol of the social value and importance of an individual or group. It consequently becomes reasonable to conclude that film stars, sports figures, and billionaire CEOs are so highly paid because they contribute so much to our society, while those who are not well compensated contribute less. And soon the ideas expressed by wealthy individuals are also viewed as more valuable than those expressed by lesser mortals.

Social fields are characterized by disparities in wealth and power, which are played out in the lives of individuals within those fields and in the larger society. The ideas and taken-for-granted assumptions that permeate fields, which reflect those power differences, constitute the environment on which social actors depend, so that sensemaking and action are possible. Throughout the life course, individuals enter fields that are already in existence and that shape their thoughts and actions: the educational system, work life in different organizations, and spheres of activity within communities and societies. As individuals adapt and adjust within different fields, their worldviews and identities change and align with the larger constructions and frames characteristic of those fields. If we focus on contemporary corporate life, for example, where money holds sway and being wealthy forms an intrinsic part of an individual's identity, cultural concepts such as field, habitus, and doxa help explain why an investment banker who receives $25 million per year in compensation might consider himself underpaid, given what an executive of his caliber ought to be making; why a lower-level counterpart who earns $3 to $5 million annually might develop a sense of worthlessness; and—more appropriate for the topic addressed here—why such individuals might find irresistible the lure of highly risky investment strategies that hold the promise of a bigger payday.

We inhabit a socially constructed world that acts back upon us in very concrete ways, even in cases in which constructions do not square with facts. That idea was articulated well nearly one hundred years ago by sociologist W. I. Thomas, who observed that situations that are defined as real are real in their consequences (Thomas and Thomas 1928). In the aftermath of the terrorist attacks of September 11, 2001, al-Qaeda operatives were not lurking in every city and town in America, waiting to strike—the organization's membership was simply not that large and the network was not that well resourced—but U.S. leaders acted as if the risk of additional terrorist attacks constituted a genuine existential threat to the nation, and in turn those actions had real-world effects in the form of presidential directives, laws and policies, and massive allocations of financial support for terrorism prevention and consequence management. Prioritizing terrorism as a public policy concern also meant that other risks, such as the risk of a catastrophic hurricane in the Gulf of Mexico striking a vulnerable city like New Orleans, fell off the radar. And that was just domestic policy. The social construction and framing of the struggle against terrorism as a war triggered two major overseas conflicts that sapped the nation of blood and treasure. Situations that are defined as real are real in their consequences, both intended and unintended.

CULTURAL ASSUMPTIONS, BELIEFS, AND RISK PRODUCTION
Nature, Growth, and Progress

Embedded within the cultural DNA of the United States and other modern industrialized societies is a complex set of beliefs about the physical and natural world that promotes both material progress and the production of risk. These ideas construct the physical and natural world as essentially a collection of resources over which human beings hold dominion. A key element within the modern worldview is that nature exists to be exploited. Land, water, forests, gemstones, other minerals, fish, mammals, and other living things all constitute resources that can and should be extracted for the benefit of human beings. This is of course not the only way contemporary societies think about nature; nature also exists to be appreciated, conserved, and sustained. However, such concerns are typically assigned a lower priority than the basic need to acquire resources and transform them in beneficial and profitable ways. The natural world is also constructed as a sink—that is, as a place to deposit wastes and other unwanted materials. Framed in these ways, nature exists to yield resources for human use and as a repository for things that have been used up, including vast amounts of waste and toxic materials.

Cultural ideas concerning the need for continual growth and progress coexist well with the construction of nature as a resource pool and sink. Growth and progress bring benefits such as increased wealth, higher living standards, new infrastructure systems, and broader opportunities. Analysts like Aaron Wildavsky (1988) also argue that risks decline as wealth increases. This claim has some validity, especially for macrolevel comparisons. Many fewer people die in earthquakes and tropical cyclones in well-off nations than die in poorer ones, for example. However, the "richer is safer" argument has a number of flaws. First, not all communities and groups have the opportunity to reap the benefits of the wealth derived from natural resource exploitation and pro-growth activities, nor do they have an equal opportunity for safety. Second, scholars like Lee Clarke (1989) point out that wealth per se does not result in lower levels of risk and may create new risks unless the social systems in question are also characterized by democratic forms of government that encourage transparency and accountability. As I discuss later, wealthy nations like the United States and Japan have a long way to go in this respect.

Justifying JARring Actions

One reason why societies and scholars tend to overlook the ways in which ideologies of growth also result in the growth of risks is that growth-related decisions often move risks around in time and space. For example, recent scholarship has called attention to a set of risk-expanding practices known as JARring actions—activities that *j*eopardize *a*ssets that are *r*emote (Kousky and Zeckhauser 2006; Berger, Kousky, and Zeckhauser 2008). The essence of JARring actions is that they yield benefits for particular actors in the present and near future while off-loading risks onto other groups, other geographic locations, and the distant future, including future generations. JARring activities undertaken in the name of "growth," "progress," "jobs," and other values at one point in time or at one location set in motion processes that produce vulnerabilities at a later time or somewhere else. When a triggering event does occur, the losses are assumed by other entities—private households and businesses, government agencies, and the insurance industry. As an illustration, Carolyn Kousky and Richard Zeckhauser characterize as a series of JARring actions the various activities that resulted in the loss of wetlands and other ecosystem services along the Mississippi River, its delta, and the Gulf of Mexico. These actions, carried out for private gain, were key contributors to the massive losses incurred in both the 1993 Mississippi River floods and Hurricane Katrina. The authors also note that JARring actions involve perverse incentives because those actions

are undertaken for the private benefits they bring, as the entity taking the action has no incentive to consider the harm it brings to others, particularly since those others are remote. There is a gulf between the recipients of benefits and the recipients of costs. (2006: 65)

JARring actions that produce risks and result in disasters are difficult to prevent precisely because their consequences are remote—temporally, spatially, socially, and causally—and therefore those who undertake such actions generally cannot be held responsible. Kousky and Zeckhauser argue that such actions continue unless those who undertake them can be made to internalize the risks that they currently externalize successfully. These authors offer many other examples of JARring actions, but they highlight activities that are producing climate change as perhaps the best example of the concept, as climate change affects people and communities worldwide—including those that have contributed infinitesimally to climate change—as well as succeeding generations.

Returning to the concepts of social constructionism, framing, fields, and doxa, one reason many JARring actions are easy to undertake is that they receive cultural support; put another way, such actions draw upon and are justified by socially constructed ideas—and not just any ideas but those that favor economic and political elites. Communities at risk from flooding quite frequently demand flood protection in the form of levees and other protective works. However, once levees are built or improved, this encourages more development in areas "protected" by levees. Such development is seldom opposed, because the idea of growth as a positive community value is taken for granted—and besides, "everyone knows" that areas behind levees are safe for more intensive development. However, as more and more communities build levees to protect themselves, rivers are increasingly constrained and natural protections are lost due to that channeling, so that when flooding does occur levees are breached or overtopped, resulting in ever-larger losses, because in the meantime populations and structures near levees have also increased.

Engineer and flood expert Gerald Galloway, chair of the presidential committee that produced the definitive report on the 1993 Mississippi River floods (Interagency Floodplain Management Review Committee 1994), has observed that there are two kinds of levees: those that have failed and those that will fail. The riskiness of relying on levees for property and life safety protection is well understood within the engineering community, and the consequences of the levee effect have been well documented. Levees are subject to failure for a wide variety of reasons, and building levees encourages development behind them, raising the risk of larger future losses. Levee building is a classic example of the moral hazard problem, in which measures designed to contain risk end up encouraging riskier behavior. However, ideas like those articulated by Professor Galloway do not fare well against the strong pro-growth sentiments that are common in American communities. Development is socially constructed as universally beneficial despite the fact that many development projects constitute JARring actions that generate private benefits while producing and distributing additional risk.

Technology Will Save Us

Accompanying cultural constructions about nature, growth, and progress is a strong cultural preoccupation with the unalloyed benefits associated with technology. That technological advances bring benefits is inarguable; they have created enormous wealth, saved numerous lives, and improved our overall quality of life. In light of such advances, being a Luddite is simply not an option; technology is a massive force for good. At the same time, however, technologies can also generate new risks. One hundred years ago, American society did not have to contend with incidents like Three Mile Island, and the human race was not threatened with nuclear

Armageddon. Nor did it have to decide what to do with nuclear waste. Disasters involving hazardous chemicals are more common today because there are now many more such chemicals in use, and also because of the large scale on which they are now produced and processed. The existence of massive oil tankers helped make the *Exxon Valdez* oil spill and its aftermath possible, and deep-water drilling technology helped to produce the 2010 BP oil spill. New threats are continually emerging; for example, many people, both inside and outside government, are spending large amounts of time trying to assess and reduce the risks associated with complex interdependent infrastructure systems, such as the cyber-infrastructure upon which contemporary society depends.

More relevant to discussions here, unquestioning faith in technology, another key element in the contemporary mind-set, can lead to both the discounting of risk and to its subsequent expansion. Levees and the levee effect are one such example, in which the appetite for growth and belief in the safety of protective systems converge. The city of New Orleans literally exists because of unquestioning faith in levees—even though that faith is largely misplaced.

This is not an argument against seeking technological solutions to problems societies face. It is an argument against technological hubris, or blind faith in the idea that technology can solve any and all problems, combined with collective unwillingness to consider arguments to the contrary. In the sections that follow, we explore two seemingly disparate but closely comparable examples of technological hubris and how it could lead, or has led, to calamity: the preoccupation with constructing ever-taller buildings, and the confidence placed in financial engineering in the years leading up to the financial crash of 2008.

TO ENGINEER IS HUMAN, PART I:
EXTREME ENGINEERING

Readers may recognize that the title of this section is the same as that of an acclaimed 1985 book by engineer, historian, and author Henry Petroski, which has long been appreciated for its readability and erudition. The full title of the book, *To Engineer Is Human: The Role of Failure in Successful Design*, tells a lot about its overall theme. Petroski observes that human history has been marked by numerous engineering advances but that engineering and engineered structures can never be fail-safe, because they are human productions. As he puts it, an engineering project is a kind of hypothesis; engineers, architects, and builders hypothesize that the project will not fail under conditions they expect it to encounter. When a project does fail, the hypothesis is disproved. Central to this argument is the idea that failure teaches important lessons. The science and art of engineering thus progresses just as much through its failures as through its successes, as reasons for failure are discovered, calculations are changed, and designs are modified on the basis of actual occurrences.

We live in a time of astounding engineering accomplishments, so much so that engineering advances that were unthinkable ten or fifteen years ago—tiny, hand-held devices that store and make accessible massive volumes of information and enable ubiquitous and instantaneous communication, for example—are now taken entirely for granted. At the same time, however, we can also begin to take for granted that technology will never fail in major ways, or put another way, that projects which incorporate technology involve certainty rather than carrying at all times some probability of failure. Of course, we do have experience with numerous technologies that are highly reliable and robust—which further increases faith in technology.

However, problems can and do emerge when that faith extends to extreme and bleeding-edge engineering and technology and to projects and processes that, if they fail, will fail catastrophically. The design professions and the public alike are fascinated with tall buildings, and a trend toward constructing super-tall skyscrapers began in the mid-1990s. For a time, the twin Petronas Towers in Kuala Lumpur held the title of the world's tallest buildings, but the towers were quickly surpassed by other super-talls such as Taipei 101 (101 stories), the Shanghai World Financial Center (101 stories), the Hong Kong International Commerce Center (118 stories), and by the massively tall Burj Dubai, now the Burj Khalifa (160 stories). The projected tallest building in the United States, set to be completed in 2014, is One World Trade Center, formerly known as the Freedom Tower. It will be the same height as the original One World Trade Center, which was destroyed on September 11, 2001. Also under construction are the Abraj al Bait Towers in Mecca. The largest tower in that complex will become the second-tallest building in the world (after Burj Khalifa), the tallest hotel in the world (a title now held by a hotel in Dubai), and the largest building, by square footage, in the world. There are numerous other super-tall skyscrapers worldwide, but these examples suffice to show that designing and building such structures has great cultural and symbolic importance. Their developers, architects, and engineers, as well as the nations and communities in which they are located, want very much to send a message with these super-structures—quite often a message about their own importance and capacity for innovation. To the backers of massive projects, bigger is always better, and whether such projects are economically viable and sustainable is of less importance.[1]

The proposed Transbay Development in San Francisco is one example of how technological hubris is reaching (pardon the pun) new heights, with risky consequences. The plan for the Transbay Development, which will be located in the city's financial district, consists of a major transportation hub, which among other things will replace the CalTrain terminal and extend the line, and a complex of thirteen skyscrapers, including three super-tall buildings. The development will be mixed-use, accommodating residences and hotel and office space. Major buildings in the complex represent the visions of two international "starchitects," Renzo Piano and Cesar Pelli. Two of the super-tall skyscrapers, currently called Renzo Piano 1 and 2, will be 101 stories each and will be situated within a five-tower complex. Cesar Pelli's Transbay Transit Center and Tower will be approximately the same height. That building alone will contain 1.6 million square feet of usable space. The tallest buildings in the Transbay complex will be 330 feet taller than the city's iconic Transamerica Pyramid.

The design group for the Transbay Transit Center, Pelli Clarke Pelli, also designed the International Financial Center in Hong Kong, and before that the Petronas Towers. The Pelli Clarke Pelli web site describes its transit center complex as "designed to be graceful, luminous, welcoming and safe," adding that its design includes a "robust concrete-and-steel system, which is engineered for performance in the event of severe earthquakes." What critics call the "Manhattanization" of San Francisco has been under way for decades, and the buildings in the Transbay complex are only some of the skyscrapers that have recently been built or that are planned for the city. The intention seems to be to overcome the small geographic size of San Francisco by building vertically with a vengeance.

What about earthquake and fire hazards in a city that was nearly destroyed by both in 1906? Over the decades, earthquake engineering advances have been substantial, and many of San Francisco's new buildings, those under construction, and those that are planned represent the state of the art in earthquake-resistant design. That is the good news. But there is potential bad news to contemplate as well, for several reasons. First, San Francisco is at risk from major earthquakes originating both on the San Andreas Fault and on the Hayward Fault in the East Bay. Ground shaking intensities and peak ground accelerations for many projected earthquake scenarios on those faults will be high in San Francisco. The area where the Transbay Development is located is especially vulnerable to a Hayward Fault event with an epicenter near Oakland. Second, although the public may not realize it, earthquake-resistant design codes promise one outcome, and one outcome only: that buildings designed appropriately and built as designed will not collapse under expected earthquake loads. Period. The codes do not guarantee that a building will not experience major damage, damage to its nonstructural elements, such as windows and internal partitions, or to its contents. Moreover, the codes are entirely silent on the question of whether well-designed and -constructed buildings will be able to *function* following a major earthquake. Put another way, codes are intended to ensure that buildings will not fall down—not that they will be operational after an earthquake strikes.

Third, skyscrapers like those that will compose the planned Transbay Development and like the hundreds of other tall buildings in San Francisco depend very significantly on the performance of the lifeline systems that serve them, particularly electricity and water systems. Yet those systems are very vulnerable to large earthquakes. One recent report observed that the utility infrastructure of the Bay Area is "extremely susceptible to damage from a major Hayward Fault earthquake as the fault crosses every east-west connection that the Bay Area depends upon for water, electric, gas, and transportation" (Grossi and Zoback 2010: 15). What would happen if a large earthquake were to occur during normal business hours, and what if the earthquake were followed by large-scale power and water outages? This is not farfetched; such outages occurred in San Francisco when the Loma Prieta earthquake struck in 1989. What if fires began to break out in tall buildings in San Francisco, and what if sprinkler systems suffered earthquake damage in some of those buildings, allowing the fires to spread? What if hundreds of people were trapped in elevators because of power outages, and what if residents of ultra-high-rise condominiums, apartments, office buildings, and hotels were stranded in those structures without water? San Francisco's beautiful new skyscrapers contain huge amounts of glass. What if some proportion of that glass were to be smashed and sent kiting downward by the forces of a major earthquake? What might happen to the people on the ground?

There are other equally serious problems. In addition to the new ultratall buildings, San Francisco contains many other structures that were not built to current codes, including many old collapse-hazard buildings. Those structures would become death traps in a major earthquake, and ruptured gas lines would ignite numerous fires.

San Francisco residents would come to one another's aid in the event of a major earthquake, but clearly the San Francisco Fire Department and other emergency services agencies would have their hands full trying to respond to such an event. Their sworn duty to save lives would make search and rescue, the provision of emergency medical care, and fire suppression top priorities. The San Francisco Fire Department is a highly professionalized and capable organization, but what if some firefighters were lost in the earthquake or unable to report for duty in a timely way? Equally important for this discussion, how would a firefighting and rescue force that has not grown significantly in past years be able to respond to so many problems at once—including problems that could develop in the city's ever-growing inventory of buildings that soar skyward for many dozens of stories?

Significant fires in super-tall buildings are difficult to fight, even without an earthquake to complicate things. The Burj Khalifa complex experienced two fires while it was still under construction, one of which was a major blaze that burned for over ten hours. Fires in tall buildings place almost superhuman demands on firefighters, who are typically unable to use elevators and must therefore climb, loaded down with gear and air cylinders, to where the fire is located. To give just one example, a fire that broke out in the First Interstate Bank Building (now the Aon Center) in Los Angeles in May 1988 started on the twelfth floor of that sixty-two-story steel-frame structure and burned the four floors above before it was extinguished. Fully one half of all on-duty members of the Los Angeles Fire Department were needed to fight that one fire. The firefighters faced extremely dangerous conditions, including heavy smoke on various floors and falling glass and debris outside the building, and the logistical challenges of fighting the fire were described as "massive" (U.S. Fire Administration 1988). This for a fire that was not high in the building, and in a structure that was occupied by only about fifty people when the fire broke out. Compare that incident with the immensely daunting challenges firefighters faced in the World Trade Center during the September 11 terrorist attacks—such as the need to climb up dozens of stories loaded down with equipment, assist with emergency evacuations, and contend with counterflow, or people evacuating down the stairs as firefighters were going up. This is the kind of scenario emergency workers would face in earthquake-induced fires in fully occupied high-rise buildings.

Fire, police, and other emergency services agencies in San Francisco have mutual aid agreements that enable them to provide assistance to one another in the event of a major emergency. But what about an emergency that simultaneously affects both San Francisco and neighboring jurisdictions, including those across the bay, as would happen in any severe Hayward Fault earthquake? How much help would actually be available, and how soon? And the possibility of major earthquake damage, deaths, injuries, and fires in San Francisco raises another interesting issue with respect to mutual aid. The Oakland Hills firestorm of 1991 in the East Bay was one of the most devastating urban conflagrations in American history. One of the problems that was identified in the response to the firestorm was that converging fire agencies from other jurisdictions often could not connect their hoses to fire hydrants, because hydrants and hose connections were not standardized. California subsequently passed a law requiring such standardization, meaning that now when one jurisdiction's fire department aids another, there won't be compatibility problems. However, one city got itself exempted from the law. That city is San Francisco. In what was billed in the media as a sound cost-saving strategy, the city has provided adapters to fire departments in some Bay Area cities, and in the event of a major fire requiring mutual aid, it plans to hand them out to incoming firefighters who don't have them. Whether this will work or not in an actual emergency is anyone's guess. What does seem certain is that San Francisco emergency workers, and especially its firefighters, will have to be very lucky to avoid unnecessary loss of life in the next big earthquake. To paraphrase Henry Petroski, the gorgeous new skyline of San Francisco is a hypothesis waiting for a test that will be undertaken at some future time—or perhaps already has, after this writing.

Another problem is that massively tall structures make attractive terrorist targets. In the United States, most estimates rank New York City as having the highest terrorism risk, followed by Chicago, Washington, D.C., San Francisco, and Los Angeles (Willis et al. 2005). Population size and density are important parameters for determining terrorism risk, but other factors clearly include the presence of large iconic structures, such as the Empire State Building and the buildings under construction at Ground Zero in New York, the Willis Tower (formerly the Sears Tower) in Chicago, and the Transamerica Pyramid and now many more tall buildings in San Francisco. The ability to obtain insurance on such properties is one indicator of how markets socially construct risk. It was easy to insure buildings against terrorism prior to September 11, 2001, but it became very difficult after the 9/11 terrorist attacks, and the United States and many other countries had to pass legislation in order to make such insurance available and affordable.[2] Yet even now in the United States, with more terrorism insurance available and premiums dropping, one 2010 report noted that "capacity is restricted in Chicago, New York City, and San Francisco. Some corporate insurance policyholders in high-risk areas still have difficulty obtaining coverage with sufficient limits" (President's Working Group on Financial Markets 2010: 17).

Of course insurance only provides compensation for terrorism losses after the fact. Another way to protect iconic buildings is to prevent attacks, or prevent them from achieving their objectives. The world learned in 2011 that with those goals in mind, the United Arab Emirates is financing and housing in Abu Dhabi a mercenary force, operated by a company owned by former Blackwater chairman Eric Prince, to increase regional capability to (among other things) protect the Burj Khalifa from terrorists (*New York Times*, May 15, 2011). Sociologist Charles Perrow, whose work will be discussed in subsequent chapters, argues that one major way to discourage terrorist attacks is to "shrink targets" (Perrow 2007), so that even if terrorist acts do succeed, terrorism will not produce its desired catastrophic effects. Instead, what is actually happening is that many cities around the world seem bent on providing even more tempting and target-rich environments for terrorists.

Difficult to finance, design, build, make profitable, insure, maintain, and protect, ultra-tall buildings continue to proliferate worldwide because of what they symbolize: money, power, prestige, influence, and in cases like the new One World Trade Center, pure defiance in the face of terrorism.[3] Such structures represent an unerring faith in progress as socially constructed within the global system. Many super-tall buildings are beautiful and awe inspiring, but an alternative framing is that they reflect societal arrogance and the desire to triumph symbolically over the laws of gravity and other laws of nature. However, if recent years have taught us anything, it is that it can be highly risky to bet against nature.

TO ENGINEER IS HUMAN, PART 2:

FINANCIAL ENGINEERING AND THE ALCHEMY OF RISK

One online dictionary presents the following definition of the concept of alchemy:

1. a form of chemistry and speculative philosophy practiced in the Middle Ages and the renaissance and concerned principally with discovering methods for transmuting baser metals into gold and with finding a universal solvent and

an elixir of life. 2. any magical power or process of transmuting a common substance, usually of little value, into a substance of great value.

Looking at the beliefs and cultural practices of the financial sector in the period leading up to the financial collapse of 2008, it is difficult not to conclude that philosophical speculation and belief in magic were alive and well on Wall Street and in government, at least for a time. I have already mentioned the subprime mortgage bubble, but in this chapter we focus on the social constructions that fueled the bubble, many of which received support from the relatively new field of financial engineering, as embodied in "quant culture." Here again, trust in technologies and tools associated with the quantification of risk, and also in the people who were able to employ them, tells part of the story of why so many individuals, organizations, and institutions came to share the belief that it was possible to transform large amounts of highly problematic material—various genera of subprime mortgages and the exotic instruments that theoretically made it possible to rearrange risk—into the gold of massive profits for investors and traders.

The conceptual foundations of financial engineering are sound. Indeed, if quantitative analytics did not exist within the financial sector, markets would be unable to function. Contemporary societies need financial engineering just as much as they need civil, structural, and computer engineering, and there is no question that much can be learned through the quantitative analysis of the behavior of markets, equities, and securities over time and within sectors of the economy. "Quants" rightly inhabit a respected niche within the financial services sector, and used appropriately, financial engineering is a powerful risk management tool.

At the same time, boundless faith in the power of financial engineering was one of the factors that led the United States and the world to the brink of financial catastrophe. The definitive history of the financial crash of 2008 has yet to be written, but enough has been published already that it is possible to indicate in broad outline how so many were so wrong about so much, and to the detriment of so many others.

The crash has many cultural roots, and it would be a major mistake to oversimplify its causes. However, following the constructivist analytic framework laid out at the beginning of this chapter, we start with the cultural mind-set that animated the financial sector in the last two decades or so. One important social construction or frame that shaped ideas and behavior has to do with the concept of the "New Economy." This über-frame drove the dot-com bubble of the 1990s and maintained its influence even after that bubble burst. The guiding frame of the New Economy, which has been written about extensively, boils down to a few axioms: new economic formations have emerged that are based on information and knowledge, not on manufacturing and production; traditional ways of valuing stocks, such as assessing their price-to-earnings ratios, are therefore outmoded because the New Economy operates according to rules that differ from those of the Old Economy; and the provision of services—including a wide array of financial services—is now the most important driver of the economy. This last-mentioned piece of the New Economy frame both reflected and reinforced the ongoing large-scale expansion of the nation's financial services sector. Popular books like *Dow 36,000* (Glassman and Hassett, 1999) promoted the idea that because the New Economy was so fundamentally different from what came before, stocks were actually undervalued by many orders of magnitude.

Science and engineering are always on a restless hunt for the new and innovative, and financial engineering was no exception. After the bursting of the subprime mortgage market of the 1990s and of the dot-com bubble, money had to go somewhere. In tandem with increased demands, novel and ever more specialized and esoteric financial products were developed and made available to fuel the market: collateralized debt obligations, synthetic collateralized debt obligations, credit default swaps, BISTRO (Broad Index Secured Trust Offering, a synthetic swap first developed in 1997 by J. P. Morgan), and other products for which the market was hungry. Such instruments were phenomenally well suited to the residential mortgage bubble that began to expand as the dot-com bubble deflated, and indeed many were created specifically to smooth the operation of the subprime mortgage market.

Let's home in on the cultural force that confidence in new financial instruments and financial engineering exerted within the economic field, or in other words, how the doxa of the financial sector so pervaded the thinking of corporate actors that shrewd institutions and business leaders felt compelled to go all in on enormously risky ventures.

The thinking that drove the subprime mortgage bubble flew in the face of the long-standing maxim that trees do not grow to the sky; risks were created and allowed to balloon on the assumption that housing prices would always go up, along with the assumption that the potential losses that were being produced across vast portfolios would never occur, even though—and this is key—those risks were staggeringly massive and highly correlated with one another. This socially constructed reality ignored the fact that there had already been a subprime mortgage boom in the 1990s that went bust, as all bubbles inevitably do, and it also "forgot" not only about the recent dot-com crash but also about the busts that followed past bubbles, such the hard landing that put an end to the Japanese real estate boom of the 1980s. Animating the boom was the social construction that enormous correlated risks that were packaged and renamed would inevitably turn into enormous moneymaking opportunities for participants in a boom that would never end—in short, that baser metals could be turned into gold.

The sociological field of collective behavior focuses on the analysis of emergent social behavior, including crazes, booms, and bubbles. Social-structural conditions enable the emergence of these forms of collective behavior, but culture and ideas are also important. Like other types of collective behavior, crazes, booms, and bubbles are energized by shared beliefs—social constructions—that encourage participation. In essence, like other forms of collective behavior, these waves of acquisition are animated by norms that emerge in specific situations. As these forms of collective behavior gather steam, they become very compelling, strongly influencing nonparticipants to join in or risk losing out, both financially and reputationally. This dynamic was clearly present in the lead-up to the collapse of the subprime bubble. In *All the Devils Are Here* (2011), Bethany McLean and Joe Nocera explain in detail how one by one, otherwise stable and even conservative financial institutions were drawn into the boom mentality and how they became voracious consumers of ever more speculative financial products. In the authors' telling, a key turning point that was followed by an increase in frenzied speculation was when the government-sponsored entities (GSEs) Fannie Mae and Freddie Mac entered the subprime mortgage market. By their actions, the GSEs signaled that they supported the frame that constructed enormous investment in subprimes as legitimate and necessary business activity. What could be more solid than the endorsement of such practices by the GSEs? And so the belief grew among more cautious entities that investment banks, hedge funds, and other entities had found the key to taming risk through the wholesale application of financial engineering.

Another idea that fueled the subprime boom, which was articulated strongly by the federal government regardless of which party was in power, was the notion that home ownership is an important American value deserving of support across government and the financial services sector alike. A critical element in this narrative was that owning a home was part of the American Dream, even for those who were only marginally able to afford one, including particularly members of minority groups who had previously encountered structural barriers to ownership. This government-supported view meshed seamlessly with the socially constructed reality that held sway over Wall Street in the first years of the new millennium, including the idea that financial engineering had succeeded in managing risk. As the bubble expanded, key institutions transgressed basic tenets of borrowing and lending, such as the idea that the size of a loan should be proportional to the recipient's ability to pay that loan back. However, like the rules of the New Economy, the new norms that drove the subprime frenzy said otherwise.

Here we find yet another example of a principle presented earlier: situations that are defined as real are real in their consequences, but that does not mean that empirical reality does not exist. Like all booms, the subprime craze greatly increased the fortunes of many investors, but like all booms it had to end. Taking on enormous volumes of strongly correlated high risks, dividing them into tranches, and engineering new ways to sell or hedge them, from the so-called super-senior to the mezzanine tranche (which in fact was the subbasement), did not make those socially produced risks anything other than what they were, as the world found out to its utter dismay in 2007 and 2008. People who cannot afford their mortgages will default on their mortgages, and when financial entities worldwide went all in on selling and securitizing those mortgages, that reality did not change. Participants in the boom only believed that it did—or hoped that they could chalk up enormous profits before the party ended. Similarly, during the craze, numerous citizens of Iceland, a country of about 300,000 people whose economy is historically based on fishing and farming, did not suddenly turn into brilliant bankers. But those citizens believed they had and acted on the basis of that socially constructed reality, and now the country is bankrupt. The same is essentially the case for Ireland, which also went bust when the boom ended.

Publications on the crash are full of stories of individuals who monitored what was happening during the boom and figured out for themselves that catastrophe was on the way. For example, in *The Big Short* (2010), Michael Lewis profiles several investors who bet against the dominant Wall Street consensus. In Lewis's account, these individuals seem to have three things in common. First, they were skeptical of the zeitgeist that held that people could indefinitely use their homes as ATMs and that the bubble would expand indefinitely. Second, they were obsessed with numbers, with the most minute details of the financial instruments and transactions that made the bubble possible, and with the sheer scale at which risk buildup was occurring. Third, and tellingly, they did their own independent research on the behavior of investors and markets, and what they found astonished them—although sociologically speaking it probably shouldn't have. Through conversations with individuals whose activities were fueling the bubble and through attending various meetings around the country at which participants gave and received advice, shorters found that a substantial majority of bubble investors literally had no idea how the mortgage market functioned and how much risk was being created. Participants either did not understand the intricacies of the deals they were making, or thought that they were cleverly spreading risk, or completely overlooked and even denied that massive and correlated risks were a problem. Like people in Iceland, those who took part in the craze evidently believed that they had all suddenly become financial geniuses and tamers of risk. From the perspectives of social constructionism and collective behavior, that is not particularly surprising. Culture provides ways of seeing and ways of not seeing.

BLINDED BY BELIEFS: IGNORING "THE WORST"

The Black Swan by Nassim Taleb (2007) has received a great deal of attention because the core of its argument is so compelling: grounding our expectations in experience, we completely overlook the possibility of statistical "outliers" or rare events that have large impacts. Then, if such events do actually occur, we engage in retrospective interpretation to show that we knew all along that they could happen. Taleb describes the terrorist attacks of 9/11 and the 2004 Indian Ocean earthquake and tsunami as Black Swan events. The book is refreshing in many ways, but the processes it describes had already been thoroughly mined by risk researchers. For example, in the previous chapter I discussed cognitive heuristics, such as myopia and the optimistic bias, which frame individual, social, and cultural perspectives on the world. There is also an extensive literature on issues associated with perceptions regarding low-probability/high-consequence events. That literature focuses, for example, on why such events are so difficult to contemplate, why there is a tendency to discount their likelihood, and why, as a consequence, people tend not to plan for them.

The difficulty people have in thinking about and dealing with Black Swans, also called "fat tail" events, stems from the simple and entirely understandable fact that perceptions, frames, and social constructions of the world are strongly shaped by past experience. This is as true for cultures, institutions, and organizations as it is for individuals, and if it were not the case, the human race probably would never have survived. Many economists and decision scientists still cling to the rational actor paradigm of decision making, but the force of that conceptual frame is diminishing because there is simply too much evidence that contradicts it, based on research on institutions, naturalistic or real-world decision making, and dual-processing theories of perception and decision making. Past experiences are both embedded in and shapers of socially constructed views on risk, the manner in which risks are framed, and the mental models that are employed to understand and explain risk, and it is these elements of culture that drive both thought and action with respect to risk.

In the previous chapter we observed that research on perception and decision making continually discovers new heuristics, and here I suggest yet another cognitive frame that influences decision making at all levels: the continuity heuristic. The continuity heuristic refers to the tendency of people, organizations, and institutions to believe and act as if the future will resemble the past—or better put, that the future will resemble the past as socially constructed and framed. This is not to say that people are unaware that social change is occurring, because clearly they are. They are even capable of constructing realities, like the New Economy, which emphasize discontinuity. Rather, the continuity heuristic involves thinking about future events as composed of elements that are already familiar, as well as the belief that future events can be prepared for and responded to in tried-and-true ways based on past experience. For example, one old saying is that the military prepares itself well to fight the previous war, and disaster researchers have also found that communities organize their future planning around their last significant disaster. In other words, even though responding to future challenges involves foresight, people and institutions operate on the basis of hindsight and on the idea that future events will more or less resemble those that have occurred in the past. They are often correct, but they are sometimes wildly off base.

Along these same lines, future risks, including catastrophic ones, are always in the process of being created, but people and institutions are in many respects incapable of thinking about future risks, except in ways that reflect their past experience. This is particularly true with respect to worst cases. If we recall earlier discussions on the anchoring heuristic, people anchor on past experiences, extrapolate from those experiences, and view worst cases as similar to those experiences, only more so. Or they devise solutions for future crises to address the socially constructed causes of past ones and then conclude that future risks have been managed. After the Black Monday stock market crash of October 1987, for example, trading "circuit breakers" were instituted to prevent runaway programmed selling, which was identified as a key cause of that crash. That solved one problem but did nothing to address the risks that caused the massive crash of 2008.

The continuity heuristic may blind us to Black Swans, but it serves some parties well. For example, the notion that the future will be similar to the past, only distinguished perhaps by the appearance of new technological miracles, is an idea that is exploited aggressively by the climate-change denial industry and its political adherents. The scientific consensus that climate change is occurring and that human activity is a major contributor to that change, often captured in the expression "stationarity is dead," has been widely acknowledged by scientists and policy makers. Nonetheless, the denial industry wins many policy battles, largely on the basis of a discursive strategy that mixes a heavy dose of the continuity heuristic with an equally large helping of conspiracy theory (witch hunt, anyone?), then adding large portions of religion and traces of the idea that technology, in the form of nuclear power and geoengineering, will serve up ready solutions to any climate-induced problems that might arise. In this case, the continuity heuristic does yeoman's duty in frames that are intentionally constructed to eclipse a potentially catastrophic global threat.

As the climate-change example shows, the continuity heuristic often leads to misestimation of other risks. One of the themes throughout this volume is that risk is the outcome of social, institutional, and organizational forces that are continually in flux. Demographic forces such as migration matter, as do global economic trends, national policies, local politics, population vulnerabilities, and organizational behavior. Although they are culturally constructed and framed in a variety of ways, and for a variety of purposes, risks do exist "out there," and even as some threats decline, others emerge or expand. One thing that the study of risk makes clear is that while past data provide useful guidance in some risk arenas, such as the health risks associated with smoking, they can be badly misleading in others, such as fat-tail events. Exhibit A in this argument is Japan's 9.0 earthquake and deadly tsunami in 2011, which led to not one but multiple partial core meltdowns at the Fukushima nuclear facility—a scenario even disaster movie producers would have a hard time thinking up.

Recent scholarship sheds light on the challenges inherent in constructing appropriate visions of worst-case events. In *Never Saw It*

Coming: Cultural Challenges to Envisioning the Worst (2008) Karen Cerulo brings together a large body of research to support the notion that human beings and social groups find it extremely difficult to envision worse cases, and that this difficulty is cultural as well as cognitive in nature. Cerulo argues that individuals, organizations, and groups show a marked tendency toward what she terms "positive asymmetry," meaning, in simple terms, that they are cognitively and culturally much more comfortable with upside thinking than with downside thinking. Focusing on organizations, for example, she locates blindness to worst cases in cultural practices and institutional logics that lull members into ignoring the potential for catastrophic failures. Perhaps more important, however, she highlights the practices societies, institutions, and organizations employ both with worst cases and with those who raise questions about worst cases. She refers to these practices as eclipsing, clouding, and recasting practices. Ways of rendering the worst invisible include banishment; shunning; shadowing, or emphasizing high points so low points become less visible; and rhetorical recasting, a practice in which negative events are reinterpreted in a positive light. But even more tellingly for our purposes, Cerulo makes the case that it is elites that have the ultimate say in what constitutes the worst, in that they have the power to define the parameters of which risks warrant consideration and which should be discounted. Because those who hold power are generally loath to give it up and are looking for ways to expand it, it is unsurprising when elites' ideas about risks align with their own interests.

Lee Clarke points to similar limitations in the ability to envision the worst, including other collective cognitive habits that blind us. Most relevant to the current discussion is the socialized and trained capacity of organizations to think primarily in probabilistic rather than "possibilistic" terms. While probabilistic thinking focuses on the socially constructed likelihood of disaster, possibilistic reasoning is concerned with the impacts that could occur as a consequence of disaster events and the use of risky technologies, even if those impacts are unlikely (Clarke 2006a, 2008). In other words, it focuses on the worst that could happen, not solely on what is viewed as most likely to happen. Clarke argues, for example, that the inability to think in possibilistic terms was behind the federal government's flat-footed response to Hurricane Katrina (Clarke 2006b). As Katrina approached, government officials felt quite confident that everything that could be done to prepare for a major hurricane was being done; the possibility that Katrina might be not just a major hurricane but a near worst case was not considered by those in charge, despite the fact that a Category 3 event had been identified as potentially catastrophic by many scientists, journalists, and other observers.

The use of probabilities in attempting to forecast potential disaster impacts is so well institutionalized that it goes largely unquestioned. Following the 2011 Japan disasters, for example, the *New York Times* ran a front-page article whose basic theme was that Japan did not foresee the catastrophe because it was using "old science" in its risk management strategies (Onishi and Glanz 2011). The old science referred to in the article was how the authors and sources characterized Japan's tendency to base its disaster mitigation and preparedness measures on scenarios, or characterizations of what would happen in a particular earthquake disaster, in which a specific magnitude and epicenter and other details were specified. The article quoted various experts who described scenario-based planning as outdated and argued for the superiority of probabilistic risk analysis (PRA), which would have simultaneously taken into account multiple likely earthquake events and their impacts. The general message of the article was that probabilistic analyses would have enabled disaster planners to better envision the massive March 11 earthquake and the catastrophic tsunami that followed.

The claims made in the article were erroneous for a variety of reasons. Disaster risk analysis in Japan does employ probabilistic methods in addition to scenario-based ones; further, scenarios based on single events can be very useful for planning purposes, provided they are the appropriate ones. Indeed, scenarios may be especially well suited to envisioning worst-case impacts. In the United States, disaster scenarios are used extensively for public education, training and exercises, disaster loss estimation, and preparedness planning. Examples of such scenarios include the earthquake scenario used in the Great California ShakeOut of 2009, California's ARKStorm scenario and disaster exercise of 2011, impact and loss projections for the San Francisco Bay Area in the event of a repeat of the 1906 earthquake, and the "Hurricane Pam" disaster exercise conducted in Louisiana a year before Hurricane Katrina. But more important, a key point the article missed is that probabilistic approaches for analyzing the likelihood and impacts of earthquake and tsunami events in Japan would have resulted in the complete discounting of the events that did happen in 2011, because such events would have been considered a highly unlikely statistical outlier.

In fact there had already been at least one massive earthquake-tsunami sequence in that very same area during recorded history. The 869 Jogan Sanriku earthquake, estimated at a magnitude of 8.6, caused an enormous tsunami that among other things spread inland onto the Sendai Plain for two and a half miles. Probabilistic risk analyses would have ignored a repeat of that event because they tend to emphasize what would occur in a "maximum probable" or "maximum credible" event, and not in a worst case. Nor would standard analyses even have considered the chain of events that the earthquake triggered. In other words, probabilistic risk analysis is just what its name implies: it is probabilistic in its emphasis, not possibilistic. And here again, because what is constructed as probable is framed in terms of what has occurred relatively frequently in the past—in terms of fault locations, earthquake occurrences and magnitudes, and impacts on structures, lifelines, and their components—I cannot conceive of any probabilistic risk analysis and loss estimation activities that would have centered on a 9.0 earthquake event off northern Honshu island and its subsequent impacts. In essence, PRA is a form of "backcasting" that is based on the continuity heuristic, that explains future disaster impacts on the basis of what is known about past impacts, and that directs attention away from worst cases. Even though PRA techniques are spectacularly bad at anticipating Black Swans, belief in PRA is so firmly rooted in the culture of entities that manage risk that its methodologies are entirely unquestioned (Tierney 2010).

Cultural barriers against envisioning the worst can be so powerful that they can even prevent organizations from taking into account and incorporating into their risk and consequence calculations things that have already happened. For example, in her brilliant book *Whole World on Fire: Organizations, Knowledge, and Nuclear Weapons Devastation*

(2004), Lynn Eden describes in great detail why over decades the nuclear war plans of the U.S. military establishment only took into account the blast effects of nuclear devices, while overlooking the massive losses that would result from the large-scale fires that nuclear explosions would generate. How could such a systemic oversight occur, given that the military had dropped nuclear bombs on Hiroshima and Nagasaki and knew that those detonations had resulted in massive firestorms? How was it possible to exclude from impact analyses fire damage resulting from bombs, when during World War II the world had already witnessed the consequences of incendiary warfare in cities like Dresden and Tokyo? How did it happen that fire-related impacts continued to be ignored by war planners for decades, even though those impacts were no more difficult to model and assess than blast damage? What were the roots of this form of risk gerrymandering?

Eden argues that institutional blindness to the possibility of nuclear conflagrations can be traced to two sources, which she terms "knowledge-laden organizational routines" and "organizational frames"—the latter used in the same sense as it is in this chapter. Knowledge-laden routines consist of sets of activities, undertaken by specialists and experts, that consist of "solutions to problems that those in organizations have decided to solve" (Eden 2004: 3); while organizational frames are the problem-solving strategies that organizations employ, which include "how problems are chosen and represented, how strategies are developed to solve them, and how constraints and requirements are placed on possible solutions" (3).

One of Eden's most important contributions to the study of risk is the recognition that routines and frames are built up over time, constituting the doxa or stock of knowledge which guides routines within fields, and that once established, routines and frames become part of the taken-for-granted reality of those fields. Modeling blast effects resulting from nuclear detonations was emphasized to the exclusion of fire effects because that type of modeling was part of a constellation of well-established activities that included aircraft design, bomb making, target selection, and other organizational routines. Based on data from earlier conflicts like World War II, the interest in blast effects had already been well established within the military prior to the development of nuclear weapons. A focus on blast impacts was also consistent with the skill sets of many analysts who specialized in the dynamic loading of structures; these were civil engineers as opposed to fire protection engineers. It was also consistent with military doctrine that stressed the targeted bombing of enemy facilities, as opposed to widespread bombing that would kill large numbers of civilians. Further, in line with my earlier argument that frames represent the cultural embodiment of institutional interests, overlooking the massive destruction that nuclear firestorms would create and concentrating on blast effects meant that more bombs would need to be produced in order to prevail in a nuclear exchange. Simply put, the reality of nuclear war was socially constructed in ways that made it easy and even normative to exclude the risks posed by massively deadly fires induced by nuclear bombs.

But the knowledge-laden routines of the nuclear war establishment went even further, as Eden stunningly observes:

[T]hrough omission, abstraction, classification, disembodiment, a focus on physical forces, specialized vocabularies, and whole systems of knowledge, nuclear war planners engage in a social construction of the asocial. . . . As if to anticipate the effect for which they plan—the utter effacement of human society—the environment they consider is abstracted from and devoid of the buzz and hum of human activity. The world of nuclear weapons damage is generally an unpeopled one of physical objects—structures, installations, and equipment. (290)

Just as our medieval forebears constructed a world in which witches and demons intervened for evil purposes in the lives of human beings, enabled by embedded institutional routines such as the practices of the Inquisition, contemporary war planners constructed a world of which human beings were not a part, even as they devised weapons to incinerate them. Such is the power of socially constructed and institutionally reinforced reality.

A DIFFERENT FRAME

This chapter and the previous one have pointed out that most research on risk perception and on the cultural dimensions of risk tends to focus

on the public side of the topic: why the public misperceives risk and wor-
ries about the wrong things; how factors such as social class, race, and
gender influence the perception of risk; what factors are involved in the
social amplification of risk, and so on. These are important subjects,
and research in these areas has yielded significant insights. However, my
position is that perceptions and culture are important in other ways, in
that cultural frames such as those involving nature, technology, growth,
and progress, along with the perceptions, beliefs, and cultural practices
associated with those frames, are strongly implicated in the social production of risk. Social constructions that justify JARring activities; culturally supported hubristic efforts to continually push the envelope of
safety; collective behavior processes that create the social climate that
fuels booms and crazes; and other beliefs and practices that place cognitive limits on people and institutions so that they are blind to worst cases
are all causal factors in the creation and growth of risk.

Risk-related frames, constructions, and practices do not suddenly
spring from nowhere. As we have seen here, they are often generated
and embraced by social actors that stand to gain from those particular
framings as opposed to others, and at other times they prevail in more
taken-for-granted ways through cultural and institutional inertia or
gradual changes in institutional and organizational routines. Frames and
social constructions are only part of the picture, however. Culture doesn't
create risk—social entities do. The buildup of risk is the result of sins of
commission and sins of omission on the part of powerful and influential
social actors. It is a consequence of well-established knowledge-related
practices such as those discussed by Eden, but it is also the product of
intentional organizational efforts to cut corners in pursuit of profit, and
sometimes of out-and-out criminal activity. The magnitude and distribution of risks result from processes that are social in nature and that
operate on local and global scales. In the next two chapters, we look in
more detail at the parties and processes that produce risk.

CHAPTER 5

Organizations, Institutions, and
the Production of Risk

UNTIL NOW, WE HAVE BEEN MAINLY CONCERNED with the perception of risk and with the cultural factors that encourage the expansion of risky technologies and practices. In this chapter, the discussion turns to the social-structural, organizational, and institutional forces that result in an increase in risk. We tend to think of risks and disasters as somehow inherent in the natural order of things: some hazardous substances are simply more dangerous than others, and some communities and regions are vulnerable to natural disasters by virtue of their location in harm's way. In doing so, we lose sight of the extent to which organizational and institutional decisions and practices are implicated in the occurrence of disasters. Many coastal communities in the United States are subject to hurricane threats, but New Orleans was uniquely vulnerable to a large hurricane, mainly as the result of decisions made and actions undertaken by a variety of entities in the New Orleans area. Levee boards and the U.S. Army Corps of Engineers were responsible for the weak condition of many levees. Oil companies that carried out operations in the Gulf played a key role in wetlands depletion, which left New Orleans with fewer natural hurricane protections. Boosters of the Mississippi River Gulf Outlet failed to consider the fact that the ship channel on which they had pinned so many hopes might also serve as a "hurricane highway," delivering storm surges into vulnerable areas of the city. In July 2004, officials from the Federal Emergency Management Agency, Louisiana's emergency management agency, and other organizations took part in the scenario-based "Hurricane Pam" exercise, which was designed to boost preparedness for a major hurricane that could strike New Orleans. After the exercise, an action plan was developed to enhance preparations, but the plan was never implemented, and a second major preparedness exercise scheduled for 2005 was cancelled. Local, state, and federal government agencies were ill prepared to respond to a major hurricane, and when they had to mobilize, their efforts were ineffective and even counterproductive. In different ways, these and other organizational entities contributed to the buildup of risk that unfolded into catastrophe when Katrina struck.

Katrina was of course not unique in this respect. Studies of disasters of all kinds locate their origins in actions that organizations and groups of organizations have either taken or failed to take. The discussions in this chapter are again meant to show the ways in which the origins of risk, harm, and loss are primarily social, not natural or technological. Driven by their own interests and bolstered by the kinds of cultural assumptions discussed in the previous chapter, powerful organizational and institutional actors often drift into unsafe practices, especially when there are no countervailing forces preventing them from doing so. As subsequent discussions will show, safety is often given a lower priority than other goals that social actors value, and risks tend to expand as a consequence of the ways in which those actors pursue those goals. The potential for disaster also increases in organizational environments in which checks on risky practices are weak or transparency and account-ability are lacking. Of course, this is not the same as saying that societal actors consciously decide that they will permit disasters to occur, or that they act in total disregard of safety. Rather, in the course of pursuing other priorities, in particular productivity, profits, efficiency, and freedom from regulation, they fail to (or are unable to) consider ways in which those competing priorities may compromise safety.

RISK IN ORGANIZATIONS AND ORGANIZATIONAL FIELDS

Organizational risk taking comes in a variety of forms. Business owners may pursue strategies that put their businesses at risk from failure, for example by expanding too rapidly or by making injudicious investments. However, our concern here is not with these forms of organizational conduct, which generally have negative consequences only for the orga-nizations in question. Rather, our focus is on the kinds of organizational actors that can create large-scale, severe risks that when actualized, affect entire communities or societies in disastrous ways. Examples include entities that operate facilities which process or store large amounts of hazardous substances, manage risky technologies, operate and maintain critical infrastructural systems, develop and enforce disaster risk-reduction efforts, and are charged with taking steps to protect employees and the general public from harm. Like all organizations, these kinds of organizations have multiple goals. And like all organizations, they do not possess infinite resources, which means that key decisions always involve trade-offs among different goals and strategies. Their performance is also influenced by the environments in which they operate—the other entities with which they interact and exchange resources on a routine basis—as well as by information signaling the preferences of their leaders and others whose directives govern their activities.

Risks can thus be thought of as generated and managed through processes that involve decisions among competing goals, influences from broader organizational networks or fields of interaction, and intraorganizational interactions and signals. As we have seen, organizational culture matters. However, culture, organizational structure, and organizational processes are interactive and mutually constitutive, and the manner in which organizations structure their activities can act as an independent force that influences levels of risk. Put another way, some types of organizational arrangements and practices seem to attract risk. The sections that follow discuss organizational and institutional conditions that play a role in the expansion of risk, and I provide examples of when these conditions have contributed to the occurrence of disasters.

SIZE, CONCENTRATIONS, AND RISK BUILDUP
Bigger Targets: Systems and People

We are concerned about some places and some hazards more than others, and generally this is because of the large vulnerabilities they represent. Sociologist and über-risk expert Charles Perrow has written extensively on the ramifications of concentration, a condition that is more characteristic of contemporary globalized societies than of earlier times. In *The Next Catastrophe* (2007), he focuses on three different types of concentrations that represent an increased potential for disasters: concentrations of hazardous activities and facilities (what he terms "concentrations of energy"), those of populations, and those of political and economic power. Concentrating in a single location large quantities of dangerous substances, processes, and industrial facilities essentially guarantees that when things go wrong, they will do so on a large scale; yet such concentrations are becoming more common, owing to growth in the size of industrial entities and to efforts to increase profits through economies of scale. The significance for risk levels can probably be best seen in the March 2011 Fukushima Daiichi disaster. Rather than consisting of one or two nuclear reactors, the Fukushima Daiichi plant had six; nearby Fukushima Daini, which was part of the same facility, contained four reactors. Because of this high degree of concentration, the Fukushima nuclear complex represented a substantial threat to workers and the public if a major accident were to occur. That threat was realized when the 2011 earthquake and tsunami caused partial core meltdowns in three reactors. A nuclear incident on the scale of the Fukushima disaster was only possible because Tokyo Power (TEPCO) had decided at an earlier time to load up a particular piece of oceanside real estate in a highly seismic area with large-scale nuclear power generation capabilities.

These kinds of physical concentrations are risky in several ways. Large size almost always means increased complexity, and in complex systems small anomalies and minor malfunctions can proliferate and lead to large-scale failures that are all the more serious because of the sheer number of structures and quantities of substances that are at risk. Large, complex, and failure-prone technology systems are also vulnerable to hazard events, and to the potential for what researchers call "na-tech" (natural-technological) disasters. During Russia's 2010 heat wave, for example, large fires threatened the Novovoronezh nuclear power plant and its three reactors. While the plant has systems that protect it from fire, concerns were raised that the fires could affect offsite electrical power transmission and distribution systems, thus endangering those systems. In the United States, the 5.8 earthquake that struck the East Coast in August 2011 caused physical damage and a loss of power to the two-reactor North Anna power plant, which was not far from the quake's epicenter, forcing an automatic shutdown. It was later found that the ground shaking at the site was far in excess of the plant's design specifications (Koch 2011). Flooding on the Missouri River in the summer of

2011 threatened both of Nebraska's nuclear power plants. The protective berm surrounding the Fort Calhoun plant collapsed, and the entire facility was flooded. There was a loss of electrical power, and for a time spent fuel rods could not be cooled (Ananda 2011). Fort Calhoun is the designated spent fuel storage facility for the state, with a reported 840 metric tons of rods on site in 2010. As global climate change moves inexorably forward, it seems prudent to ask whether protecting facilities like Fort Calhoun from flooding is feasible over the long term.

The potential for catastrophic earthquake impacts exists in the New Madrid Seismic Zone (NMSZ) in the central United States, where a series of mega-earthquakes occurred over a three-month period in late 1811 and early 1812. The 1811–1812 events were the largest earthquakes to occur in the contiguous United States since records have been kept. A large NMSZ earthquake is the prototypical "low-probability/high-consequence" event for the United States—a worst case even compared to Hurricane Katrina. Damage and loss estimates for a magnitude 7.7 New Madrid earthquake event indicate that impacts would be extensive over an eight-state area, with the most severe damage centered in Tennessee, Arkansas, and Missouri. Cities such as Memphis and St. Louis, which have many collapse-prone masonry buildings, would be especially hard hit. There could be as many as 86,000 deaths and injuries, and 7.2 million people would be initially displaced from their homes—a nightmare scenario should the earthquake occur during the winter months. A 7.7 New Madrid earthquake would damage over 700,000 buildings and 3,500 bridges, and fifteen major bridges in the region would have to be closed on account of damage. Oil and natural gas pipelines that serve the eastern United States traverse the New Madrid Seismic Zone, and damage estimates indicate that a major earthquake would cause 425,000 breaks and leaks in interstate and local pipelines. The 1811–1812 earthquakes were followed by hundreds of aftershocks, and the same will be the case for the next large New Madrid event; ongoing aftershocks will create additional damage, hamper relief and restoration efforts, and further traumatize victims.

There are fifteen nuclear power plants in the NMSZ, and it seems unreasonable to assume that none of those plants would sustain damage or be forced to shut down in a major New Madrid event. The Nuclear Regulatory Commission (NRC) has been conducting studies to assess the seismic safety of nuclear plants in the central and eastern United States, especially in light of new information on seismic hazards in those regions and in the wake of the Fukushima tragedy. However, as is typical of risk analyses for nuclear plants, those studies focus strictly on potential earthquake impacts on the plants themselves. For the New Madrid Seismic Zone, that means that NRC analyses ignore the damage and disruption a major earthquake would cause throughout the New Madrid region, even if that damage would have consequences for nuclear plant safety—which would clearly be the case. Loss estimation analyses indicate, for example, that electrical utility lifelines will experience damage and disruption on a large scale and that

[p]ower outages are likely to extend beyond the eight-state study region, particularly if damage near the rupture zone causes a substantial failure of the electric grid. If this occurs, lengthy power outages may persist over numerous states east of the Rocky Mountains. (Elnashai et al. 2009: 133)

In other words, for an extended period of time nuclear plants in the NMSZ region could be without the electrical power they need to operate safely. Moreover, in the event of a large-magnitude quake, all modes of transportation, including air, rail, and water, would be seriously compromised within the eight-state impact region, meaning that if an emergency were to occur, needed personnel and resources would almost surely not arrive in a timely manner. Planning scenarios for a large NMSZ event suggest that after a large earthquake, approximately forty thousand personnel would be needed *just to conduct search and rescue activities.* With so much damage, it will be a challenge to move that many rescuers when and where they will be needed.

NMSZ damage and impact scenarios strongly suggest that should a nuclear plant emergency occur following a major earthquake, help would be long in coming. Putting this potential megadisaster into comparative context, it is important to remember that when the 2011 tsunami churned through the Fukushima Daiichi nuclear plant, its effects were utterly devastating, but they were still relatively focused geographically.

The absence of serious earthquake damage in inland areas of adjacent prefectures and not-too-distant cities like Tokyo meant that emergency workers and supplies could converge on the damaged plant, and also that residents could evacuate out of the most heavily irradiated areas, although the evacuation itself was badly bungled. Given what researchers have found regarding the impacts of future New Madrid events, if an earthquake were to cause an emergency at any of the fifteen nuclear plants in the NMSZ, the scenario would be entirely different.

Continuing with the problem of concentrations, Perrow points out that very large population concentrations are another source of ballooning disaster vulnerabilities and losses. The movement of people into geographic places that are vulnerable to disasters is a worldwide trend. In the United States, research shows that disaster losses are growing not because extreme events are becoming more intense—although owing to climate change that is actually the case for some types of events—but more importantly because so many people and so much wealth are increasingly concentrated in high-hazard areas. Focusing on coastal areas that are vulnerable to hurricanes, for example, Roger Pielke and his collaborators have shown that over the period between 1900 and 2005, the main force driving hurricane losses has not been hurricane frequency or intensity but rather population increases and the growth of the built environment in coastal regions. They argue that if the nation wishes to avoid paying for ever more expensive storms, something needs to be done to slow down the rate of population growth in vulnerable areas, improve construction standards, and find additional ways of making structures more disaster resistant. Among their conclusions is that

[u]nless such action is taken to address the growing concentration of people and properties in coastal areas where hurricanes strike, damage will increase, and by a great deal, as more and wealthier people increasingly inhabit these coastal locations. (Pielke et al. 2008: 38)

The expanding potential for loss caused by population concentrations is the reason why private insurers became reluctant to offer earthquake insurance after experiencing large losses in the 1994 Northridge earthquake, and why they retreated from the Florida insurance market midway through the first decade of this century after several successive damaging hurricane seasons. Growth and population concentrations had simply pushed their exposures to untenable limits.

High population concentrations are associated with high disaster death tolls in less developed nations and large dollar losses in developed ones. With the focus again on earthquakes, the population of Port-au-Prince constituted one third of Haiti's population—three million people—at the time of the 2010 earthquake. This high degree of concentration virtually ensured that any major disaster affecting Port-au-Prince would exact catastrophic losses and cripple the nation. Port-au-Prince is only one example of primacy, a common phenomenon in the developing world in which large numbers of people reside in or migrate to one or two urban centers within a country. Primacy and the forces that drive it are major causes of disaster vulnerability.

In 2011, Japan experienced what was likely the costliest disaster in history in terms of economic losses, but the Great East Japan earthquake wasn't even Japan's "big one." Government leaders and the public rightly fear the coming Great Tokai Earthquake, which will occur not far from Tokyo, where the Philippine Sea Plate is sliding under the Eurasian Plate in a vast subduction zone in the Nankai Trough. Large earthquakes have been occurring along the Tokai segment of the subduction zone at intervals of around 100 to 150 years, most recently in 1707 and 1854 when earthquakes in the neighborhood of Richter magnitude 8.4 occurred. On the basis of this record, experts argue that a large quake is overdue, placing the likelihood of a magnitude 8 Tokai earthquake in the next thirty years at 87 percent. Like earlier earthquakes, the Great Tokai event will also spawn a large tsunami (Central Disaster Management Council 2005; Stein et al. 2006). The aging Hamaoka nuclear power plant, with its five reactors, is located close to the presumed focal region of the Great Tokai event, which led former prime minister Naoto Kan to order the plant to suspend operations following the March 2011 earthquake. But here again, as the Fukushima events have shown, even reactors that are in shutdown mode present a radiation risk under the right (or wrong) set of conditions.

The cause of this catastrophic earthquake loss potential is not the subduction zone itself but rather the high concentration of people and wealth that are at risk from a Tokai event. The Tokyo-Yokohama metropolitan region is currently home to 33.2 million people, or about one fourth of Japan's population, and is responsible for generating the lion's share of the nation's economic activity. Owing to this massive degree of concentration, the coming Tokai earthquake, tsunami, and possible nuclear plant and other industrial accidents are certain to have devastating impacts. Depending on the characteristics of the next Tokai earthquake (magnitude, depth, shaking intensities), the time of day it occurs, the season in which it occurs, tsunami wave effects, and levels of disaster preparedness in affected areas, tens of thousands could be killed. Direct property damage is expected to exceed $310 billion—and that is likely a low estimate. As Japan remains in the economic doldrums following the 1997 Asian financial crisis, and given the massive losses incurred by the 2011 triple disaster, a Tokai earthquake in the near future could well render the nation insolvent.

Like large-scale hazardous facilities, large population concentrations don't just happen. They are the result of social forces such as migration, other historic population trends, development policies and practices, and decision making (and nondecisions) around land-use issues. These forces operate largely independently of hazard-related concerns. Indeed, it often seems that decision makers go out of their way to ensure that growth takes place in ways that ignore potential disasters.

More Power: Power Relationships
and the Social Production of Risk

Perrow is also concerned with a third form of concentration: the concentration of economic and political power that enables a small number of actors to make decisions that affect the safety and security of large numbers of people. Power concentrations have always existed, but they have become increasingly significant because of the global scale on which many economic entities operate and the frantic pace of mergers, acquisitions, and industry consolidation, and also because overall regulatory controls on size and economic might have been weakened over a period of decades. The end products of these concentrating forces include banks that are deemed "too big to fail," giant energy conglomerates, food supply chains that are dominated by a shrinking number of large-scale agribusinesses, and highly consolidated media that are controlled by a few major corporations. Economic power on this scale is easily translated into political power, with important consequences for risk buildup.

The relationship between untrammeled power and risk plays out in several ways. First, economic actors use political influence to free themselves from regulatory regimes that are intended to keep risks in check. The effects of concentrated power within the financial sector were evident, for example, in its ability to bring about the repeal of the Glass-Steagall Act, an action that among other things, allowed the derivatives market to explode, in tandem with the passage of the Financial Services Modernization Act of 1999, also known as Gramm-Leach-Bliley.

Second, powerful organizational actors are able to achieve dominance over internal and external critics in ways that allow them to achieve their objectives without opposition. Possessing overwhelming power, corporations can force concessions from unions; employers can keep workers in line when they raise questions regarding risks; and industries can neutralize citizen groups and social movements that oppose their activities as unsafe.

When power imbalances persist over time, powerful entities have a greater tendency to overreach and drift into increasingly risky practices. This overreaching tendency was evident in the activities of large and powerful actors within the U.S. financial system in the run-up to the 2008 financial crash. Freed from regulation and confident of political support for their activities, banks, investment banks, hedge funds, and entities such as AIG, General Motors, and other megacorporations loaded up on ever-riskier financial tools. Because risk taking received such strong support within networks of institutional actors in the financial sector, and because it offered such high rewards, participants in the mortgage bubble ended up literally competing with one another to see how much risk they could take on. Here again, they were able to do so because of their immense concentrated power and because countervailing forces were so weak.

The implications for risk buildup of concentrated and unconstrained political-economic power are evident in many industries worldwide. The

Japanese nuclear industry is a case in point. Public antinuclear sentiment has been common in Japan owing to the nation's experience in World War II, and getting the Japanese public to accept nuclear power was initially a hard sell. Still, over time a strong coalition of government agencies and electrical power utilities has had a free hand in the siting of nuclear power facilities, primarily through its ability to offer large economic incentives to small, often remote, often economically depressed towns. As nuclear power emerged as a major source of energy in Japan, communities were essentially bribed into accepting nuclear plants, with the promise of jobs for young workers and support for schools and community projects; also, extensive propaganda efforts were launched (Aldrich 2005, 2008; Nelson 2011; Dunsinberre and Aldrich 2011). Then, once government and industry succeeded in getting communities to accept the presence of nuclear plants, the natural tendency was to locate multiple reactors at nuclear sites to achieve economies of scale and to avoid having to repeat costly charm offensives in large numbers of communities. The decades-long propaganda campaign favoring nuclear power was so effective that Japanese nuclear power production was not thwarted or even slowed down by the Three Mile Island and Chernobyl accidents, as it was in some other countries.

The Japanese "nuclear village," which has so successfully promoted nuclear power, consists of successive cohorts of industry and government personnel whose members studied together at Japanese universities and implicitly take for granted that they will at some point be working together. The most prestigious university in Japan, the University of Tokyo, or Todai, is a well-known pipeline for nuclear industry and nuclear ministry officials, as well as for Japan's political elite more generally. Perhaps not surprisingly, Todai has also reportedly benefited more than any other academic institution from nuclear industry research dollars. University-based relationships are important everywhere, but they are especially important in Japan and other parts of Asia.

Japan's nuclear industry and its regulators operate according to deeply rooted institutional practices that normalize their close collaborative relationships. The concept of *amakudari* ("descent from heaven") is a long-institutionalized feature of Japan's political economy that helps explain the close bond that exists between the government bureaucracy and industry in Japan (Colignon and Usui 2003). Technically, the term refers to the system through which ministry officials who reach retirement age move on to assume lucrative positions in industries that they formerly regulated, such as the nuclear industry. However, there are also other forms of *amakudari* that involve the movement of high-level bureaucrats into public corporations (often for short periods, after which they then transfer to the private sector) and successive movements from one sector to another—the latter known as *wataridori,* or the "migratory bird" pattern of employment. A form of academic *amakudari* also exists in which university professors go on to find jobs in the industries for which they conducted research; such moves are common in part because the mandatory retirement age from Japan's public universities is sixty.[1] The economic and political rationales that are commonly offered for this system are that it facilitates the smooth operation of both government and the private sector and manages their interrelationships. However, according to Colignon and Usui (2001), among its other consequences is the creation of what the late sociologist C. Wright Mills called a "power elite," consisting of homogeneous policy and practice networks.

In Japan, the cozy relationships fostered by common educational backgrounds and institutionalized career ladders led to situations in which there were few countervailing forces that could effectively keep hazards in check or protect worker and public safety. Japan's worst nuclear accident prior to the Fukushima event, the September 1999 Tokaimura criticality incident, was considered the world's third-most serious peacetime nuclear incident (after Three Mile Island and Chernobyl) at the time it occurred.[2] In that accident, two workers at the Tokaimura uranium reprocessing facility died from massive radiation exposure, a third was seriously irradiated, and an estimated four hundred workers and community residents were also exposed. The company that operated the Tokaimura facility, JCO, a subsidiary of Sumitomo Mining Company, had been in violation of numerous safety rules. After the accident, it was found, for example, that JCO doctored government-approved worker safety manuals in order to make its divergent procedures seem legitimate, and that the severely exposed workers had not been wearing dosimeter badges at the time of the accident. The facility was not equipped with an alarm that would signal a criticality condition, and as the emergency began to unfold, local officials and residents were not informed of the accident in a timely manner—perhaps no surprise, since the Tokai city government had not conducted a nuclear emergency exercise for eight years prior to the accident. For its part, Tokaimura's regulator, the Japanese Science and Technology Agency (STA), had not conducted an inspection at the facility in ten years.[3]

CAPTURE, REGULATION, AND RISK

The Japanese government-industry nuclear complex is a clear example of regulatory capture, a situation in which those charged with policing the operations of an industry are incapable of doing so, typically because the industry wields overwhelming power. In fact, the report issued by the Japanese Diet, or parliament, following the Fukushima triple meltdown explicitly pointed to regulatory capture as a root cause of the disaster (Kurokawa 2012). Capture's influence is often subtle, as regulators develop social relationships with industry officials and come to share industry values and priorities, thus compromising their ability to regulate effectively. Forces of capture are also strong because the financial rewards offered by the private sector can serve as a lure for regulatory officials, who often perceive themselves as underpaid compared to private-sector employees. Such rewards are all the more compelling in a culture like that of the United States, which equates public service with financial sacrifice and in which it is expected that hard-pressed public officials will at some point find it necessary to leave government service "to make money." Capture can also be a reflection of the structural conflicts of interest that are built into industry-government relationships. For example, critics of the Japanese "nuclear village" and its *amakudari* tradition point out that the mission of Japan's nuclear regulatory entities, like that of the industry itself, is to promote nuclear power and argue for its being safe. The Nuclear Industry Safety Agency is part of Japan's Ministry of Economy, Trade, and Industry, and in the years leading up to the March 2011 disaster both agencies were actively collaborating with the nuclear industry to promote the construction of nuclear plants in

Vietnam and other nations in Southeast Asia.[4] Thus, rather than acting as a disinterested, independent entity, the regulatory agency acted as a booster for the industry.

THE U.S. CASE: FOSSIL FUELS
AND REGULATORY CAPTURE

Although the ways in which the "nuclear village" and *amakudari* have facilitated regulatory capture are unique to Japan, it is impossible not to see parallels in the United States. The revolving door between the financial services industry, particularly firms such as Goldman Sachs, and U.S. government agencies like the Treasury Department is one case in point, as are numerous examples of members of Congress who leave public service either to join industries over which their committees had jurisdiction, or to hire on at lobbying firms that work on behalf of those industries. If we refer back to earlier discussions of how shared cultural frames influence the behavior of actors within institutional networks, under such circumstances it is easy to understand how government and corporate officials come to view the world in similar ways and to behave accordingly.

The relationship between U.S. Minerals Management Service (MMS) and the oil and gas industry had already been identified as a potentially dangerous case of regulatory capture long before the occurrence of the 2010 *Deepwater Horizon* explosion and oil spill. Like the Japanese nuclear regulators who made common cause with the nuclear industry, the MMS had mixed motives: it was expected to regulate the oil industry but also to collect royalties from it. Investigations have revealed extensive misconduct on the part of the agency that can be traced directly to regulatory capture and to the conflicts of interest that were inherent in its structural position vis-à-vis the industry. In the Gulf region, offshore drilling was permitted without the necessary environmental permits, and MMS staff members were regularly overruled when they raised issues about the safety of drilling operations and their potential environmental impacts. A March 2010 investigative report on relationships between the Lake Charles, Louisiana, MMS district office and Island Operating Company (IOC), an oil and gas production company that operates oil platforms, documented extensive ethical violations on the part of MMS employees, who reportedly accepted gifts, meals, and airline and football tickets from oil companies and took part in skeet-shooting contests, hunting and fishing trips, and football tailgate parties and games with company employees. Regulatory officials permitted oil industry personnel to fill in their own inspection reports in pencil, then later traced them over in pen before submitting them. Industry and MMS employees also took illegal drugs together, including crystal methamphetamine and cocaine. Indicative of a revolving-door relationship, IOC tried to recruit inspection personnel from MMS, and active MMS employees sought jobs at IOC (Office of the Inspector General 2010). Louisiana was far from an isolated case. In 2008, an investigation by the office of the Department of Interior's inspector general reported remarkably similar activities in the Royalty-in-Kind Program of the Minerals Revenue Management division of the Denver MMS office. Eight officials in the royalty program accepted gifts that included golf and ski outings, meals, and concert, football, and baseball tickets. Among the report's other revelations were that MMS officials used marijuana and cocaine and had sexual relationships with employees of the oil and gas companies they were charged with regulating, which included Shell, Chevron, and other major corporations (Savage 2008). One official was later convicted of felony conflict-of-interest charges, because soon after he retired from the MMS he set up a consulting company, and almost immediately got a contract from the agency. While working at the MMS, the former director of the royalty program obtained an unauthorized paid consulting job with a company that provided technical services to the oil industry, and in that capacity steered some of the companies with which he worked in his official position to that firm.

One telling revelation from the Denver investigation was that when questioned about their activities and confronted with their ethical violations, the MMS employees showed no signs of remorse. Despite the fact that ethics briefings covering conflicts of interest and illegal gifts were given on a regular basis by the agency, employees evidently believed they had done nothing wrong. In their view, the social events they attended and the meals, drinks, and drugs they shared with industry representatives were simply part of the job of becoming familiar with people in the companies with which their agency was doing business. Such reactions are only understandable in an institutional milieu in which regulatory capture is a taken-for-granted way of life.

The National Commission on the BP Deepwater Horizon Oil Spill and Offshore Drilling cited regulatory capture and pervasive mixed incentives as key factors in the BP disaster, noting that "[f]rom birth, MMS had a built-in incentive to promote offshore drilling in sharp tension with its mandate to ensure safe drilling and environmental protection" and that as a consequence "[r]evenue generation—enjoyed by both industry and government—became the dominant objective" at the expense of safety (National Commission on the BP Deepwater Horizon Oil Spill and Offshore Drilling et al. 2011: 56). The report also noted that even as drilling became increasingly risky, the oil industry fought regulation at every turn, and that while investing in oil and gas development and production, it did little to improve safety in drilling operations or emergency response and spill containment procedures.[5] After the BP spill, in what appears to be an example of organizational learning, the MMS was divided into three separate agencies, including one devoted only to revenue collection, in an effort to resolve previous conflicts of interest.

Regulatory capture is a form of rent seeking, or activity that aims at influencing government policies and activities in ways that create advantages for the groups that are exerting such pressure. First identified as an important political-economic process in the 1960s and 1970s (Tullock 1967; Krueger 1974), rent seeking ensures that those who practice it obtain larger profits and other benefits than they would realize without exerting influence within governmental institutions. Economists point out that rent seeking has an adverse effect on both economic benefits and public welfare, because rather than generating additional wealth through creativity and innovation, rent seekers manipulate public institutions in order to grab a larger share of existing wealth. In addition to capture, other forms of rent seeking include out-and-out bribery and other forms of corruption, as well as activities that rig the political and regulatory game by influencing government decision making in ways that favor special interests. Our interest here in rent seeking centers on the ways in which it contributes to risk buildup, both directly by encouraging activities that increase vulnerability and indirectly by weakening regulatory constraints on unsafe practices. As I go on to discuss social processes that increase risk in places like the Northern California Delta, New Orleans, and in corrupt societies around the world, different forms of rent seeking will again make an appearance.

ORGANIZATIONAL STRUCTURE AND PROCESS IN THE PRODUCTION OF RISK

Interactivity, Tight Coupling, and Normal Accidents

In a globalized world, many organizational enterprises have grown very large, and with enormous size come greater degrees of complexity. Large manufacturing facilities, nuclear power plants, offshore drilling operations, banking systems, cyber-infrastructures and information systems, and global supply chains operate at scales and levels of physical and organizational complexity that were simply unknown in earlier times. Often referred to as sociotechnical systems, these kinds of operations consist of a blending of human organizational and technological systems that interact in complex—and sometimes disastrous—ways.

Through the study of accidents and disasters, researchers have identified features of sociotechnical systems that render risks less manageable and mishaps more likely. Charles Perrow's *Normal Accidents* (1984), a seminal text on the organizational origins of disaster, made its debut thirty years ago. Inspired in part by the 1979 Three Mile Island nuclear plant accident, Perrow's study focused on high-risk sociotechnical systems, such as nuclear plants, chemical processing facilities, and marine transport, in an effort to identify factors that make some systems tolerably safe and others more dangerous. His analysis identified two key factors that make major accidents more likely: interactive complexity and "tight coupling," the latter defined as the extent to which a problem or failure in one element of a system straightforwardly triggers problems in one or more additional elements. Complexly interactive systems can be contrasted with linear ones, in which a problem, a "component failure," that develops in one component or phase of system operations remains independent of and isolated from others. In complexly interactive systems, different components and operations are related to one another—for example, through feedback loops—in ways that allow for many types of failures to occur, and also for unexpected interactions among failures. When such systems are also tightly coupled, failures in one component or process within a system can then cascade, leading to rapid catastrophic failures. Perrow identified nuclear power plants like the Three Mile Island facility and the Fukushima plant as exemplars of complexly interactive and tightly coupled systems that are subject to runaway processes of destabilization and degradation, often as a consequence of relatively mundane component failures. In a subsequent book, *The Next Catastrophe* (2007), he also discussed the electrical power grid, focusing in particular on the massive blackout that occurred in August 2003 in the Midwest and northeastern United States and Canada, a classic normal accident in which a few otherwise small problems (sagging power lines, untrimmed trees) led to a rapidly cascading regional power loss.

Normal Accidents 2.0: It Isn't Only System Design

The financial crash of 2008 can also be viewed through the lens of normal accidents theory. This is the perspective advanced by Guillen and Suarez (2010), who argue that over time the global financial system had become so complex and tightly coupled that it was inherently prone to cascading failures. For example, financial institutions were wildly diversified, and securitization enabled them to offer ever more exotic financially engineered products that were themselves highly complex. The global system was also so highly leveraged (that is, tightly coupled) that once initiated, perturbations rippled very rapidly throughout the system, with catastrophic effects. Although the buildup to the meltdown occurred over time, the 2008 Lehman Brothers bankruptcy was the final triggering event in what became a rapid cascade of financial failure that can be traced directly to the structural properties of the system. The strength of interconnections also mattered in the meltdown; in contrast with Western nations whose financial systems were very tightly coupled, China fared relatively well during the crash, owing to its relative lack of integration into the global system.

Perrow himself disagrees with the idea that normal accidents theory should be used to account for the financial crash. Instead, he argues that while the requisite system characteristics were indeed present, the meltdown was the consequence of the behavior of financial elites, who were aware of the risks inherent in their activities but acted in disregard of their own institutions, their clients, and the public (Perrow 2010). In light of what is known about the ethics of the financial services sector (if that is not an oxymoron) during the period in question, this argument is valid. However, a third perspective would acknowledge the complex, interactive, and tightly coupled structural characteristics of financial markets as the source of the scale and severity of the meltdown, while also highlighting, as we have here, the political-economic and cultural milieu that enabled financial institutions to continually push the risk envelope, accompanied by the failure of regulatory institutions to take steps to address the unsustainable buildup of intercorrelated risks. Indeed, far from worrying about the system's potential for cascading collapse, regulators, with the backing of Congress and influenced by the industry's gargantuan lobbying efforts, went out of their way over decades to unleash financial institutions so that they could pursue ever-larger profits while courting ever-larger risks.

This brings us back to the notion of capture and rent seeking. As highlighted by Baxter (2011), capture within the financial sector was so far-reaching in the period leading up to the crash that it encompassed not only the prosaic kinds of conflicts of interest that characterize many regulatory relationships but also what Baxter calls "deep capture," a culturally and socially supported melding of perspectives and worldviews that renders the regulator and the regulated virtually indistinguishable. Taking into account the revolving door that has long existed between the financial services sector and its regulators (or, as they say in Japan, the practices of "migratory birds"), the result of deep capture is interpersonal and interorganizational relationships that are so close that, in Baxter's words, they constitute a type of "consanguinity," and perhaps even "co-dependency." Because of deep capture, it mattered little whether an individual was the CEO of an investment bank, a lead economic advisor, a Federal Reserve official, or an employee of the Treasury Department.

All players in the financial system's organizational ecology shared a common worldview and stock of knowledge that permitted financial risks to increase unchecked.

Unleashing Risk: Organizational Structure and Process

Continuing with this line of thinking, sociotechnical systems can be seen as consisting of three elements: physical components; intra- and interorganizational structures and relationships, such as task-related divisions of labor, power relationships, organizational interdependencies, and lines of authority; and the social processes that are involved in managing, carrying out, and sustaining the activities of the entity in question, such as training, communication, coordination, and decision making. Organizational processes also include the exercise of formal and informal social control over organizations and their members, as well as sensemaking and meaning-making activities that continually take place within and also among organizations. The management of risk within complex sociotechnical systems requires attention to all three elements, as well as to their interrelationships. Unfortunately, with increasing size and complexity this becomes more difficult, and when there are misalignments and imbalances within the elements that make up sociotechnical systems, the potential for disaster increases.

One clear insight from research on disasters is that the manner in which relationships are structured within and among organizations can render risk management efforts ineffective. For example, in complex sociotechnical systems, one challenge is to identify the optimal structural placement for entities having loss-reduction roles, such as safety and risk management units. Increases in complexity can also distort organizational processes such as information sharing in ways that have ramifications for overall system safety. NASA's experience with the *Challenger* and *Columbia* space shuttle accidents is a textbook example of both of these problems. The two catastrophic failures were initiated by physical problems with components embedded in highly complex technological systems—O-rings in the case of *Challenger*, and foam insulation in the case of *Columbia*. However, official postaccident investigations and research on the two accidents generally identified organizational structural factors and organizational processes, not technology, as critical contributors to NASA's failure to maintain safe operations.

The shuttle accidents are case studies on the many factors that lead to risk buildup, but here the discussion will focus only on certain elements of structure and process as key contributors to the *Challenger* disaster. Sociologist Diane Vaughan spent more than ten years studying that incident and later served as a researcher and writer for the *Columbia* accident investigation panel. Her research on *Challenger* found that while the agency had been aware of potential problems with O-rings for years prior to the disaster, organizational structural factors, such as NASA's ties with its regulators, as well as flawed organizational processes created conditions that led NASA to downplay those problems. One of her key analyses focused on the structural features and interactive processes that characterized NASA's relationship with its three regulatory bodies, two of which were internal to the organization and one, external. One internal body, the Safety, Reliability, and Quality Assurance Program (SR&QA), had the most responsibility for the oversight of safety at NASA. This team, which consisted primarily of engineers, was never particularly good at performing its problem-reporting functions. For example, it did not do a good job of communicating its safety-related findings upward through the NASA hierarchy, nor did it formulate a coherent system for reporting in-flight anomalies. In other words, processes for collecting and disseminating information critical to shuttle safety were flawed. Additionally, the SR&QA program was not represented on the critical prelaunch conference call when Morton Thiokol engineers cautioned against launching the shuttle during cold weather because of possible O-ring problems, nor was the program represented when the Mission Management Team made its final decision on the *Challenger* launch. Vaughan also noted that as opposed to being independent of the agency, the SR&QA team was wholly dependent on NASA for resources, which NASA had been steadily cutting, and that its staffing was inadequate to monitor safety issues throughout NASA's complex web of contracting relationships. A second internal body, which had responsibility for crew safety, was similarly dependent on NASA, and its influence was diluted when it was merged with another panel.

Its ultimate influence on crew safety was moot, because it went out of existence five years before the *Challenger* launch.

The relationship between NASA and its external regulator, the Aerospace Safety Advisory Panel (ASAP), was also characterized by problems related to structure and process. ASAP was directly dependent on NASA for its very existence, and it also suffered from a chronic shortage of resources, especially in light of its very extensive responsibilities. However, more important in Vaughan's view is the fact that ASAP was so dependent on NASA for the information it required in order to do its job that its ability to act as a regulator was compromised. ASAP was not able to oversee day-to-day NASA operations, and thus obtained its information from NASA either through formal reporting mechanisms or through informal contacts with NASA and contractor personnel. This information dependence and the interpersonal relationships it fostered between ASAP members and personnel in the shuttle program made ASAP understandably reluctant to advocate for strict sanctions in cases where questions regarding safety were raised. More important, ASAP did not actually have the power to impose sanctions on its own. That was the sole responsibility of NASA. However, NASA's need to comply with externally imposed performance expectations, combined with its dependence on its contractors, weakened its own ability to exert social control in areas related to safety. In an organizational context characterized by huge technical complexities, organizational structure and process were misaligned in ways that allowed risk to expand. In Vaughan's words,

[t]he space agency created a regulatory structure and controlled its operation. Over time, however, NASA administrators altered that structure. By doing so, they altered the information available to them about hazards in the Space Shuttle Program, hence altering the bases on which still other critical decisions were made. One of them was the decision to launch the Space Shuttle *Challenger*. (1990: 253)

Complexity, Sensemaking, and Risk

Sensemaking and meaning making are critical processes within organizations, and this is especially true for organizations operating in complex environments, such as those that manage risky technologies and respond when disasters strike. These kinds of organizations must detect, process, and interpret a wide variety of informational signals, often on the fly, and must arrive at collective understandings in ambiguous situations. Risk expands when such processes are distorted by organizational forces. For example, Vaughan (1996) calls attention to various sensemaking practices within NASA that resulted in what she terms the "normalization of deviance," a process that led over time to reduced concern about O-ring problems, such as erosion. As she describes it, determining the safety significance of a problem like O-ring erosion was no easy task, because the shuttle continued to fly even when there was some O-ring damage. O-rings were recognized as critical system components and were rated as such, but even when damaged they appeared robust, creating ambiguity regarding how much damage was likely to be truly dangerous. Those responsible for shuttle operations recognized that a host of anomalies needed to be addressed to ensure mission safety and success, but O-ring and other anomalies were common in the shuttle program, and it was impossible to reconcile all of them. Given these ambiguities, NASA personnel developed a working consensus concerning the significance of O-ring damage—one that not incidentally allowed missions to go forward most of the time. Similarly, O-rings were known to be prone to failure at low temperatures, but NASA personnel reasoned that if a temperature-related failure were to occur in a primary O-ring system, the backup system would work as intended. The problem here was that this was merely an assumption, and additionally it was NASA's official policy not to rely on backup systems for highly critical components like O-rings. To make matters worse, concerns about the low temperature on the day of the launch were discounted. This drift into practices that were deviant from the perspective of risk management was a key contributor to the *Challenger* disaster.

Communication Processes, Sensemaking, and Risk Buildup

Communication is fundamental to managing risks and disasters, in part because it serves as a key basis for collective sensemaking. In order for social actors and entities to develop shared understandings and effectively address complex and often ambiguous situations, information must flow freely among parties that are responsible for managing risk—interpersonally, across groups, and among organizations. Yet many features of contemporary institutions, organizational structures, and organizational practices inhibit rather than facilitate the free flow of information. Here again, the sheer size and scale of organizational entities and networks makes it difficult for risk-relevant information to reach those who need to interpret and act on it. We live in an information age, but paradoxically the sheer volume of information that is generated in the course of institutional activities can make it difficult to distill information that is relevant for successful sensemaking.

Efforts to respond to terrorist threats in the United States provide an apt illustration of how size, scale, and information overload can make information sharing and collective sensemaking extremely challenging. Prior to the terrorist attacks of September 11, 2001, antiterrorism efforts were spread across dozens of government agencies and other entities such as private consulting firms. After the attacks, structurally induced problems with information sharing were highlighted in studies such as the 9/11 Commission Report, as well as in other government investigations. However, the complex system that existed prior to 9/11 was primitive compared to the vast homeland security behemoth that subsequently emerged as part of the global war on terror (GWOT). For example, in a groundbreaking investigative report entitled "Top Secret America" (Priest and Arkin 2011), the *Washington Post* provided mind-boggling statistics on the size and scope of current U.S. homeland security activities. Although the report stressed that it is literally impossible to know exactly how many people are engaged in antiterrorism-related activities nationwide, or how much those efforts cost, it appears that there are around 854,000 people working on some aspect of counterterrorism, intelligence, or homeland security in approximately 1,200 government agencies and close to 2,000 private companies at approximately 10,000 different locations around the country.

In the Washington, D.C., area alone, there are around 17 million square feet of building space devoted to intelligence activities. One huge complex is organized around the headquarters of the National Security Agency in Fort Meade, Maryland. The headquarters itself contains 6.3

million square feet of space, making it roughly the same size as the Pentagon. It is surrounded by the offices of approximately 250 other organizations, including large defense contractors, clustered in locations such as the 285-acre National Business Park.

The homeland security system is also geographically dispersed. Nationwide, the most concentrated clusters of homeland security-related organizations are located along the Interstate 95 corridor between Washington and Boston, but there are also significant concentrations in Southern California, the San Francisco Bay Area, central and southern Florida, the area around Colorado Springs, Colorado—the home of Northern Command—and smaller clusters in every state in the nation. In Texas alone, forty-one new homeland security-related offices have opened since the initiation of the GWOT. Government-sponsored homeland security agencies include just over one hundred joint terrorism task forces around the country, sixty-nine "fusion centers" that are intended to facilitate interorganizational information sharing, and around 160 city and county agencies.

The "Top Secret America" report discusses a number of problematic aspects of this cornucopia of intelligence efforts, including communication blockages caused by complex security clearance systems, duplication of efforts across agencies, excessive costs, a lack of appropriate guidance and accountability across agencies at different levels of government, and the production of so many documents, reports, memos, and other types of information that agency personnel admit to simply not having the time to review and comprehend them. The authors of the "Top Secret" report observe that even experts are astonished by the manner in which homeland security operations have mushroomed. One experienced source is quoted as saying, "I'm not aware of any agency with the authority, responsibility or a process in place to coordinate all these interagency and commercial activities. . . . The complexity of this system defies description" (Priest and Arkin 2011).

Within this vast collection of organizations, there are also numerous rules and practices that discourage information sharing, further hampering efforts to make meaning out of the bewildering array of information that is continually being acquired, processed, and interpreted.

These barriers include systems for classifying materials (for example, top secret, secret, and so on through multiple classification schemes), regulations, security clearances, and firewalls, and they also include deliberate efforts on the part of self-interested entities to avoid sharing information. It should not be surprising, then, that cues regarding terrorism-related threats have often gone undetected, both before and after 9/11. What is surprising is that there has been sufficient sharing of information that a number of potential attacks have been thwarted.

Collective sensemaking is critical during disasters but is also often difficult to bring about because of problems with the flow of information from multiple and diverse sources. Everyday practices related to information sharing and hoarding do not automatically disappear when disasters threaten or strike; in fact, predisaster patterns of sharing and exclusion have a significant influence on information-sharing behavior during crises. Because disasters are inherently dynamic, rapidly and continually updated information is critical for situation assessments and decision making. However, complex bureaucratic entities like many of those that mobilize during disasters are often ill suited for rapid information gathering and dissemination. Sensemaking is doubly problematic when the entities charged with collecting, analyzing, and sharing information are separated or geographically distant from where the disaster is taking place—which is frequently the case—and also when hierarchical authority arrangements thwart upward communication and broader sharing efforts.

The structurally induced inability to meet these kinds of communication challenges had an adverse impact on the intergovernmental response to Hurricane Katrina, with tragic consequences. Indeed, particularly with respect to the federal government level, the organizational arrangements that existed at the time could not have been less auspicious from the perspective of encouraging collective sensemaking. The hurricane occurred a scant four years after the 9/11 attacks, at a time when the nation's emergency management system was evolving rapidly. The Department of Homeland Security (DHS) had been established in 2003 through a governmental reorganization that involved twenty-two agencies and approximately 188,000 employees. The Federal Emergency

Management Agency (FEMA), formerly an independent agency, had been subsumed as a small unit within DHS. The Federal Response Plan, which had been used as the template for intergovernmental response activities at the time of the 9/11 attacks, had been judged inadequate and in need of modification. After a lengthy and somewhat contentious process, a new plan, called the National Response Plan, had been officially adopted in December 2004, after which DHS secretary and former Pennsylvania governor Tom Ridge, who had overseen the development of the plan, left the agency. He was replaced in February 2005 by Michael Chertoff, whose most recent position had been as a judge in the U.S. Court of Appeals. The nation thus entered the 2005 hurricane season with a new set of enormously complex organizational arrangements, a new plan for responding to terrorism and disasters, and a DHS secretary who was new to the job and lacked a background in disaster policy and response management. Additionally, in reaction to the 9/11 disaster, the federal system for responding to large-scale crises had tilted so far in the direction of managing terrorism-related threats and incidents that disaster-related issues and management expertise had been seriously marginalized (Tierney 2006).

When Katrina struck, additional problems with collecting, interpreting, sharing, and disseminating information further compromised collective sensemaking capabilities and hampered response activities. The earliest and perhaps most fundamental error was the failure of the DHS leadership to understand that any large hurricane coming even close to making a direct hit on New Orleans would likely have catastrophic effects, even though that potential was well known in government and scientific circles. The newly minted National Response Plan included procedures for responding to what it termed an "incident of national significance," but there was no general understanding among key officials and agencies of the kind of event that would qualify as such an incident, except that it would probably involve a large terrorist attack. It was also unclear who could make a declaration of an incident of national significance, although the National Response Plan suggested that either the president or the DHS secretary could do so, and that under such a declaration the DHS secretary would be in charge of managing the response.

The director of the National Oceanic and Atmospheric Administration's (NOAA's) National Hurricane Center warned the president directly that Katrina's impacts along the Gulf Coast would be catastrophic, and NOAA forecasts prior to landfall contained similar warnings. FEMA director Michael Brown also emphasized to the president and secretary Chertoff that the oncoming hurricane would cause a megadisaster. DHS could have moved decisively prior to Katrina's landfall in the Gulf states to activate the elements of the National Response Plan that were developed for catastrophic events,[6] but it did not do so. Katrina was not even declared an incident of national significance until August 30, a full day after levee breaches caused massive flooding in New Orleans.

Flawed information-sharing processes during and after the hurricane's landfall were a key source of other sensemaking failures. Levees and floodwalls began to fail in New Orleans as early as dawn on August 29, and those breaches were reported to state government and FEMA officials and to other agencies in a 7:30 A.M. telephone call.[7] The federal-level Homeland Security Operations Center (HSOC), described by DHS as the "nerve center for information sharing and domestic incident management," was the entity that was charged with collecting information on the disaster from a range of sources and providing that information to decision makers such as state officials, the DHS secretary, and ultimately the president. The Transportation Security Administration reported to the HSOC at 8:00 A.M. on August 29 that the Industrial Canal levee, which was designed to protect the Lower Ninth Ward, had been breached. Shortly thereafter, the National Weather Service also received a report of a levee breach and issued a flash flood warning. At 9:00 A.M., a DHS protective security agent working in New Orleans sent an e-mail to the HSOC that floodwaters in the Lower Ninth Ward were ten feet deep. Throughout the morning, levee breaches were reported by various agencies in New Orleans. An official in the governor's office was informed of at least one breach at around 11:00 A.M. Nonetheless, in a late morning video conference that was attended by state officials, FEMA director Brown, DHS secretary Chertoff, Louisiana governor Kathleen Blanco, and others, the idea that levees were failing was discounted. Blanco indicated that the levees had not been breached. Chertoff reportedly asked no question and praised the agencies involved in the response.

Just after 5:00 P.M. on the twenty-ninth, a FEMA official riding in a U.S. Coast Guard helicopter observed the extent of the flooding, which by then was catastrophic, and about an hour later he called FEMA director Michael Brown and other FEMA officials. Brown then called the White House. The same FEMA official also organized a conference call with FEMA, state, and other officials to discuss the flooding. An HSOC report marked 10:30 P.M. Eastern Time, which the White House received at 12:02 A.M. Eastern Time on August 30, summarized the conference call. At 6:00 A.M. Eastern Time on the thirtieth, nearly twenty-four hours after initial information had been relayed, the HSOC finally issued a report indicating that levees had been breached in three locations.

Adding to the confusion, on August 29 and even August 30 major media outlets were reporting that impacts in New Orleans were not as severe as feared. One such report, on CNN Headline News on the afternoon of the twenty-ninth, evidently reassured the director of the HSOC that reports describing widespread severe flooding in New Orleans were overblown. The Headline News segment showed footage of people in the French Quarter drinking and having a good time. This may have been why the HSOC director, Matthew Broderick, felt comfortable leaving the HSOC that evening—or so he testified later to Senate investigators. However, it also seems that despite all the information that was theoretically at his disposal, the HSOC director simply did not grasp what was happening in New Orleans and other heavily affected areas, or else thought that an event that was not a terrorist attack did not warrant his full attention. According to one report, Broderick

[w]ould also tell investigators that he rarely looked at his e-mail and had received seven hundred e-mail messages during the disaster that he had never even bothered to open. He admitted that he didn't read the New Orleans newspaper, the *Times-Picayune*, which on the day Katrina hit had treated the collapse of the 17th Street Canal as fact and had written a long story describing the scene after two reporters on bicycles had visited the area. Broderick would later say he hadn't seen Michael Brown on CNN on Monday night [August 29] referring to Katrina as a catastrophe and saying that as many as 10,000 people might be trapped in the floodwaters. (Cooper and Block 2006: 150–151)

Broderick resigned his position in early March 2006 amid severe criticism. However, even though his performance during Katrina fell far short of what would be expected for an official who was in charge of directing the nation's information "nerve center," it is clear that the problems that hampered sensemaking during Katrina were systemic and not the responsibility of any one individual or agency. Under the new National Response Plan, the interagency and intergovernmental context in which disaster response was supposed to be carried out was unfamiliar and ambiguous. DHS was a new and massively complex entity consisting of a congeries of agency entities and diverse organizational cultures. Key decision makers such as Secretary Chertoff were new to their posts, and entities such as the HSOC were also new. Those responsible for making critical decisions lacked a shared understanding of the vulnerability of New Orleans, its population, and the problems that were almost certain to develop with the levees, and they were physically distant both from the area of impact and from one another as the hurricane approached and made landfall. These were the conditions under which the nation struggled to respond to one of the worst catastrophes in its history— and failed.

PUSHING THE ENVELOPE:
PRODUCTION PRESSURES AND RISK EXPANSION

Organizations have multiple goals and cannot pursue them all with equal vigor. Over-emphasizing production and performance over other goals, such as safety, can have disastrous consequences, yet numerous organizations and interorganizational networks face strong production pressures on an ongoing basis. Private-sector entities are expected to be profitable, and the inability to produce may lead to the demise of a company or the firing of its executives. Public-sector entities are of course not immune from economic pressures; in addition to pursuing their primary functions, they also seek to expand, or at least maintain, their budgetary allocations. All organizations wish to maintain legitimacy with the public, their organizational collaborators, and their constituents and supporters.

The production pressures organizations generate can manifest themselves in various ways: stepping up schedules and setting difficult-to-reach deadlines; allowing and even encouraging workers to take shortcuts as they perform their tasks; sending implicit or explicit signals that avoiding regulations is necessary to maintain production schedules; excessive cost cutting; attempts to carry out tasks with insufficient personnel and other resources; and punishing those who resist or question such pressures. Too often, production pressures foster a drift toward riskier practices and ultimately toward disaster.

Evidence of the significance of production pressures for risk buildup comes from diverse sources. For example, such forces were present in the Tokaimura nuclear accident that was discussed earlier. Prior to the criticality incident, management had been pressuring employees to produce larger quantities of uranium fuel, which led to efforts to find shortcuts in carrying out procedures at the facility. Postaccident investigations found that on the day the incident occurred, workers had bypassed the measuring machines that were supposed to be used in the mixing process and were literally dumping buckets of uranium fuel by hand into mixing vessels, and also that they were using a concentration of uranium that was three times the recommended one (Wilford and Wald 1999). Workers at the facility had been poorly trained, and operator error was doubtless a factor in the accident. However, it was management that allowed poorly trained personnel to handle deadly nuclear material, produced operations manuals that deviated from industry standards, called for higher rates of production, and allowed safety and emergency preparedness practices to deteriorate severely over time.

Offshore oil drilling is an inherently hazardous activity, and also one that is characterized by high levels of production pressure. The deadly 1988 *Piper Alpha* offshore drilling platform fire, which killed 165 workers, has been studied extensively. Writing about that disaster and also about offshore drilling more generally, Mary Elisabeth Paté-Cornell has discussed how production pressures in the oil drilling industry contribute to high levels of risk taking:

In an organization that rewards maximum production, operates most of the time in a rough and generally unforgiving environment, and faces a demanding world market, the culture is marked by formal and informal rewards for pushing the system to the limit of its capacity. Production increases sometimes occur with little understanding of how close one is or might be to the danger zone. . . . In such a cultural and economic environment, the star is thus the one who shows unflinching optimism and wins the battles of "us" (the production people) vs. "them" (the safety inspectors, the government regulators, and others who tend to slow down production). (1993: 227–228)

If risk reduction involves achieving an appropriate balance between productivity and safety, postaccident investigations of drilling disasters reveal an industry and a set of regulatory controls that were seriously out of balance. For example, investigations indicate that production pressures and a subsequent lack of attention to accident prevention and disaster response were key factors in the 2010 BP drilling platform explosion and oil spill. The presidential investigative commission's report notes that revenue generation was the primary goal pursued by both BP and the MMS, and that throughout that regulatory body's existence its leadership devoted little attention to safety operations, sending a clear signal to personnel about the importance of earnings over safety. The entire report details a history of regulatory capture and a host of institutional weaknesses within the MMS that enabled BP and its contractors to focus on production at the expense of safety and environmental protection. The National Academy of Engineering's report on the BP accident and spill concluded that BP lacked a vibrant, effective safety culture and that industry research and development efforts had historically focused in an unbalanced way on technologies and practices related to oil exploration and production at the expense of research on improving safety processes. The picture painted by these postaccident studies is one of an industry determined to focus on productivity, avoid regulatory constraints, and invest as little as possible in safety and disaster preparedness practices.

The *Exxon Valdez* oil spill is typically characterized as a classic case of operator error. The ship's master is usually described as a heavy drinker who was not available to monitor ship operations and who put an inexperienced crew member in charge, resulting in the grounding of the supertanker and the spilling of 11 million gallons of oil. However, various reports present a more nuanced perspective on the circumstances that led up to the spill. One important set of factors involved Exxon's approach to vessel staffing. The *Valdez* accident had been preceded over time by significant reductions in crew size. The Coast Guard is responsible for establishing requirements for the size of shipping vessel crews, and it had determined that Exxon supertankers needed to have a minimum crew size of fifteen, down substantially from prior numbers. These lower manning requirements were in part the result of Exxon's misstatements about the amount of overtime crew members were routinely expected to work. Key crew members were suffering from fatigue at the time the *Valdez* accident took place, and this was not unusual given the time pressures and increasingly smaller crew sizes associated with marine shipping.

Crews on the *Valdez* routinely worked twelve-to-fourteen-hour shifts, plus overtime. Exxon did not have procedures in place to identify drinking problems with ships' masters and other personnel, nor did it undertake measures to ensure that crew members received adequate rest. The *Valdez* supertanker had on board a collision avoidance radar system that might have helped to avert the accident, but the system was not in use at the time of the accident because it was broken, and the company had failed to have it fixed (Tasca 1989; Alaska Oil Spill Commission 1990; National Transportation Safety Board 1990). Here again, we see evidence of an industry that was more concerned with productivity and cost cutting than with safety or the environment.

Other industries routinely pressure their employees to the point of fatigue and beyond. Commercial aviation is a case in point. The crash of a Colgan Air flight outside Buffalo in February 2009 revealed a great deal about performance pressures in today's airline industry and the ways those pressures can produce disastrous results. On approach, the flight crew was unaware how much the plane was slowing down, and when the in-flight warning system was tripped, the captain reacted incorrectly, resulting in a crash that killed forty-nine people on the plane and one person on the ground. Subsequent investigations centered on the ways in which Colgan's personnel practices contributed to the deadly accident. Like the underpaid pilots who lost their lives in the crash,[8] other Colgan pilots often commuted cross-country before flights and flew while they were sleep deprived. Various company policies actually encouraged long-distance commuting before and after flight duty. Additionally, pilots earned only a half day of sick time for each month they worked, which discouraged calling off sick; in fact, the first mate on the Buffalo flight appeared to be suffering from a respiratory problem at the time of the crash. She had also commuted overnight from Seattle to Memphis, and then from Memphis to Newark, Colgan's hub, prior to starting on the Buffalo flight (Wald 2009).

A 2010 report by Canada's Transportation Safety Board noted that pilot fatigue was a factor in six deadly crashes and six other aviation accidents over the previous decade. Fatigue was especially common among personnel working for smaller regional airlines, who reportedly felt pressured by their employers to work beyond legal limits and to falsify records about the length of time they had been working.

In December 2011 the U.S. Federal Aviation Administration issued a rule designed to reduce airline pilot fatigue by setting new limits on flight times and mandating a ten-hour rest period between flights. While hailing the new measures as a good first step, critics such as the U.S. Transportation Safety Board argue that they do not go far enough (Lieberman 2011). Cargo pilots, who fly mainly during nighttime hours, are exempted from the rule's requirements, and the regulations do not address directly the issue of pilots who commute prior to and after their assigned flights. Time pressures often force flight crews to sleep in airport crew lounges, even though that is forbidden by regulations, and the new FAA requirements also ignore the risks posed by the practice.

Public entities are of course not immune from performance pressures. For example, such pressures were cited as factors in both the *Challenger* and *Columbia* space shuttle disasters. After the *Challenger* accident, there was a short spike in funding for NASA, which was later followed by budget cuts. At a time when its contracting relationships were becoming more complex and difficult to manage, and as its resources dwindled, NASA continued on with tight launch schedules under the agency mantra of "faster, better, cheaper"—until it overlooked one too many safety issues. Vaughan (2006) observes that over time the culture of the NASA shuttle program shifted from one that focused on the primacy of technical expertise to one that placed significantly more emphasis on productivity: keeping to launch schedules; emphasizing efficiency and a "can do" attitude toward space flight; and doing more with less, in terms of budgets and in particular safety personnel and oversight.

DON'T THEY EVER LEARN?
INTERPRETING SIGNALS, LEARNING FROM EVENTS

Thinking about NASA's early problems with O-rings and foam leads us logically to question why organizations and institutions are often unable to perceive, understand, and act on cues that signal impending danger. For NASA that was often difficult, for both technical and organizational reasons. As discussed earlier, signals regarding faulty system components were ambiguous, and there were incentives for shuttle personnel to normalize those sorts of problems and drift into deviant practices. And indeed such behavior is not uncommon in situations involving complex, risky technologies, in which anomalies can be common and do not usually lead to catastrophic failures. After all, NASA had a good safety record, and *Challenger* had flown successfully with O-ring problems, right up until the time it exploded upon launch. Problems with foam loosening and debris had been identified *even before shuttles began to fly*, but they were defined merely as maintenance issues, not occurrences that could cause catastrophic losses (Vaughan 2006). Foam problems were persistent and had been the subject of extensive research. Paté-Cornell and Fischbeck (1990, 1993) had conducted analyses on the implications of such problems for shuttle flight safety and had made a number of recommendations for corrective action a decade prior to the *Columbia* accident. Some of those recommendations were followed, while other critical ones were ignored by NASA. Those risk analyses were taken into account in studies of the overall safety of the shuttle orbiter,[9] but their meaning was not absorbed by NASA at the management level. According to Paté-Cornell, because her analyses revealed that the foam issues posed significant flight safety risks and because NASA thought otherwise, the agency found another contractor that determined the risk to be lower by a factor of three. NASA lost track of its copies of Paté-Cornell's earlier risk-analytic reports and later had to ask her to provide new copies. That request was made on February 2, 2003, the day after the *Columbia* disaster (Paté-Cornell 2006).

NEAR MISSES AND RISK BUILDUP

It seems reasonable that organizations might err when anomalies that could signal potential disaster are ambiguous. However, ignoring risk is more difficult to understand when signs of impending doom are more clear. Yet organizations routinely ignore or misconstrue such signals. Near misses, or close calls that could have led to disaster but for lucky circumstances, are one case in point. Near misses and related anomalous events are commonly conceptualized as sitting at the broad base of a "safety pyramid" whose apex consists of actual accidents or disasters. Theoretically, organizations should be attentive to such danger signs and should make appropriate adjustments. In fact, on the basis of this rationale, various industries have developed complex systems for the reporting and analysis of near-miss and accident precursor events. The aviation industry has the Aviation Safety Reporting System; the nuclear industry has the Accident Sequence Precursor Program; and similar systems are common in medical settings, chemical process industries, fire-fighting, and marine safety. The basic assumption is that when organizations attend to signs of things that could go wrong, they will fix those problems and achieve higher levels of safety. Too often, however, they do neither.

We know how the process should work. For example, since 2000 the Wharton Risk Management and Decision Processes Center at the University of Pennsylvania has been studying near misses and near-miss programs and has developed guidance on how such programs can be improved (Phimister, Bier, and Kunreuther 2004). That framework consists of seven steps: identification; reporting; prioritization and distribution of information on the near miss to those responsible for follow-up action; causal analysis, ideally focusing on the so-called root causes of the incident; solution identification; dissemination of information on follow-up corrective action; and resolution of the problem that caused the near miss.

This seven-step approach is a useful way of conceptualizing how organizations can learn from close calls, provided they have both the will and the capacity to do so. However, the formulators of the framework also acknowledge that each step in the near-miss management process can be problematic. For example, because near-miss identification is fundamental to all efforts to learn and change, it is important that an organization have an appropriate and shared definition of what constitutes a near miss. However, conceptions of what constitutes a near miss may differ among front-line workers, supervisors, upper management personnel, and collaborating groups—as happened, for example, in the case of the *Challenger*'s O-ring problem, which was seen as very significant by Morton Thiokol engineers but not by NASA management. It is also critical that close calls are reported, but numerous barriers to reporting exist, such as formal and informal sanctions against those who wish to make reports and insufficient incentives for reporting. Additional constraints appear at later stages in the near-miss management process, and here again where production pressures are ascendant, activities that are defined as having the potential to slow down production processes or to require costly fixes will generally be frowned upon by management. Unfortunately, efforts to subject near misses to close scrutiny and to correct the root causes of such incidents can be easily framed that way.

In thinking about why organizations fail to learn and change even when there is evidence that they should do so, we need to look further at near misses and how they are treated in real-world contexts. The recent track record of BP Corporation offers insights into those processes. The multifatality BP *Deepwater Horizon* explosion and oil spill of 2010 was preceded just five years earlier by a major explosion at the BP Texas City, Texas, refinery that killed fifteen people and injured nearly two hundred. Evidently BP learned little from that disaster—which, as we will see later, is not unusual—but the key point for now is that the 2005 Texas City explosion itself was preceded by no fewer than six close calls in the previous ten years *in the same refinery system*. These were by no means minor incidents, and they were investigated at the time they occurred, yet those investigations had essentially no impact on plant operations.

Andrew Hopkins (2010) identifies several reasons why things worked out that way at BP. First, safety programs at the plant focused primarily on avoiding worker accidents and injuries, and not on overall system safety. Senior managers were assessed in terms of their efforts to maintain a safe working environment—defined again as low worker injury statistics—rather than on reducing the risk of facility-wide disasters. The corporate CEO was also focused on worker safety as opposed to the buildup of disaster risks, and because the Texas City plant had a good record in that respect, it may have appeared that there was little cause for concern. The steps that need to be undertaken to avert major disasters involving high-risk technologies cannot be equated with procedures to ensure that workers do not slip and fall while on the job, but that appears to be exactly what BP did in Texas City.

Second, even though the Texas City refinery was profitable, it was not seen as profitable enough by management. In other words, the refinery was operating under severe production pressure. Cuts had been extensive during the years leading up to the 2005 disaster. To squeeze out additional profits, the plant cut back on maintenance and avoided investing in equipment that would have made refining processes safer. In this context, as Hopkins bluntly puts it, "there was not a lot of point in attending to close calls because the company was not willing to make the capital investments that were necessary to respond effectively to them" (2010: 5). The U.S. Chemical Safety Board's investigation of the Texas City disaster was also blunt about the influence of BP's cost-cutting measures on the treatment of close calls at the plant. According to the board's chair, Carolyn Merritt,

[t]he combination of cost-cutting, production pressures, and failure to invest caused a progressive deterioration of safety at the refinery. Beginning in 2002, BP commissioned a series of audits and studies that revealed serious safety problems at the Texas City refinery, including a lack of necessary preventative [sic] maintenance and training. These audits and studies were shared with BP executives in London, and were provided to at least one member of the executive board. BP's response was too little and too late. Some additional investments were made, but they did not address the core problems in Texas City. In 2004, BP executives challenged their refineries to cut yet another 25% from their budgets the following year. (Chemical Safety Board 2007)

Third, in yet another example of how structural arrangements within organizations contribute to risk buildup, there were safety experts in high positions in the corporation, but they were located in the home office in London and they had responsibility only for establishing the company's safety standards, not for enforcing them. Enforcement was the responsibility of management at various BP plants, over whom corporate safety officials had no authority. Additionally, the safety official at the Texas City plant, who was very concerned about the close calls and about overall system safety, was able to exert little influence over management. How much headway can any safety advocate expect to make in the face of a 25 percent budget cut?

We should also recall that the meanings assigned to events like close calls are not simply "out there" to be automatically perceived. Rather, such meanings are the product of social definition processes. This means that near misses need not necessarily be socially constructed as accident precursors at all. This is the conclusion reached by Georgetown University's Robin Dillon and her collaborators, who have been conducting research on group perceptions of events involving near misses. One of their key findings is that near misses can engender complacency rather than concern. In one experiment involving students and NASA personnel, they found that subjects rated a hypothetical manager as successful when his space mission succeeded but also when the mission succeeded despite a near miss that could have had catastrophic results. This effect is known as outcome bias—a focus on positive outcomes at the expense of the (flawed) processes through which those outcomes were achieved. Interestingly, subjects expressed surprise about the successful outcome in the near-miss condition, indicating that they were aware the mission could have failed. However, this did not stop them from defining the completed mission as a success, or seeing the manager as successful. The Dillon group also found that managers' experiences with near misses can encourage more extreme risk-taking behavior, in part because, being defined as successes, near misses do not count against them (Dillon and Tinsley 2008).

Dillon and her colleagues have also found evidence of such effects in the realm of natural hazards. In experiments, they found that in groups that included students and risk experts, information on previous near misses had a negative effect on groups' interest in purchasing flood insurance. Similarly, in an experiment involving hurricanes and hurricane damage, study participants who were told that their homes had experienced storms in the past but no property damage were less likely to decide to evacuate under warning conditions than those who did not receive information on previous storms. Put another way, near-miss information caused subjects to be more likely to opt out of recommended protective actions, putting themselves at greater risk (Dillon, Tinsley, and Cronin 2011).

These kinds of findings remind us that group and individual perceptions of the meaning of near misses can be the opposite of what might be desirable from the perspective of risk reduction. Viewed in tandem with knowledge about how organizational structures and processes influence definitions of and responses to close calls, they help explain why brushes with catastrophe are so often discounted.

LEARNING FROM DISASTERS?

Ambiguous cues and near misses are one thing, but shouldn't organizations and institutions learn and change following major disasters? When disaster strikes, people may die and organizations that perform poorly are singled out for opprobrium. Doesn't that provide a powerful incentive for change? As it turns out, not necessarily. As discussed earlier, NASA appeared not to have learned key lessons following the *Challenger* disaster; inquiries following the *Columbia* explosion identified contributing organizational factors that were essentially identical to those cited in studies on the *Challenger* incident (Vaughan 2006). BP did not alter its practices significantly after the Texas City disaster, even though it was brutally criticized for its focus on productivity and cost cutting and its deficient safety culture.

Within the disaster research community, political scientist Thomas Birkland is the foremost authority on the extent to which institutions and policy systems learn from the experience of disaster. In two books and several other publications (Birkland 1997, 2004, 2006, 2009), he explores why some disasters lead to some degree of learning and change within policy systems, while others—the majority, in fact—do not. On the basis of analyses of events as varied as hurricanes, earthquakes, oil spills, aviation disasters, and the 9/11 terrorist attacks, Birkland has isolated factors that cause some disasters to become focusing events capable of changing institutional agendas and promoting learning. Typically, the disasters that lead to change are large, serious ones that are also socially defined as representing major policy failures that need to be remedied. What then follows is a search for lessons learned and policy remedies. Here again, both the lessons of disaster and proposed solutions to disaster-related failures are socially constructed, and advocacy groups and policy entrepreneurs are typically active in suggesting solutions. Following John Kingdon's work on the policy process (2002), as well as the "garbage can" model of organizational decision making (Cohen, March, and Olsen 1972), the putatively disaster-related problems that new policies need to solve are often defined in terms of solutions that already exist within the policy system or that are advanced by interest and advocacy groups and the media.

Borrowing a term originally coined by Lee Clarke (1999), Birkland argues that many organizational and institutional after-action reports and lessons-learned reports can be viewed as "fantasy documents" that do little to stimulate learning or to address the fundamental causes of disasters. Efforts to extract lessons learned are often nothing more than a knee-jerk response to the fact that things have gone badly wrong, and even efforts to bring about institutional change are biased by powerful interests. After major disasters,

[o]pportunities for learning and change come because these are extreme events, and therefore gain the attention that routine events do not. These events gain a great deal of media attention and, therefore, public attention. . . . With public attention comes pressure to do something about the event. *What that "something" might be is often very murky, because focusing events not only raise an issue on the agenda; they also elevate the manifold constructions of the issue on the agenda. Only those constructions that somehow resonate with the public or elites are elevated, even if these constructions are, in the causal sense, wrong.* (Birkland 2009: 148; emphasis added)

Research by Birkland and others (see, e.g., Alesch, Arendt, and Petak 2005, on California's hospital seismic safety policies following the 1994 Northridge earthquake) provides many examples of how efforts to address disaster-related problems often go awry. Solutions to socially constructed problems that appear to be revealed by disaster may be largely symbolic. Even serious, nonsymbolic efforts may not actually reduce future risks. Implementing lessons learned may prove too costly or may be blocked for other reasons, or the change process may be hijacked by actors who are motivated solely by economic or political motives. For these and other reasons, organizational and institutional efforts to learn and change following disasters are typically laden with difficulty.

Yet learning and changes do sometimes take place in the aftermath of disasters, often because disasters open policy windows, by forcing key actors to acknowledge long-standing problems, by revealing unanticipated threats, and by temporarily suppressing forces that support the status quo. For example, after the 1933 Long Beach earthquake, which caused severe damage to school buildings, the state of California passed the Field Act, which mandated seismically safe construction for public schools (Alesch and Petak 1986). The Oil Pollution Act of 1990 followed closely on the heels of the *Exxon Valdez* spill. The Katrina catastrophe led to the passage of the Post-Katrina Emergency Management Reform Act. The 9/11 terrorist attacks ushered in numerous legal, policy, and institutional changes that were meant to address lessons learned. Many of those changes were, to put it mildly, ill advised and, as Birkland would say, "in the causal sense, wrong," but the impact of 9/11, for good or ill, is undeniable. After the BP oil spill, the federal government finally did take steps intended to reduce regulatory capture in the oil drilling industry. The government of Japan did the same thing with the nuclear industry after the Fukushima disaster.

Some communities do learn from disasters, even if many do not. After experiencing a series of severe floods, the city of Tulsa, Oklahoma, embarked in the 1980s on an ambitious flood mitigation program that is now recognized as a model of its kind. Along the Gulf Coast, although not well publicized, many recovery projects that developed in the aftermath of Hurricane Katrina reflect significant learning on the part of property owners, neighborhoods, and communities (for details, see Smith 2011). Elsewhere, other efforts seek to apply new learning in the aftermath of future disasters. For example, some communities engage in predisaster planning for postdisaster recovery, focusing on changes they deem necessary for successful recovery and the effective reduction of future risks and vulnerabilities.[10] Efforts like these may prove in time to have only limited effects, or even perverse ones, but they hold out hope that learning is indeed possible.

This chapter has focused primarily on the production of risk within organizations and organizational ecologies. In the next chapter, I broaden the analysis to include risk production at community and global scales.

CHAPTER 6

Communities and Societies at Risk

THIS CHAPTER SCALES UP FROM the organizational level of analysis to community, national, and global levels in a further effort to explore the forces that are implicated in the social production of risk and vulnerability. It characterizes risk production and buildup as consequences of the operation of political-economic forces at these different levels. At the local community level, elevated disaster risks are one consequence of the activities of "growth machines," and rent-seeking practices again emerge as drivers of risky behavior. Differential group vulnerability is also tied to the political economy of place, in that exposure to hazards and disaster impacts is structured by and through social processes that help dominant groups and powerful political actors realize their aims at the expense of the less powerful.

Similarly, for nations, the magnitude and severity of disaster risks and vulnerabilities are closely linked to economic and political conditions. As later discussions will show, disaster risks are not so much a function of geographic location and hazard exposure as they are of societal conditions such as poverty and poor governance. While losses from disasters take place at particular points in time, the social and economic processes that create those losses evolve over much longer periods. The current era of megadisasters reflects the buildup over time of unaddressed catastrophic risks.

RISK PRODUCTION AT THE COMMUNITY SCALE
Growth Machine Politics and the Production of Risk

To gain insight into the production of risk at the community level, a useful starting point is to think about land—that is, land that can be turned into real estate, developed, and redeveloped. There is only so much land; unlike other types of property and capital, generally speaking, we cannot create more of it. There are exceptions, of course, as anyone knows who has seen the artificial islands in Osaka Bay, Port and Rokko Island; or the real estate in San Francisco's Marina District, which was created literally from the debris of the 1906 earthquake. But original or manufactured, existing or reclaimed, land is finite. Land is also a commodity, and one very important way to generate wealth is through intensified land speculation and development.

Urban researchers in the United States have long pointed to the central role played by development interests and their boosters in local politics. In fact, it is not an exaggeration to say that growth and development are the central focus of local politics. Local "growth machines" (Molotch 1976; Logan and Molotch 1987) consist of coalitions that seek to make their communities attractive for investment, which may be generated within the community itself but increasingly comes from external sources, such as national or multinational corporations seeking office or industrial space and opportunities for profit. Growth machine coalitions typically consist of landowners, property developers, and leaders of key industries, as well as other entities that profit directly from development, such as banks. Alliances between business elites and political decision makers are a common, taken-for-granted element in local politics. Pro-growth interests possess systemic power (Stone 1980) that enables them to form strong and lasting coalitions with political leaders in order to advance their agendas. Governments encourage development in various ways, such as offering tax incentives and other subsidies and providing infrastructure services in order to stimulate growth. Public-private development partnerships are increasingly common—and increasingly touted as the model for how development should proceed worldwide.

Communities compete with one another to attract activities that spur growth and "job creation," although good jobs are not necessarily created through pro-growth schemes. The push toward developing and strengthening engines of growth takes many forms. Some cities opt for casinos, convention centers, and sports venues. Others organize development around theme parks, leisure and recreation, or publicly funded facilities such as agency headquarters, public universities, national labs and other research facilities, and military bases. Even prisons are framed as attractive from the standpoint of "job creation." Also common is development centering on what John Hannigan (1998) calls the "fantasy city" model of growth, based on the colocation of various forms of entertainment, best exemplified by cities such as Las Vegas and Orlando and places such as the Mall of America, Universal City in Los Angeles, and San Diego's Gaslamp Quarter.

Some communities have rejected the pro-development gospel in favor of growth limits, open space protection, and urban planning concepts such as smart growth and compact development. Similarly, some neighborhoods slated for more-intensive development have successfully opposed such plans. However, these communities and neighborhoods are atypical, and the fact that community residents find it necessary to organize antigrowth community movements is itself a testimony to the entrenched political power of pro-growth coalitions.

Growth machine politics and rent seeking are essentially inseparable. Recall that rent seeking involves activities on the part of organized groups to mold governmental policies and expenditures in ways that are profitable for those groups. Rent-seeking practices take different forms, but what they have in common is the use of political power to shape governmental decisions and actions in ways that generate rents, or profits for particular groups—in this case, local growth machines—that are in excess of what they could have generated without such action.

Growth machine politics, growth promotion, and the rent-seeking activities they generate have several consequences for disaster risk and vulnerability. First and most basic, pro-growth actors want as few limitations on profitable forms of development as possible, even in situations involving development in potentially hazardous areas. They prefer to operate in environments in which they are not constrained by land use plans, zoning and code requirements, and environmental regulations. They generally oppose regulations and requirements that would add to the cost of building and infrastructure construction and maintenance, including hazard reduction requirements, and they seek to comply only minimally with existing mandates. Second, growth machine coalitions deemphasize the risks associated with places and spaces, focusing instead on the amenities provided by those locations. The general pattern is to downplay the fact that many high-amenity places—coastal communities, areas adjacent to rivers and streams, and the wildland-urban interface—can also be high-hazard areas.

Third, growth coalitions have few incentives to pay attention to hazards. With some exceptions, communities and homebuyers do not demand protection against disasters; in fact, the public may oppose such measures as too costly, or as interfering with property rights. One reason pro-growth interests discount disaster risks is that the ultimate costs of development in risky locations are not borne by those who profit from development activities in the short term. Rather, those costs are borne by others: individual property owners, communities, insurance providers, and taxpayers. Finally, even when disasters occur, giving stricken communities the opportunity to act decisively to reduce future disaster losses, those opportunities are frequently missed, and gains that are made tend to be rolled back over time. Long-term risk reduction efforts have succeeded in only a limited number of cases, which again attests to the lasting influence of pro-growth interests.

There are many examples of how the activities of the pro-growth sector result in expanded disaster vulnerability. The Sacramento–San Joaquin River Delta, also known as the Northern California Delta, is one such example. The delta is vast, stretching from the Pacific Ocean eastward beyond Sacramento. Throughout the delta, more than fifty "islands" are protected from flooding by more than 1,300 miles of aging earthen levees, many of which are subsiding or are in poor repair. Levee failures have been occurring in the delta on a regular basis since construction originally began on the system in the 1800s—so much so that the increasingly fragile delta region is thought to be the site of the next Katrina-like catastrophe. Studies indicate that levees in the delta will fail catastrophically in the event of a major Bay Area earthquake, that the entire delta region is under threat from winter storms and flooding, whose effects will intensify with sea-level rise, and that current strategies for managing risks in the delta are unsustainable (URS Corporation 2009, 2011; see also Galloway et al. 2007). However, these conditions have not prevented an explosion of residential development behind levees and in flood-prone areas throughout the delta region. Estimates indicate that by 2020, 1.3 million people will be living behind levees in Sacramento, San Joaquin, and Yolo counties alone (Burton and Cutter 2008).

One of the most notorious examples of development behind the levees is an area called Natomas, which is part of the Sacramento metropolitan area. The Natomas basin has a long history of flooding and is often described as a "sink" or "bathtub" that would fill rapidly to a depth of twenty feet, and even higher in some spots, if any of the approximately forty miles of substandard levees surrounding it should fail. However, the basin has also long represented a development opportunity owing to its location within and adjacent to the city of Sacramento. Significant building began in the late 1980s, when the Arco Arena (now the Powerbalance Pavilion) was constructed and the National Basketball Association's Sacramento Kings took up residence. The 1990s and early 2000s were marked by land specu- lation, intense residential development, and residential growth within the basin, which currently has a population of around 80,000.

The Katrina catastrophe led federal agencies to take a closer look at flood hazards in the Northern California Delta and the Sacramento area, particularly Natomas. In 2008, in recognition of the levee system's many vulnerabilities, the Federal Emergency Management Agency (FEMA) raised the flood-risk rating for the basin significantly, making insurance coverage mandatory for property owners with federally backed mort- gages and increasing residential flood insurance premiums. Predictably, the new requirements were met with opprobrium on the part of local elites and residents of Natomas, and in the face of intense opposition, FEMA reversed itself in 2010 and permitted a temporary reduction in premiums. However, the Natomas area remained under a de facto build- ing moratorium because any new construction would have to be elevated to federally specified safe levels of flood protection.

At issue in the 2008 FEMA decision was the fact that the Natomas levees did not meet the minimum federal standard for protection against a one-hundred-year flood, which is defined as a flood that has a 1 percent chance of being equaled or exceeded in any given year. Use of terms such as "one-hundred-year" to describe flood probabilities is misleading for several reasons. Some areas within one-hundred-year flood zones will flood more frequently and deeply than others, and flood projections always contain some uncertainty. As scientific measures have improved, flood probabilities have been adjusted upward or downward. Communities can experience one-hundred-year floods two or more years in a row, or even more than once in a single year. Perhaps a better way of expressing the one-hundred-year flood concept would be to say that such a flood has a 26 percent chance of occurring over the life of a thirty-year mortgage. However, those wishing to promote development and downplay risks benefit from the one-hundred-year terminology, implying as it does that there is little cause for concern regarding events that putatively happen so rarely.

Responding to the federal government's revised flood probabilities, Natomas embarked in 2007 on a multiyear levee improvement program that was designed to provide one-hundred-year flood protection, which would enable property owners to continue to have access to flood insurance at standard rates and allow the lifting of the building moratorium. Since that project began, the U.S. Army Corps of Engineers adopted stricter levee safety standards; as a consequence, what was originally estimated as a $414 million series of levee improvements is now projected to end up costing $780 million for two-hundred-year flood protection. There is currently no clear indication, in the face of falling home values, foreclosures, and a governmental fiscal crisis in California at local and state levels, of how Natomas and the state will be able to make up their share of the shortfall.

The Natomas case is interesting in many respects, not least of which are the ways it illustrates how growth machines operate. The Natomas area has flooded many times in the past. Until fairly recently, the area mainly consisted of agricultural land, and experts consistently warned against more intensive development because the risk of flooding was so high. However, over the last few decades Natomas became a classic example of rent seeking on the part of local development elites and their political allies. Although the levees nearly failed in a major flood in 1986, prompting stricter flood insurance requirements, growth promoters continued to press for commercial and residential development, and they ultimately prevailed. Fortunes were made as the price of land skyrocketed in areas slated for development. The building boom in

Natomas contributed in a major way to population growth in greater Sacramento, increasing the region's overall vulnerability to floods. But the real genius of development strategies in Natomas and elsewhere in the Northern California Delta was the way they generated profits for rent-seeking interests at the expense of virtually everyone else. Landowners, developers, and their political allies achieved their growth objectives against weak opponents such as conservation groups. Moreover, they were able to do so by getting other parties to pay for the levee upgrading that made further intensive development possible. Under the current levee improvement scheme, affected local jurisdictions need to generate only 12.5 percent of project costs, while the state and the federal government will provide the remainder. Revenues at the local level are being raised through property assessments, in effect requiring property owners to pay for the privilege of living in one of the most flood-vulnerable areas in the nation. Improvements in flood protection constitute a major subsidy to development interests, and when Natomas floods, as it inevitably will—and probably sooner rather than later, under our changing climate regime—U.S. taxpayers will foot the bill for recovery through federal flood insurance payouts, FEMA assistance to government-owned properties, small business loans, and other forms of aid.

Government programs to reduce losses from floods have made little headway in the face of development pressures. As documented by Pinter (2005), government efforts to buy out at-risk properties and relocate residents in the aftermath of the massive 1993 Midwest floods have been more than offset by more-intensive development within those same floodplains, particularly in the state of Missouri and around the St. Louis area. Levee improvements by the Army Corps of Engineers have encouraged such development, even though levees that are certified as safe do not prevent large-scale flooding and actually undermine natural flood protections such as wetlands. The weak floodplain management policies that exist in many states have done little to stem the tide of development.

To put present-day flood risks in context, levee building and flood control projects in general have historically been undertaken to provide protection for profitable economic activities, increase land values, and allow for more-intensive development in floodplains. From the nineteenth century to the present, throughout the nation, including the Northern California Delta and cities along the Mississippi and numerous other rivers, the federal government, primarily through the Army Corps of Engineers, has acted at the behest of local elites to put flood control projects in place. Indeed, federal action to provide flood control systems in response to the demands of economically powerful groups was an important element in the emergence of the U.S. state itself (O'Neill 2006). Legislation such as the 1917, 1928, 1936, and 1944 flood control acts and major floods such as the catastrophic Mississippi River floods of 1927 firmly institutionalized the federal government as the protector of the interests of economic elites in New Orleans, Memphis, and other major river cities (Barry 2007; O'Neill 2006). Over time, the composition of elite power blocs shifted; on the lower Mississippi River, for example, the early beneficiaries of levee construction were planters, merchants, and shippers, while later beneficiaries were land developers and the fossil fuels industry. What remained constant, however, was the search by growth promoters for ever-stronger flood protection.

As described earlier, the late geographer Gilbert White, who is known as the father of floodplain management for his research and contributions to flood loss-reduction programs like the National Flood Insurance Program, was a strong critic of federal flood control policies such as extensive levee and dam building. In his dissertation, published in 1945, and in subsequent publications, White called attention to what he termed the "levee effect"—the idea that levees actually increase flood losses rather than decrease them, because the presence of levees encourages development in floodplains. Communities that believe they are protected from floods will proceed to develop land adjacent to levees, leaving more people and property vulnerable to large floods that will inevitably occur.

Studies on normalized hurricane losses in the United States indicate that increasing losses can be traced directly to intensified development in vulnerable coastal areas (Pielke and Landsea 1998; Pielke et al. 2008). Between 1970 and 2009, seven of the world's ten most expensive disasters in terms of insured losses occurred in coastal areas. Those events include, in descending order of losses, Hurricanes Katrina (2005), Andrew (1992), Ike (2008), Ivan (2004), Wilma (2005), Rita (2005), and Charley

(2004), which together killed approximately 2,200 people and caused more than $164 billion in total insured losses (Peacock and Husein 2011). More recently, Superstorm Sandy topped all but two of those disasters (Katrina and Andrew) in economic losses. As Pielke and colleagues note in their study of 105 years of hurricane damage in the United States,

[a]s people continue to flock to the nation's coasts and bring with them ever more personal wealth, losses will continue to increase. A simple extrapolation of the current trend of doubling losses every 10 years suggests that a storm like the great 1926 Miami hurricane could result in perhaps $500 billion in damage as soon as the 2020s. (2008: 38)

Sea-level rise, erosion, and other consequences of climate change are steadily increasing exposures to hurricanes, tropical storms, and nor'easters in many parts of the United States. For example, sea-level rise has been accelerating in a one-thousand-kilometer-long "hotspot" on the Atlantic Coast stretching north from Cape Hatteras, North Carolina (Sallenger, Doran, and Howd 2012), virtually ensuring that future storms will create more extensive damage and disruption. Along with other factors, sea-level rise has been implicated in the massive losses caused by Superstorm Sandy. However, here again Sandy's damage can be attributed at least as much to imprudent development in hazardous areas, which took place without official opposition. As one investigative report noted after that disaster,

[o]n Staten Island, developers built more than 2,700 mostly residential structures in coastal areas at extreme risk of storm surge flooding between 1980 and 2008, with the approval of city planning and zoning authorities. . . . Developers built up parts of the Jersey shore and the Rockaways, a low-lying peninsula in Queens, N.Y. in a similar fashion . . . with little effort by local or state officials to mitigate the risk posed by hurricanes. . . . Ocean County, N.J., home to devastated communities including Seaside Heights and Toms River, has been one of the fastest growing counties in the nation's most densely populated state. Between 1980 and 2010, the county's population increased more than 70 percent. . . . More residential building permits were issued in the county in 2010 than anywhere else in New Jersey. (Rudolph et al. 2012)

Urban planning researcher Raymond Burby (2006) has called attention to what he terms the "safe development paradox," a pattern created by federal actions aimed at protecting areas that are at risk from disasters, which then make it possible to develop such areas. Examples of such actions include levee building, beach replenishment, flood insurance—and ultimately disaster relief. For Burby and others (see Kates et al. 2006), pre-Katrina New Orleans is the prototypical example of federally enabled activities that resulted in ballooning vulnerability. Throughout the twentieth century, major floods and hurricanes were immediately followed by greater investments in flood control, and subsequently by more-intensive development. The Army Corps of Engineers is required to justify flood-protection works using cost-benefit analysis, but tellingly, as Burby (2006) and others point out, in New Orleans and other areas, the benefits the corps calculated, which were judged to outweigh the costs of increased protection, typically reflected benefits from the protection of *future* rather than *existing* development. Put another way, flood protection expenditures could be justified from a cost standpoint only if more at-risk land was developed.

Burby (2006) also points to a second paradox of risky community action, which he terms the "local government paradox," or the observation that local communities want to be kept safe from hazards but do not want to invest in hazard loss reduction or manage development. Hazard reduction is not sufficiently salient at the local level to warrant emphasis, especially compared with the "job-creating" projects championed by development boosters (see also Mileti 1999). Burby argues that these two paradoxes result in an increase in moral hazard, or conditions in which measures originally designed to reduce risk actually increase it.

If we turn again to New Orleans, a book called *Catastrophe in the Making* (Freudenburg et al. 2009) places the failure of flood-protective works in Hurricane Katrina in broad historical context, with a special focus on the Mississippi River Gulf Outlet (MR-GO) as a classic example of rent seeking in a city that has perfected the art. In addition to profiting from more-intensive land use made possible by levees, local elites have historically sought to profit from shipping, and to that end they promoted canal building and other forms of "water pork" made possible by large federal subsidies. Over time, canals became more numerous, and they also became wider and deeper as the size of ships increased. MR-GO was a very large project that was meant to accommodate very large ships and shorten their transit distance and time between the Mississippi River and the Gulf of Mexico. It was also intended to increase New Orleans's competitive advantage over other ports in the region, such as Houston. Growth boosters promised that MR-GO would yield large economic benefits, but those benefits never materialized. Indeed, Freudenburg and coauthors (2009) provide evidence to show that even the original Army Corps of Engineers cost-benefit analysis for MR-GO, a scarcely impressive benefit-to-cost ratio of $1.45, was arrived at by ignoring many projected costs. Prior to Katrina, use of the outlet for shipping had been spiraling downward from a peak volume of 9.4 million short freight tons in 1978 to 1.2 million short freight tons in 2004 (Carter and Stern 2006). What did materialize, however, was a host of problems caused by the channel that included the need for constant dredging and widen-ing; saltwater intrusion; damage to fragile wetlands, cypress swamps, and bayou ecosystems; and wildlife and fisheries losses. Wetlands and cypress damage in turn translated into reduced protection against hur-ricanes. While it is not entirely accurate to argue, as some have, that the MR-GO channel itself conveyed Katrina's storm surge directly into the heart of New Orleans, what is clear from various studies (Seed et al. 2008; Interagency Performance Evaluation Task Force 2008) is that the presence of MR-GO created a series of conditions that increased the severity of the surge within the city, and that levee failures along the outlet led directly to the flooding of St. Bernard Parish, which is adja-cent to New Orleans. In 2012, supporting a lower court ruling, the Fifth Circuit Court of Appeals found that the U.S. Army Corps of Engineers was responsible for flooding in the Lower Ninth Ward of New Orleans and St. Bernard Parish through its failure to maintain MR-GO, and also that the corps was not immune from liability for flood damages.[1] That judgment was reversed in 2012 (Greene 2012).

The machinations of growth proponents are evident with respect to other hazards as well. In California, which has done more than any state to reduce earthquake risks, efforts to promote earthquake safety have historically been opposed by such interests. For example, California's 1972 Alquist-Priolo Earthquake Fault Zoning Act required the mapping of all active earthquake faults statewide, prohibited some types of construction in such fault zones, and required that prospective buyers be informed if the properties they wished to purchase were located in areas where faulting had occurred. The law immediately raised the ire of real estate interests, developers, and property owners, who were concerned that information on active earthquake faults might negatively affect property transactions and values. Nonetheless, maps indicating active faults were duly drawn up by the state. However, four years after the passage of the law, the maps began to be redone, and that remapping process resulted in the "disappearance" of many previously mapped faults as well as the shrinking in size of many fault zones. Approximately 160 of 708 fault maps were altered in that fashion (Johnson 2011). The process by which changes were made was complex, but the method used to make faults disappear was simple: the state simply created a new definition of what constituted an "active fault"—one that varied significantly from commonly used scientific definitions. In 2011, investigative journalists working with California Watch devoted many months to the study of these and other activities that served to undermine state seismic safety legislation. In one case documented by California Watch, an earthquake fault map for the city of Pescadero shows a fault that makes a right angle, so that it avoids the property on which the town's high school is located. An earthquake expert asked by reporters to review the map observed that "faults don't go at right angles. . . . It doesn't look right, because faults don't do this" (Johnson 2011).

Owing to lobbying by the California Realtors Association, the original Alquist-Priolo law contained many exemptions, and the disclosure materials provided to prospective buyers after the law was passed were so vague that most buyers did not understand the meaning of the information they were given. Typically, they were told that a property was in a "special studies zone" or an "Alquist-Priolo district," without any direct reference to earthquake hazards. Disclosures were made late in the purchasing process, which reduced their influence on buyer decision making (Palm 1981).

The Alquist-Priolo law has been amended over time, and disclosure requirements have been strengthened. However, there is little current research on the extent to which the law is actually working as intended. Moreover, in the case of development in Alquist-Priolo zones, responsibility for complying with the law generally resides at the local community level and with developers and their consulting geologists. Here again, growth machine politics come into play. Communities desiring growth—that is, most communities—have an incentive not to look too closely at reports generated by consultants, and developers have an incentive to shop around for favorable geological reports. This is how it happened that in Pleasanton, California, in the late 1980s a developer wishing to build on a 258-acre site could reject both state maps and a geologist's report confirming the presence of the active Calaveras Fault on the property and then find another geologist who dutifully produced a report showing that the fault stopped at the property's southern border and then continued again at its northern border (Halper 2002).

Only a tiny proportion of California's land falls within active fault zones; hazardous buildings are a much more significant source of earthquake risk, and California has many of them. Here again, development interests have been in the forefront of opposition to hazardous-building remediation programs, such as those addressing unreinforced masonry buildings (URMs). URMs have long been regarded as posing a life-safety hazard in even moderately sized earthquakes, and there has been a moratorium on their construction in high-seismic-hazard zones in California since after the 1933 Long Beach earthquake. However, for many decades URM owners and their allies resisted efforts to require seismic upgrading of existing hazardous structures. In many California cities, coalitions of property owners sought to prevent URM laws from being enacted, lengthen the time period for compliance when laws were passed, make adherence to seismic standards voluntary rather than mandatory, and exempt certain types of buildings from retrofit programs. San Francisco, for example, did not pass a URM ordinance until 1992, and rental properties of four or fewer units are exempt.

More recently, engineers and building officials have called attention to the hazards associated with another class of buildings, nonductile concrete (NDC) structures. NDC buildings also present significant life-safety hazards, and unfortunately they are also a very common building type in California and other seismically hazardous areas of the United States and around the world. The construction of NDC buildings was banned in California after the 1971 San Fernando earthquake, but thousands of older buildings remain, including numerous large high-occupancy structures. The Concrete Coalition, an advocacy group made up of engineers and other seismic safety experts, has estimated that there are 16,000–17,000 NDC buildings built prior to 1980 that are located in high-seismic-risk areas in California, including public school build-ings. For the most part, these buildings have not even been inventoried, owing in large measure to opposition from building owners and busi-ness groups (Bernstein 2005).

Building Booms, Development, and Disaster Losses

Over decades, disaster losses in the United States have been increasing steadily. This is not because the natural events that trigger disasters, such as hurricanes and floods, have become more frequent or severe. Rather, it is because of an increase in what risk specialists call *exposures*, or the number of people and amount of property at risk.

In addition to the sheer quantity of buildings and other structures that are at risk, there is also an issue of quality, or the extent to which properties that are in harm's way are designed and built to withstand disasters. The URM and NDC buildings discussed above are hazardous primarily because they are older existing structures not built to current codes, but even newer buildings can be prone to loss and damage if they are poorly designed and constructed. Issues of quantity and quality were highlighted in Florida following Hurricane Andrew, which devastated South Dade County in 1992. Population growth in Dade County and other coastal areas in Florida had been rapid in the decades preceding the hurricane. Much of the residential building stock that was added to accommodate that growth later proved to be highly vulnerable to hurri-cane damage. The problem stemmed largely from developers' disregard of appropriate building techniques for hurricane-prone areas, combined with government's inability—or unwillingness—to ensure that such techniques were being used. Although the South Florida Building Code was reasonably strict, construction practices and code enforcement were lax. Code details were not followed, appropriate materials were not used, and many builders working in fast-growing Florida communities were from outside the region and thus unfamiliar with the kinds of measures that are necessary to reduce hurricane damage. The use of nonlicensed contractors was widespread, and corners were continually cut to meet the demands of mass-scale residential construction. Grand jury investigations conducted both before and after Andrew found that the Miami-Dade County building department was not carrying out its inspection and building code enforcement duties properly; the investigations also uncovered many cases of fraud in the preparation of building inspection reports. A grand jury report filed in May 1990 highlighted various examples of slipshod and essentially nonexistent building inspection practices, such as this one involving a roofing inspector. That inspector

never climbed a ladder his entire work day. As the morning hours progressed, the length of time involved in inspections markedly decreased. While early sites were visited from between eight and twenty minutes, by 9:48 A.M. the inspector was leaving construction sites within two minutes of his arrival. In one instance the inspector only visited the construction trailer and never looked at the building to be inspected. By 11:02 A.M. the inspections were done by driving through the site without ever leaving the car. By 11:40 A.M., this inspector was home for the day. (Dade County Grand Jury 1989: 6)

Roof damage is a key source of losses in hurricanes and other wind events, so with reports like this one we can begin to see how such large-scale hurricane damage occurred in Hurricane Andrew. Elsewhere the same report bluntly stated that "[Dade County] Building and Zoning does not have enough building inspectors to competently conduct the necessary number of building inspections and they are not adequately supervised. Inspections are frequently conducted in a short, perfunctory manner and some are not performed at all" (4). As a result of such practices, some estimates indicate that as much as 40 percent of the insured property losses in Andrew were due to weak code enforcement and substandard building practices (Bragg 1999).

In Dade County, the consequences of rapid development without appropriate safeguards were vividly seen in the aftermath of Andrew, and here again it is important to keep in mind who profited from that development and who ultimately bore the costs of shoddy construction workmanship. Land speculators and developers made their money and got out before Andrew struck. Fifteen people died and 250,000 were left homeless in a disaster that produced an estimated $30 billion in property losses—at that time, the costliest disaster in U.S. history. Andrew caused the second-largest insurance property casualty loss in U.S. history, after Katrina. After massive payouts in Andrew and in subsequent Florida hurricanes, insurance companies pulled out of the Florida market, and the state had to step in to offer insurance. However, even now premiums in the state-backed insurance risk pool are not priced to reflect risk; to even suggest that rates should be higher is tantamount to political suicide in Florida. The insurer of last resort, the U.S. Treasury, has continued to pay out for losses in Andrew and later in Opal (1995); Charley, Frances, Ivan, and Jeanne (2004); Dennis, Katrina, and Wilma (2005); and other smaller hurricane events. The collapse of the real estate bubble has put an end to the construction boom in Florida and elsewhere, but the state now has a large inventory of properties—many of them foreclosed on and abandoned as a result of the economic downturn—that will be vulnerable in future hurricanes.

Politics, Economics, and the Production of Disaster Vulnerability

Vulnerability to disasters is a function of several sets of factors. Place matters: some communities are simply more vulnerable to disaster impacts than others. Also important is the disaster resistance of elements in the built environment, such as residential buildings, critical facilities, and infrastructure systems such as highways and bridges. As we saw in the New Orleans example, communities are also better off if natural systems, such as wetlands that cushion the effects of disaster agents, are healthy and able to function.

An all-important final element in disaster vulnerability involves the extent to which exposed populations are able to minimize disaster impacts beforehand and cope well when disasters do occur. Disaster impacts are most severe when large-magnitude disaster agents strike in places where the built environment lacks disaster resistance and where populations lack the ability to protect themselves and weather the effects of disasters. Disasters are often depicted as great levelers, victimizing rich and poor alike. However, research paints a very different picture, indicating that the effects of disasters on populations are anything but random. A substantial literature indicates that the disaster vulnerability of individuals and groups is associated with a number of socioeconomic factors that include income, poverty, and social class; race, ethnicity, and culture; physical ability and disability; language competency; social networks and social capital; gender; household composition; home ownership; and age. The general pattern seen across numerous studies is that many of the same factors that disadvantage members of society on a daily basis also play out during disasters. Put another way, population vulnerability to extreme events is itself socially structured. As disaster researcher Elaine Enarson notes, "[t]he everyday living conditions of the nation's poorest, sickest, most dependent, and most isolated residents directly and indirectly increase the exposure of these residents to physical hazards and to the social, economic, political, and psychological impacts of disaster events" (2007: 261).

The forces that drive disaster vulnerability operate in a variety of ways, both before and after disaster events. Low-income community residents often find themselves living in residences that are physically vulnerable, such as unreinforced masonry apartment buildings in earthquake country, mobile homes, and older, poorly maintained structures. They are therefore more likely than their better-off counterparts to be killed, injured, or left homeless when disaster strikes. Income and access to an automobile also influence evacuation options, as was tragically evident in Hurricane Katrina. Poverty in the United States and around the world is gendered; female-headed households are more likely to be poor, which limits their housing options and their ability to prepare for, cope with, and recover from disasters. Heat waves exact the highest death tolls in inner cities and among those who lack access to air conditioning (Borden and Cutter 2008).

Elderly and mobility-impaired persons are more at risk during disas-ters than younger, able-bodied members of the population. Non-English speakers do not have the same access to information on disaster safety as those who speak English, and they may not receive or understand disaster warnings that are issued in English. For example, FEMA's new commercial mobile alert system, which is designed to communicate disaster warnings in brief text form directly to cell phones, is English-only. Citizenship status determines who qualifies for disaster services and is becoming increasingly important even in access to lifesaving emergency services as states enact more anti-immigrant legislation. Homeowners have the option of purchasing hazard insurance coverage, while renters may lack coverage and are also dependent on landlords to mitigate structural safety hazards and make needed repairs when disasters occur.

Outside the United States, socially structured patterns of vulnerability are even more stark. In the December 2004 Indian Ocean tsunami, for example, mortality rates were significantly higher for women than for men. Women's high death rates were attributed to a number of factors, including the fact that many fewer women than men knew how to swim, that women were weighed down by heavy garments meant to maintain modesty, that women in many tsunami-stricken areas were confined to their homes and prevented from going outdoors without being accom-panied by men, and that many women may have died while trying to save their children (Ariyabandu 2006). As discussed later in this chapter, differences in societal levels of prosperity translate directly into differ-ences in mortality and in the economic costs of disasters.

My concern here is not with outlining the myriad ways in which social inequalities translate into differential disaster vulnerabilities. That topic is addressed in a number of other publications within the growing field of vulnerability science (for research on the United States, see, e.g., Pea-cock, Morrow, and Gladwin 1997; Enarson and Morrow 1998; Bolin and Stanford 1998; Cutter, Boruff, and Shirley 2003; Fothergill 2004; Tierney 2005; Phillips et al. 2010; David and Enarson 2012). Instead, the goal is to describe how political and economic forces have contributed over time to hazard vulnerability within the context of specific communities.

Phoenix, Arizona, is one such community. As noted, extreme heat kills more people in the United States than any other natural hazard. However, even within heat-stricken communities, some areas are significantly hotter than others. These "urban heat islands" within cities are the consequence of a number of factors, including high population density, smaller amounts of open space, and less vegetation. Sociologist Sharon Harlan and her colleagues have been conducting extensive research on microclimates and vulnerability to extreme heat in Phoenix. In addition to assessing exposures to high temperatures caused by heat island effects, they also collected data on contributors to heat vulnerability and resistance, such as building and roofing materials that are common in different neighborhoods, the types of cooling systems used in homes, and the presence of swimming pools that would give residents an opportunity to cool off during hot weather. Additionally, they employed survey data to assess the availability of social support systems across the Phoenix neighborhoods in their study, reasoning that higher levels of social support would help residents cope with extreme heat. These researchers found that parts of Phoenix that had lower median incomes, higher poverty rates, more minority residents, and residents with lower levels of education were also those with the highest heat-related hazards. Social ties were also found to be weakest in the warmest parts of the city.

Two neighborhoods in the study stood in sharp contrast with each other. The most hazardous area from the standpoint of heat was an "archetypical poor inner-city neighborhood with nearly three times the population density as the next most densely inhabited neighborhood in our sample" (Harlan et al. 2006: 2856). The neighborhood was characterized by having few trees and lawns, bare soil, an absence of parks and other green space, and homes with no air conditioning. Located adjacent to an interstate highway, the hot and dusty neighborhood was home to recent immigrants from Mexico who were overwhelmingly renters. The least hazardous place in the city from the perspective of heat, an affluent neighborhood the researchers call "Historic Anglo Phoenix," is located a mere four kilometers from the most hazardous one. But there, "[r]esidents live on palm tree-lined streets with single family houses that have grassy yards supplemented with shade trees, citrus, and dense tropical plantings" (2857). Irrigation that contributes to cooling is abundant; there are parks; homes are air conditioned; and the neighborhood's social support networks were the densest found in the study. These differences translate into very different levels of heat-related risk. On the basis of their studies of variations in heat vulnerability in Phoenix, Harlan and her collaborators concluded that

[o]ne great challenge for creating climate health equity in cities is the legacy of urban development that has left poor and minority populations in deteriorated urban spaces where there are structural constraints on improving environmental conditions. The locations of neighborhoods near transportation routes and industrial corridors result from historical patterns of enforced segregation, zoning regulations, and other municipal decisions which are part of an ongoing process of environmental inequality formation. (2861)

Poor residents of Phoenix are not just exposed to extreme heat. Sara Grineski, Robert Bolin, and their colleagues have been conducting research on patterns of exposure to air pollution and toxic contamination in the city and finding clear patterns of environmental inequality that are structured by both ethnicity and social class. Latinos are the largest minority group in Phoenix, and Grineski, Bolin, and Boone (2007) have found that census areas inhabited by higher numbers of low-income households, Latino immigrants, and renters have higher levels of exposure to pollutants such as nitrous oxide, carbon monoxide, and ozone. Additionally, historic patterns of strict residential racial segregation and decisions regarding the location of transportation corridors and polluting industries have resulted in the higher exposure of poor and minority residents to environmental toxins. Bolin, Grineski, and Collins (2005) document how Latinos and African Americans were relegated by Caucasian elites to South Phoenix, an area that later became a magnet for a long parade of polluting land uses and industries that were attracted to the city by pro-growth boosters. In the 1970s, urban redevelopment schemes led to the introduction of interstate highways, which led in turn to environmental degradation and neighborhood disruption and deterioration in areas adjacent to highways. Disparities in exposure to potential industry-related toxins are large; while 3 percent of residential areas in metropolitan Phoenix are adjacent to areas that are zoned for industrial uses, 35 percent of South Phoenix neighborhoods abut industrial zones (Bolin, Grineski, and Collins 2005).

The empirical patterns observed in Phoenix are examples of a larger nationwide pattern of environmental injustice. Here in the United States, as a consequence of pioneering books such as Robert Bullard's *Dumping in Dixie* (1990) and the activities of the environmental justice movement, it is now widely recognized that the locations of dangerous toxic dumps and hazardous facilities are correlated with the social characteristics of nearby residents. Research by sociologists such as Liam Downey, who employs sophisticated mapping techniques and statistical analyses to explore hypotheses regarding environmental inequality, leaves little doubt that racial and income disparities in exposure to technological risks are widespread. His research also shows that merely living near industrial sites is a source of stress, resulting in symptoms of depression and feelings of powerlessness among residents, even if nothing goes wrong at those facilities (Downey and Van Willigen 2005).

Environmental justice researchers have systematically focused on the ways in which patterns of exposure to pollutants and hazardous substances differ according to population characteristics such as income, race, and ethnicity, but they have been slow to recognize that the same is the case with respect to so-called natural hazards. In contrast, disaster researchers have long been aware of the influence of such factors on vulnerability, victimization, and postdisaster outcomes such as physical and psychosocial recovery (Peacock, Morrow, and Gladwin 1997; Tierney, Lindell, and Perry 2001; Tierney 2005; Bolin 2006). It took Hurricane Katrina to stimulate researchers outside the disaster field and the public at large to begin making that connection. As is now known thanks to extensive research, within the locations hardest hit by Katrina, damaged areas had higher concentrations of African Americans, renters, and poor and unemployed persons than did undamaged ones (Logan 2006). About half the white residents of New Orleans had serious flooding, as compared with three-quarters of black residents (Fussell, Sastry, and Van-Landingham 2010) When Katrina threatened, the vast majority of the residents of New Orleans evacuated, but low-income blacks were most likely to have remained in the city (Elliott and Pais 2006). Although age was the most significant risk factor for deaths in Katrina, race was also influential. Mortality rates were significantly higher for African Americans eighteen years of age and older than for their white counterparts (Brunkard, Namulanda, and Ratard 2008). There were clearly areas in which whites and better-off residents suffered severe impacts, such as predominantly white St. Bernard Parish and communities in coastal Mississippi, but those examples do not negate the significance of race and social class as predictors of hurricane losses.

This is not to say that all environmental injustice is intentional, or that some group of racists conspires to put low-income residents and people of color at risk from environmental hazards and disasters. Rather, it is more appropriate to think about differential exposures and vulnerabilities as outcomes of the ordinary workings of local political economies, in which growth machine coalitions wield the lion's share of power in decision making regarding land use and development. Practices that privilege elite groups can be overt or subtle, intentional or unintentional, but their effects on disadvantaged groups are similar. As Pulido (2000) has demonstrated in the case of Los Angeles, a variety of processes come into play in the production of environmental injustice, including practices that result in residential racial segregation; white flight from minority areas, which leaves minority group members differentially exposed to hazards; zoning laws and restrictive covenants; and decisions involving facility siting and urban redevelopment. In pursuing their own interests, community elites and their political allies may not consciously set out to expose poor and minority populations to higher levels of risk, but over time their cumulative decisions and actions have that effect. In opposing the earthquake safety ordinance in Los Angeles, landlords who owned URM buildings did not intend to impose on apartment dwellers an increased probability of being killed or left homeless in an earthquake; in fact, they contended that by refusing to take on the added expense of earthquake retrofitting, they were actually helping to keep rents affordable for their predominantly low-income tenants. MR-GO boosters in New Orleans, and entities charged with maintaining levee safety, did not consciously intend to harm poor African Americans in places like the Lower Ninth Ward, but their decisions, combined with other longer-term trends in residential land use, put those residents in harm's way—the same residents that generally lacked the ability to evacuate in advance of Katrina's landfall.

As the Phoenix research illustrates, risk buildup is a consequence of diverse decisions, made over time, that shape the urban form in ways that benefit rent-seeking interests but often put less privileged groups in harm's way. The process is self-reinforcing: once particular areas within a community become stigmatized through the presence of noxious facilities, landfills, dirty industries, and other unwanted land uses, they tend to stay that way, attracting similar facilities or leaving a residue of toxic hazards (Bolin, Grineski, and Collins 2005). This depresses property values, ensuring that those who live in such areas are essentially trapped there.

I must emphasize again that vulnerability to hazards and disasters is inseparable from more general patterns of oppression and marginalization that play out on a daily basis during nondisaster times and that have pervasive negative consequences for those who are at risk. Blacks in New Orleans experienced a long string of insults and injuries after surviving Katrina, including mistreatment and humiliation in the Superdome and Convention Center, forced relocation, the murders on Danzinger Bridge, the sometimes fatal shooting of suspected "looters," the subsequent demolition of perfectly serviceable public housing, and the closure of Charity Hospital, which had been established more than 250 years ago to serve poor and indigent inner-city residents. Those who were displaced by Katrina found themselves stigmatized in their new homes, suspected of criminal intent, being lazy, and taking advantage of the disaster relief system (Peek 2012). Although shocking in the context of a catastrophe, those indignities and others were of a piece with what many survivors had experienced before Katrina and indeed had come to expect in their dealings with the police, public officials, landlords, the educational system, and politically powerful groups in general. Such injustice has pernicious effects, not the least of which are rage against its perpetrators, helplessness and despair, and a loss of trust in institutions that, in a vicious cycle, contributes further to the vulnerability and political isolation of those who are discriminated against. We will see later in discussions concerning the social roots of community resilience that trust, the ability to connect across group lines, and a capacity for collective action are properties that enable community members to cope with hazards and disasters. Where such capacities are damaged or absent, the ability to cope is bound to suffer, to the further detriment of those who are already most vulnerable. Feelings of collective efficacy do not develop among those who have been shown again and again that they are powerless, and this is yet another way in which injustice contributes to vulnerability.

Property Rights and Disaster Vulnerability

Land-use planning is among the most effective and widely used strategies for reducing disaster losses. Properly employed, land-use-based loss reduction measures can ensure that communities avoid development in hazardous areas and develop plans for reducing existing property exposures, for example through buying up properties that have been repeatedly flooded. However, groups affiliated with the so-called property rights movement have been known to mobilize against hazard-related land-use planning, especially when land-use measures can be successfully framed as property "takings." Among other cases, the U.S. Supreme Court's 1992 decision in *Lucas v. South Carolina Coastal Commission* provides a legal justification for the movement's positions. In that case, a property owner named Lucas was denied permission to build on his oceanfront lots because the 1988 South Carolina Beachfront Management Act prohibited new construction in areas affected by beach erosion. Lucas contended that the law destroyed the value of his land and constituted a "taking" for which he needed to be compensated; the Supreme Court agreed. Since the time of *Lucas,* there has been a flurry of state-level takings bills and legislation, largely backed by the property rights movement. These laws differ, but their common goal has been to enable property owners to seek compensation for a wide range of governmental regulatory actions, such as zoning, historic building and district designations, wetlands protection measures, and building height and density requirements. The takings-related arguments made by property rights advocates continue to receive support in the courts; in 2013, the U.S. Supreme Court made several rulings favoring their interests, including an important 5–4 decision in *Koontz v. St. Johns River Water Management District*.

Although takings laws are not focused directly on hazard-mitigation activities, they have been used in that way. As geographer Rutherford Platt notes with respect to various hazards,

[t]he obvious way to prevent repetitive losses on eroding shorelines, high risk floodplains, unstable slopes, or tinder-dry forests is to prohibit building or rebuilding in such locations. But land use regulations which thwart property owners from enjoying or cashing in on splendid views, beach access, or rustic isolation are likely to be challenged as takings of private property without compensation. (2008: 4)

Recent years have seen an upsurge in property rights activities undertaken in opposition to the United Nations "Agenda 21" resolution on sustainable development. Agenda 21, which was adopted in 1992, has been framed by the Tea Party and property rights movements as the harbinger of world government, radical environmentalism, and socialism. Recently these groups have targeted the organization known as ICLEI—Local Governments for Sustainability (formerly the International Council for Local Environmental Initiatives)—an international group that seeks to promote environmentally conscious local development activities. Even the American Planning Association has been targeted by the anti–Agenda 21 movement for its programs on sustainability. According to property rights groups, the freedom of Americans is threatened by programs that emphasize smart growth, new urbanism, mixed-use housing, comprehensive land-use planning, and environmental and green codes. Agitation by the Tea Party and other groups has succeeded in influencing many communities to withdraw from ICLEI and also to pass anti–Agenda 21 legislation (Kaufman and Zernike 2012; Mencimer 2011). Although groups tend to operate under the radar, opposition to comprehensive planning for sustainability is far from being a marginal movement. In January 2012, the Republican National Committee passed a "resolution exposing United Nations Agenda 21," signaling acceptance of the Tea Party position on local land-use planning. During the 2012 primary season, presidential candidate Newt Gingrich also identified opposition to Agenda 21 as an important issue.

Anti–Agenda 21 groups oppose essentially anything they define as interfering with individual property rights, including such reasonable measures as public transportation planning. As we saw in the sections above, land-use measures such as floodplain management and restrictions on certain types of construction in active earthquake fault zones are adopted in order to protect people and property. Although this may not be their intention, property rights groups may also be making it more difficult for communities to protect themselves against hazards and climate change. We are already beginning to see how the Tea Party and related groups are reacting to local initiatives aimed at adapting to climate change. In Virginia's Middle Peninsula, for example, Tea Party-affiliated groups like the Virginia Campaign for Liberty have opposed local efforts to combat subsidence and sea-level rise that are resulting in flooding, on the grounds that climate change is a hoax and that proposed measures were part of Agenda 21 (Fears 2011). In the San Francisco Bay Area, regional land use, transportation, and greenhouse gas emission reduction plans are currently being hotly contested by groups that frame them as part of the worldwide Agenda 21 conspiracy.[2] In time, many more communities may find their hands tied by property rights activists, whether their efforts focus on climate change responses, hazard reduction, or more general sustainable planning issues.

RISK PRODUCTION IN GLOBAL CONTEXT

The social forces that act to produce risk are even more evident when viewed at a global scale. A recent World Bank/United Nations report (2010) indicates that disasters resulted in 3.3 million deaths and US$2,300 billion in damage between 1970 and 2008. While monetary losses are significantly higher for disasters that occur in developed, industrialized societies, death tolls are significantly higher in less-developed nations, and those nations typically experience greater losses relative to the size of their GDPs. Even a catastrophe as large as Hurricane Katrina resulted in relatively few lives lost (around 1,800) compared with the total population of the United States, and relatively low economic losses compared with the vast size of the U.S. economy. In comparative terms, Katrina was not as large a disaster as the Haiti earthquake, which, although exact numbers will never be known, may have killed as many as 300,000 out of a total population of nine million and wiped out more than a year's worth of Haiti's GDP in a matter of moments.

A growing body of research indicates that disaster severity—measured in lives and property lost and populations displaced—is related to the position of nations within the global political economy or world system. Decades ago, Wijkman and Timberlake (1984) argued for the importance of viewing hazards and disasters through a development lens, and over time other researchers and disaster management practitioners have emphasized that linkage (Cuny 1983; Varley 1994; Pelling 2003a, 2003b; Bankoff, Frerks, and Hilhorst 2004). Researchers also note that disasters are often the result of development approaches that are unsustainable and argue for a stronger emphasis on sustainable development as a way of reducing disaster losses (Mileti 1999; Smith and Wenger 2006). The United Nations (2005) and the World Bank/United Nations (2010) also stress the relationship between disasters and development processes and outcomes.

Countries' positions in the world system—as G8, G20, or poor nations, "developed," "less developed," and "developing" nations—relate not only to their economic and social conditions but also to their relative political power. Through international institutions such as the World Bank and the International Monetary Fund, dominant actors within the world system can impose measures such as structural readjustment and austerity programs on less powerful, less-well-off countries. Import-export agreements, foreign direct investment programs, and other global-scale interventions also have a direct effect on residents of poorer, less powerful nations. Many countries are suffering the long-term effects of colonialism while at the same time having to adjust to the forces of globalization. The variations in economic and political power that are associated with the position of nation-states within the world system are regularly played out in the landscape of disaster.

The disaster vulnerability of poorer countries is the result of a set of interrelated world-system-level processes that include rapid urbanization, the growth of informal settlements, glaring income inequalities, environmental degradation that results in the loss of natural protections against the forces of disaster, and governance failures that translate into weaknesses in disaster protections. Regarding the perils associated with rapid urbanization, I discussed in the previous chapter research by sociologist Charles Perrow suggesting that disaster losses are growing because of the increase in concentrations of people and hazardous activities—in other words, because larger "targets" mean larger disasters when environmental triggers are present. Disasters are increasing in their frequency and severity, in part because of the uncontrolled urbanization that is characteristic of many poorer countries. The growth of megacities, defined as cities with populations of ten million or more, is a prominent feature of the current world-system political economy. In 1950, there were two megacities in the entire world; in 2005, that number had grown to twenty. By 2015, there will be an estimated twenty-two megacities, of which seventeen will be located in poor countries (United Nations 2006). It is estimated that by 2050, 70 percent of the world's population will live in urban areas—most of that growth taking place in less-developed countries (United Nations 2008). Urbanization is proceeding rapidly in many places that are already highly vulnerable to hazards; these expanding urban agglomerations are outside the core of the world system: Cairo, Caracas, Dhaka, Istanbul, Jakarta, Lagos, Manila, Mexico City, Mumbai, Tehran, and others. As populations increase in urban areas, most of that growth involves people who are very poor and increasingly forced to settle in high-hazard areas—on hillsides, in floodplains, and near hazardous facilities and toxic dumps—and in fragile structures. As a consequence, the urban poor in the developing world are affected disproportionately when disaster strikes.

Urban growth in poor countries involves several dynamics that are directly related to physical disaster vulnerability. Migration into urban areas fuels rapid, speculative building booms and creates increasing pressure to build on marginal land. Even where efforts are made—and typically they are not—controls on the quality of construction are weakened. Densities increase in both existing and new construction. Informal settlements proliferate and grow. One United Nations report estimated in 2003 that 40 percent of urban dwellers in developing countries were living in slums (United Nations 2003), and that percentage has undoubtedly increased during the current global economic downturn. In his eye-opening book *Planet of Slums* (2006a), Mike Davis offers numerous sobering statistics regarding the explosion of informal settlements around the world: one million poor people living permanently in Cairo's City of the Dead; 1.6 million living in one thousand slums and squatter camps in Bangkok; four million dwelling in the slums of Mexico City; war-displaced migrants streaming into slum settlements in Kabul and Karachi; a slum population in Delhi that is expected to exceed ten million by 2015. The expansion of unregulated informal settlements is especially intense in sub-Saharan Africa and in Asia. Indicative of the scale on which slums exist in the latter region, Davis notes that "the five great metropolises of South Asia (Karachi, Mumbai, Delhi, Kolkata, and Dhaka) alone contain 15,000 distinct slum communities whose total population exceeds 20 million" (2006: 26).

Rapid urbanization is invariably accompanied by the depletion of natural resources, including those that offer protection against disasters. As one researcher who studies the disasters-development nexus observes, in areas where urbanization has intensified, environmental damage has inevitably followed:

Consumption of natural assets (trees for fuel, ground water, sand and gravel) and the overexploitation of natural services (water systems and air as sinks for sewerage or industrial waste) have modified the environment through deforestation and slope instability within and surrounding cities, the contamination and silting of water courses, the lowering of water tables followed by salt intrusion or land subsidence, and the loss of mangrove ecosystems with consequent coastal erosion. (Pelling 2003a: 27)

This kind of environmental devastation virtually ensures that when triggering events such as earthquakes, intense rain events, and tropical cyclones occur, disaster losses will skyrocket.

The Venezuelan capital of Caracas is one of many examples of ballooning urban disaster vulnerability. Located at the juxtaposition of the South American and Caribbean plates, the Caracas area is prone to earthquakes; major earthquake events occurred in 1812 and 1967. The population of the greater Caracas area has increased dramatically over the last several decades, as people have moved into the area from other parts of Venezuela and from other South American countries in search of jobs in the oil and tourism industries. As migration increased, informal settlements expanded. An estimated 50 percent of the capital district's 5.9 million residents currently live in slum conditions in extensive *barrios*. Located in a mountainous region, Caracas is at risk from flash flooding, landslides, and debris flows. Vulnerability to earthquake and flood hazards has increased as a result of the influx of migrants into hilly regions and the removal of vegetation and extensive construction on unstable hillsides. Unregulated development has also taken place in dry riverbeds and alluvial plains despite obvious flood hazards. In 1999, fifteen days of intense rainfall caused flash flooding and massive debris flows in and around Caracas that killed an estimated 20,000 people and left tens of thousands homeless (Arnold et al. 2006). After that disaster, residents returned to establish dwellings in damaged structures and to rebuild in areas that had been devastated by the flooding. In a 2004 report, a Caracas engineer who had long advocated for stricter controls on building in hazardous areas was quoted as observing that "[e]very year the people are building and developing in the creeks and the hills, vulnerable to landslides and flows. . . . It's easy to see that many people here could die. But nobody does anything. No central government authority goes to tell them 'You cannot live here'" (McCarthy 2004).

The Philippine archipelago is one of the most disaster-prone regions on earth. The country is vulnerable to earthquakes, volcanoes, landslides, typhoons, heavy monsoon rains, and flooding. The urban area that includes the capital, Manila, has experienced very rapid population growth and is now considered the fifth-largest urban region in the world, with an estimated population of around 21 million and an estimated slum population of 9 million. Flooding has always been common in Manila, but flood vulnerability has increased dramatically owing to factors that include deforestation, the erosion of topsoil and subsequent silting of the area's rivers, the deterioration of sewer and drainage systems, and increased development in low-lying areas and marshlands. Population increases have been accompanied by "suburbanization," as areas outside the city core have been developed. As the capital region became more heavily urbanized, road construction resulted in a higher volume of impermeable surfaces, which also contributed to more-intense flooding. At the same time, accelerated pumping of groundwater has led to subsidence. Under intense population pressure, canals and other waterways have become clogged with trash and human waste that government agencies have proved incapable of managing (Bankoff 2003). Current conditions are such that large portions of the Manila metropolitan area are inundated on a regular basis. In 2009, flooding triggered by a tropical storm affected 80 percent of the city, killed nearly 250 people, and caused hundreds of thousands to flee their homes.

Risk-producing processes repeat themselves across the so-called developing world, with devastating consequences: the Indian Ocean earthquake and tsunamis of 2004; an earthquake in China's Sichuan province in 2008 that killed an estimated 68,000 people and injured around 374,000; flooding in Pakistan in 2010 that inundated one fifth of that nation's land area and directly affected twenty million people; flooding in Thailand in 2011 that swept over sixty-six of the country's seventy-seven provinces and the capital, Bangkok, affected over thirteen million people, and severely disrupted global supply chains in the automobile and computer industries.

Because the underlying social forces that produce risk and vulnerability continue unabated, so will disaster losses. A recent United Nations report on risk and vulnerability in the Asia-Pacific region had little positive to say about efforts to reduce disaster impacts in that region, concluding that "[d]isaster risks are increasing exponentially, as a result of the compounding effects of inequitable growth patterns, population pressures, and extreme climatic events" (United Nations 2010: vii). This is not because well-intentioned groups and institutions are failing to take steps to reduce disaster risks; it is because they have so little real control over the broader forces that are causing risks to expand in the poorer nations of the world. In thinking about the task that disaster loss reduction advocates have set for themselves in the poverty-stricken regions of the world system, various images come to mind: bailing with a thimble, putting a Band-Aid on an amputated limb, bringing a knife to a gunfight. The vulnerabilities created as a result of world-system dynamics are far outstripping the ability of contemporary institutions to deal with them.

The kinds of governance and institutional problems that are characteristic of nations outside the wealthy core of the world system are also implicated in the growth of disaster risks. At the worst end of the continuum are the societies that are commonly referred to as "failed states" and states that are in critical danger of failing. Such nations—essentially nations in name only—lack control over their own territory, cannot provide basic services for their populations, have few or no institutions that are accorded legitimacy, and are frequently characterized by internal conflicts such as interethnic violence and civil wars (Rotberg 2003a, 2003b). Somalia, Chad, and Sudan are currently the most prominent examples of failed states. Countries like Central African Republic, Afghanistan, and Pakistan also suffer from extremely severe governance deficits, and Haiti also ranks among the nations that are least able to carry out the most basic of governance functions (*Foreign Policy* 2012).

A significant feature of the present-day world system is the extent to which many nations, while not international basket cases like those mentioned above, exhibit fundamental weaknesses in areas of governance such as the rule of law, transparency and accountability, public participation in political institutions, and the ability to limit corruption and to deliver basic safety, security, and critical services. Stable, well-governed nations are a distinct minority, and such societies also tend to be significantly better off economically.

Although correlated with other risk-generating factors such as poverty and rapid social-demographic change, governance quality and capacity also have a significant independent effect on risks and losses. Kahn (2005), for example, has shown that when disaster occurrences and severity are held constant, the presence of democratic forms of government is associated with lower disaster death tolls. Government and general societal corruption also contribute to disaster losses—for example, when officials look the other way or accept bribes for allowing construction to take place in hazardous areas and codes to be ignored. In Turkey following the 1999 Marmara earthquake, which killed an estimated 17,400 people, protests developed as the public began to recognize that high levels of damage and loss of life were attributable in part to government corruption and complicity in shoddy, unregulated construction (Jalali 2002; Green 2005). In the first round of parliamentary elections after the earthquake, both incumbent parties and those who had been in office before the earthquake were roundly defeated—an outcome researchers attribute to public outrage against corrupt government practices (Akarca and Tansel 2008). Turkish voters were fortunate in being able to express their outrage at the polls; citizens of many other countries lack that power.

Turkey is of course not an isolated case. Escaleras, Anbarci, and Register (2006) analyzed data on 344 major earthquakes that occurred in forty-two countries between 1975 and 2003 and found that public-sector corruption, as measured by standard indices that take into account practices such as bribery, was positively and significantly associated with earthquake death tolls. Finding a similar pattern, Nicholas Ambraseys and Roger Bilham (2011) note that while poverty predicts earthquake death tolls, impacts have been particularly severe in cases in which poverty was accompanied by high levels of corruption. This is in part because where corruption is endemic, the construction industry has a free hand in using inferior and inappropriate building materials, cutting corners to increase profits, and siting structures without taking hazards into account.

Shoddy building practices and inadequate code enforcement were major factors in the collapse of school buildings in the 2008 Sichuan earthquake, in which an estimated seven thousand students and teachers were killed. Families who lost children were outraged, blaming government officials for failing to ensure that school buildings were constructed to resist earthquake forces. The Chinese government moved quickly to quash criticism, but reports of structures built without adequate steel reinforcement and extensive corner-cutting continue to circulate. The use of the terms "tofu dregs" and "tofu projects" to describe the region's weakly reinforced, poorly built school buildings became widespread. In 2009, the dissident artist Ai Weiwei mounted a retrospective in Munich called "So Sorry"—a reference to official apologies regarding the loss of life in schools in the impact region. In that exhibit, a large installation entitled "Remembrance" featured nine thousand children's backpacks.

Different-colored backpacks were used to spell out in Chinese characters the words "she lived happily for seven years in this world"—a quote from a mother who lost her beloved daughter when her school collapsed in the earthquake.

This discussion is not meant to imply that corruption is strictly a Third World phenomenon. As earlier discussions on essentially nonexistent building code enforcement in Florida and disappearing earthquake faults in California indicate, corrupt practices exist even in prosperous, well-governed societies. Endemic corruption played a major role in the financial meltdown of 2008, which originated in the United States and other wealthy industrialized countries. Differences do exist, however, between situations in which corruption is exposed and penalized and those in which it has become a routine fact of life, simply part of the cost of doing business, as is the case in many countries around the world.

Aside from out-and-out corruption, other governance deficiencies that are common in countries outside the core of the world system also contribute to the buildup of risk. These range from a simple lack of expertise in scientific hazard assessment and disaster management capability to the inability to amass sufficient monetary resources and political will to carry out effective mitigation, preparedness, response, and recovery programs. Even basic resources are in short supply in many nations throughout the world, and nations that are hard-pressed to meet the basic health and safety needs of their citizens on an everyday basis may understandably accord a low priority to disaster risk reduction, especially when they know they can rely on international disaster assistance in severe disaster events. "Fix upon failure" is the default mode for many less-well-off societies as well as better-off ones, even though pre-event mitigation and disaster prevention are more cost effective in the long run.

The 2010 Haiti earthquake is the quintessential example of how the pathologies of so-called underdevelopment manifest themselves in the context of disasters. Haiti is a textbook case of the confluence of multiple risk-producing forces: poverty and income inequality, rapid urbanization and slums, dense concentrations of people in dangerous structures and disaster-prone locations, pervasive corruption, and abject state failure. Ill served and repressed by a succession of kleptocratic dictators, plagued by hunger, AIDS, and endemic violence, victimized by disaster after disaster, the long-suffering people of Haiti must now continue to endure a protracted recovery process punctuated by tropical storms, floods, and cholera outbreaks. Because the conditions that exist in Haiti are common in many parts of the "less-developed" world, albeit in attenuated form, disaster losses will continue to increase.

But against this bleak backdrop there are success stories as well; not all less-well-off countries are poorly governed or unable to take positive steps to reduce disaster losses. In February 2010, Chile experienced a magnitude 8.8 earthquake—the sixth-largest earthquake ever recorded, more than five hundred times larger than the January 2010 Haiti quake. Despite its enormous size, the earthquake killed only 486 people, largely because Chile had been able to put in place appropriate seismic building codes and to enforce those codes. A 2011 United Nations report notes that even though Chile is not a prosperous nation, levels of corruption are low and governance structures are by and large effective (United Nations 2011). As a society, Chile has been able to learn from its many experiences with earthquake disasters and to mobilize to reduce disaster risk. Put another way, Chile is one of many countries that have embarked on the road to becoming more resilient in the face of disasters. The two chapters that follow will explore the concept of disaster resilience, review research that provides insights on what makes organizations, communities, and societies resilient in the face of disasters, and discuss strategies for improving disaster resilience.

CHAPTER 7

Defining Resilience in Relation to Risk

DISASTER RESILIENCE:

FAD, OR IDEA WHOSE TIME HAS COME?

Within the fields of disaster research and policy, no concept has caught on as fast or diffused more widely than that of disaster resilience. Scarcely mentioned in scientific and policy discourses on disasters and hazards prior to the beginning of this century, the importance of community and societal resilience in the face of disasters has taken center stage in less than a decade. Internationally, the concept of resilience plays a prominent role in influential documents such as the 2005 United Nations Hyogo Framework for Action and in subsequent efforts of the United Nations International Strategy for Disaster Reduction. Nationally, driven in part by the nation's experiences in the September 11, 2001, terrorist attacks and in Hurricane Katrina, the importance of community and societal disaster resilience has been emphasized in a variety of policy initiatives and agency activities. At the federal government level, it has been emphasized in a multiagency document entitled *Grand Challenges for Disaster Reduction* (Subcommittee on Disaster Reduction 2005), which argued for the need to develop infrastructure systems that are disaster resilient and also for methods and measures that can help the nation assess resilience. The concept was further highlighted in the 2007 National Strategy for Homeland Security and was subsequently incorporated into various U.S. Department of Homeland Security programs such as those focusing on infrastructure protection. Under the Obama administration, resilience was emphasized as a national goal in the 2010 National Security Strategy, and elements of the National Security Council that had been responsible for preparedness, protection, and response policy issues were merged into the National Security Council's Resilience Directorate. Resilience was also prioritized in the 2010 Quadrennial Homeland Security Review as one of three key dimensions of a comprehensive approach to homeland security. Updating the Bush administration's Homeland Security Presidential Directive 8, which was aimed at improving the nation's disaster preparedness, Presidential Policy Directive 8 (National Preparedness) emphasizes the need for collaboration among governmental, private-sector, and civil society institutions and organizations in achieving societal resilience. A parallel effort, the Voluntary Private Sector Preparedness Accreditation and Certification Program, known as PS-Prep, focuses on activities to improve business disaster resilience. An emphasis on achieving societal disaster resilience is also evident in the Federal Emergency Management Agency's (FEMA's) recently formulated "whole community" approach to disaster risk reduction, and in other programs such as the agency's Disaster Resilient Universities initiative. On the international front, in 2011 the United States took a leading role in the Asian Pacific Economic Cooperation's High Level Policy Dialogue on Disaster Resiliency, in which participants committed to a series of activities directed at enhancing community and societal disaster resilience capabilities. The concept has gained such currency that a group of analysts recently argued that "[t]he idea of building resilience to natural and man-made disasters is now a dominant strategic theme and operational goal in the current U.S. national security policy discourse" (Longstaff et al. 2010: 1).

A host of other activities signals a growing emphasis on resilience as a fundamental strategy for disaster risk reduction. Research in disciplines concerned with disasters and their impacts has increasingly focused on the conditions for and characteristics of resilience, strategies for improving resilience, and outcomes resulting from resilience-enhancing activities. The National Academy of Sciences and National Research Council recently carried out two studies on disaster resilience, one focusing on private-public partnerships as vehicles for improving community disaster resilience (National Research Council 2011), and the other dealing with general issues related to resilience conceptualization and measurement (National Research Council 2012). Dozens of centers and initiatives focusing on disaster resilience have sprung up in the United States and around the world, at universities and in the private sector. Through its Coastal Services Center and Sea Grant programs, the National Oceanic and Atmospheric Administration (NOAA) has sponsored research and supported the development of coastal and regional resilience networks. The U.S. Department of Agriculture and the National Science Foundation have partnered to support research on disaster resilience in the rural United States, and the latter agency has also sponsored research on improving the disaster resilience and sustainability of infrastructure systems. The Community and Regional Resilience Institute, which is largely funded by the Department of Homeland Security, is conducting pilot projects in communities around the country that are intended to increase community resilience; the Red Cross has recently launched similar programs. Researchers have made substantial advances in defining and measuring disaster resilience at different levels of analysis and have developed tools such as the Coastal Resilience Index and the Community Assessment of Resilience Tool to aid communities in self-assessments that can identify resilience-related strengths and weaknesses.

The meteoric rise to prominence of the concept of disaster resilience has come with a downside. There is a good deal of divergence in how the concept has been defined and operationalized by researchers as well as a lack of clarity and agreement concerning its relationship to concepts such as adaptation and sustainability (Cutter et al. 2008; Rose 2009). Several years ago, one review article (Norris et al. 2008) provided a sample of twenty-one definitions of resilience that have been used in analyses of different types of systems (for example, physical, ecological, social) and at different scales (such as individuals, communities)—variations that reflect the multidisciplinary origins and diverse applications of the concept. Another review of the literature found forty-six different definitions of the concept (Plodinec 2009). In policy discourse, resilience terminology is often used so broadly that it could apply to just about any conditions or activities that are concerned with reducing disaster losses, raising questions about whether the concept increases our understanding of how to manage and cope with disaster risks or merely adds another term to an already large lexicon. Resilience is often derided as a buzzword used more for its faddishness than its empirical and practical value.

These concerns have some validity, but it is also clear that resilience-based theory and research provide important keys to understanding how societies and communities can reduce the frequency of disasters, respond when disasters strike, and recover in ways that render them better able to cope with future events. This chapter and the one that follows provide an overview of current theory and research in the area of disaster resilience as well as examples of resilience in action. These discussions will demonstrate how increased resilience can serve as an antidote to the forces of risk production discussed in earlier chapters—forces that will exact ever-larger tolls unless societies and communities around the world develop and implement strategies for becoming more resilient. However, even with all the emphasis that is currently placed on resilience-enhancing measures, as I argue later, true resilience can only result from genuinely transformative ideas, policies, and practices concerning how societies go about reducing risk.

HAZARDS, DISASTERS, AND RESILIENCE: ANATOMY OF A CONCEPT

In their important paper on community disaster resilience, Norris and colleagues (2008) observe that the term *resilience* is fundamentally a metaphor that has been used by many scientific disciplines to describe properties that contribute to the ability to withstand stressors of various kinds and to bounce back or adjust under subjection to stress. In engineering, the term was originally employed to describe the flexibility or elasticity of different types of materials, but more recently the phrase "resilience engineering" is being used to describe research and practice that focus on risk management within complex engineered systems (Hollnagel, Woods, and Leveson 2006). Further, the concept has a long history in the field of psychology, where research sought to answer questions such as why some individuals are better able to withstand stress and adjust to adverse circumstances and events than others, and what personality traits, cognitive styles, and coping strategies are associated with positive adjustment and adaptation in the face of life's difficulties (Rutter 1987; Masten 2001; Luthar, Cicchetti, and Becker 2000). Research on psychological resilience has addressed both chronic, persistent threats to psychological well-being such as growing up in poverty or having a mentally ill parent (Garmezy 1993) and a wide range of potentially traumatic events and experiences, including disasters (see, e.g., Norris, Friedman, and Watson 2002; Norris et al. 2002; Bonanno et al. 2010). This dual-edged quality of the term has been incorporated into most formulations on disaster resilience.

Resilience has been a major theme in research on ecological and social-ecological systems, first gaining prominence in the work of Holling (1973) and later extending to a larger body of research on global environmental change (Adger 2000; Folke et al. 2002; Janssen et al. 2006). A key idea expressed in Holling's original definition is that resilience is a "measure of the persistence of systems and their ability to absorb change and disturbance" (1973: 14). Another (and for our purposes more useful) formulation on social-ecological system resilience is more specific:

Resilience, for social-ecological systems, is related to (a) the magnitude of shock that the system can absorb and remain within a given state, (b) the degree to which the system is capable of self-organization, and (c) the degree to which the system can build capacity for learning and adaptation. . . . More resilient social-ecological systems are able to absorb larger shocks without changing in fundamental ways. When massive transformation is inevitable, resilient systems contain the components needed for renewal and reorganization. (Folke et al. 2002: 7)

The Resilience Alliance, a research network established in 1999, focuses extensively on the resilience of social-ecological systems, although very little of that work has addressed issues of disaster resilience.

Economists have also employed the concept of resilience in studies on how economies respond to external shocks such as resource shortages (see, e.g., Dhawan and Jeske 2006; Park, Cho, and Rose 2011). The most frequent and sophisticated uses of the concept are in the subfield of ecological economics, where resilience is seen as a major contributor to environmental sustainability, and in hazard economic loss estimation (Rose 2009).

Regardless of discipline, the literature generally stresses the idea that resilience involves both absorptive capacity, or the ability to resist disruption and remain relatively stable, and the ability to bounce back, regroup, and restore the activities of disrupted systems. The thinking in various fields also indicates that resilience involves not merely a return to or replacement of some prior state, but reorganization, change, and under certain conditions major system transformations.

Research focusing specifically on disaster resilience developed largely independently from resilience research in other fields while employing the resilience metaphor in many of the same ways. The use of the term in the hazards and disasters context represents an evolution in thinking regarding strategies for containing disaster losses. Until almost the end of the twentieth century, concepts of hazard and disaster management in the United States and around the world focused on the importance of effective *responses* to disaster, such as protecting life and property and providing immediate disaster relief and recovery assistance, although the importance of predisaster loss reduction measures was not entirely ignored. Then, during the 1990s, research and policy discourses began to stress making communities disaster *resistant* through more effective predisaster loss reduction measures, such as sound building practices, in order to contain disaster-related damage and disruption (Geis 2000). Three Federal Emergency Management Agency programs during that decade, the National Mitigation Strategy, the Pre-disaster Mitigation Program, and Project Impact, were examples of the new federal priority placed on increasing what was then called disaster resistance.

Toward the end of the 1990s, a new discourse emphasizing *resilience* began to emerge. Why the concept of resilience supplanted the notion of resistance so quickly is something of a mystery but is likely related to efforts to link disaster risk reduction with sustainability and sustainable development. In the United States that linkage formed the centerpiece of the Second Assessment of Research on Natural Hazards, which advanced the idea that sustainable development practices and resilient communities are the key to disaster risk reduction (see Mileti 1999 for a summary). The same argument was made internationally in the activities and publications of the United Nations International Decade for Natural Disaster Reduction. Cutter and colleagues sum up this connection succinctly:

The resilience of a community is inextricably linked to the condition of the environment and its treatment of resources; therefore the concept of sustainability is central to studies of resilience . . . an environment stressed by unsustainable practices may experience more severe environmental hazards. (2008: 601)

This growing emphasis on disaster resilience also meshed logically with emerging frameworks that focused on better understanding disaster vulnerability. In fields concerned with social-ecological systems and global environmental change, knowledge domains regarding resilience and vulnerability evolved somewhat independently of one another but began to develop closer connections over time (Janssen et al. 2006), and subsequently these literatures had an influence on disaster research, particularly through the work of geographer Susan Cutter and her collaborators (Cutter 1996, 2001; Cutter, Boruff, and Shirley 2003). Vulnerability and its various dimensions have been discussed earlier, but for this discussion recall that the concept of vulnerability represents the *potential* for experiencing damage and loss; that is, vulnerability represents a condition or state that may or may not be actualized. Two obvious reasons why this is the case is that a hazard may not be present, or a disaster event may not actually occur that exploits preexisting vulnerabilities. However, another reason why losses and harm might not be experienced, or not experienced severely, is that affected units of analysis may be able to absorb and cope with the impacts of disasters that do occur—in other words, they may be resilient. Like ecological researchers, disaster researchers began to recognize that while resilience is not quite the obverse of vulnerability, the two concepts are related, each contributing to an understanding of disaster impacts and consequences.

DEFINING DISASTER RESILIENCE

Resilience in the face of disasters and crises has been defined in various and not always consistent ways, but definitions of the concept are beginning to converge. One general definition sees resilience as "the capacity to adapt existing resources and skills to new situations and operating conditions" (Comfort 1999: 21). Norris and colleagues conceptualize resilience as "a process linking a set of adaptive capacities to a positive trajectory of functioning and adaptation after a disturbance" (2008: 130). In *Disasters by Design*, Dennis Mileti argued that

[l]ocal resiliency with regard to disasters means that a locale is able to withstand an extreme natural event without suffering devastating losses, damage,

diminished productivity or quality of life and without large amounts of assistance from outside the community. (1999: 32–33)

My own interest in the concept of resilience began in the late 1990s when I was a member of a team from the National Science Foundation-funded Multidisciplinary Center for Earthquake Engineering Research (MCEER), a distributed consortium of researchers headquartered at the State University of New York at Buffalo. When MCEER was funded in 1996, its original goal, consistent with current disaster loss reduction discourse, was to conduct research that would enhance the disaster *resistance* of communities. However, within a year or two our research team began a shift in thinking toward exploring the more inclusive concept of resilience, one element of which was disaster resistance. Our unusually diverse group spanned a variety of specializations in engineering and social science disciplines, including structural, systems, and risk and reliability engineering, sociology, economics, and regional science. Our substantive focus was on earthquakes, but our theoretical and conceptual interests were broader. In our early work on resilience conceptualization and measurement, we defined earthquake resilience as

the ability of social units (e.g., organizations, communities) to mitigate hazards, contain the effects of disasters when they occur, and carry out recovery activities in ways that minimize social disruption and mitigate the effects of future earthquakes. (Bruneau et al. 2003: 735)

This intentionally broad definition was meant to be applicable at different scales or levels of analysis—a household, business, or neighborhood can be resilient and so can a nation, and similarly an individual structure or an entire inventory of structures can exhibit resilience—and to span the "hazard cycle," from pre-event loss reduction efforts to recovery activities. That inclusive framing is also reflected in other definitions, such as one advanced by Cutter and colleagues, which characterizes resilience as

the ability to survive and cope with a disaster with minimal impact and damage . . . [encompassing] the capacity to reduce or avoid losses, contain the effects of disasters, and recover with minimal social disruption. (2008: 600)

Similarly, a National Research Council report on disaster resilience defines resilience as "the ability to prepare and plan for, absorb, recover from or more successfully adapt to actual or potential adverse events" (National Research Council 2012: 1).

Definitions remain somewhat inconsistent, and disaster researchers have also used the term in conceptually varying ways, for example to denote capacities, processes, or outcomes (National Research Council 2012). These kinds of divergences are also common in other disciplines that employ the resilience metaphor. For example, writing about the field of psychology, where the concept has been examined and critiqued extensively, Luthar, Cicchetti, and Becker observed that "[t]he theoretical and research literature on resilience reflects little consensus about definitions, with substantial variations in operationalization and measurement of key constructs" (2000: 3). Similar sentiments were expressed by Brand and Jax (2007) in the use of the term within the interdisciplinary field of sustainability science. They argue that while the concept of resilience serves well as a "boundary object" that allows diverse disciplines to converse with one another, that very property can lead to conceptual blurriness and scientific misunderstandings. Clearly, regardless of discipline, resilience theory, measurement, and applications are still in the process of evolving.

DIMENSIONS AND DOMAINS OF DISASTER RESILIENCE

As part of that evolution, researchers have endeavored to identify the elements that constitute and contribute to resilience. The framework developed by the MCEER team characterized resilience as consisting of four dimensions: (1) robustness, or the ability to withstand stresses and demands without loss of function; (2) redundancy, or the degree to which other units of analysis or elements can be substituted for those that are lost or disrupted when disaster strikes, while still maintaining functionality; (3) resourcefulness, or the ability to identify problems and subsequently to mobilize material, informational, monetary, and other resources to address those problems; and (4) rapidity, or the time it takes to restore the units of analysis to the level of functionality they exhibited before they experienced disruption.

The multidisciplinary literature on resilience is consistent in emphasizing the notion of *robustness*, resistance, or strength as a key element of resilience, whether the robustness factor in question is a personality trait that insulates a child from the negative consequences of trauma or a set of engineering techniques that prevents a building from collapsing when subject to earthquake forces. The importance of *redundancy* is also highlighted in diverse literatures. In ecological systems, species diversity provides a type of redundancy, and researchers have emphasized the connections that exist between diversity and resilience in ecological and social-ecological systems. In their book *Resilience Thinking*, for example, Walker and Salt argue that diversity involves

variety in the number of species, people, and institutions that exist in a social-ecological system. . . . The more variations available to respond to a shock, the greater the ability to absorb the shock. Diversity relates to flexibility and keeping your options open. A lack of diversity limits options and reduces your capacity to respond to disturbances. (2006: 121)

Perrings (2006) also argues for heterogeneity and diversity as contributors to resilience in ecological systems, drawing an analogy with the importance of portfolio diversity in financial management. Redundancy, which as used here includes diversity, substitutability, and heterogeneity, is an important element of resilience because it increases options; lack of redundancy reduces them. This is why safety engineering stresses the need for backup systems and why contingency planners advise businesses and agencies to store critical data off-site and plan to operate from alternative locations in the event of a disaster. Disasters can of course destroy backup safety-related systems as well as primary ones—we only need think about the Fukushima nuclear plant and the Tohoku earthquake and tsunami to realize that—but that is not an argument against the importance of redundancy in helping to allow systems to continue to function under conditions of disturbance. As Longstaff and colleagues put it,

[r]edundant resources provide a failsafe, or back-up, when any individual unit fails. Redundancy is also a form of operational slack, or buffering from external shocks. Having many hammers provides a high degree of redundancy for

sinking nails. If one breaks, there are more to use. Likewise, emergency savings accounts are a form of redundancy in financial terms and allow for the continuance of an individual or family's lifestyle in the event of a job loss or unexpected event. (2010: 6)

Disaster events provide evidence of the benefits of redundancy. For example, when the 1989 Loma Prieta earthquake struck the San Francisco Bay Area, it damaged the Bay Bridge, the key transportation artery linking greater San Francisco to Oakland, Berkeley, and other cities in the East Bay, rendering the bridge unusable for more than six months. This could have been a nightmare for commuters and a major blow to business and government operations in the region, but fortunately the Bay Area transportation system had built-in redundancies. The Bay Area Rapid Transit (BART) subway system remained operational despite the earthquake, and the region was also able to augment its existing transbay ferry system. These redundant modes of transport geared up to accommodate a much larger ridership, making it possible to compensate for the disruption caused by the loss of the Bay Bridge.

At the time of the September 11, 2001, terrorist attacks on New York City, both landline and cell phone service were lost over a large area surrounding Ground Zero, owing to physical damage and extreme congestion. However, the internet did not experience disruption because its network structure provided redundancy and allowed for rapid rerouting of data (Townsend and Moss 2005). More recently, text messaging is being recognized as a critical means of communication during disasters, providing redundancy when cellular telephone communications are disrupted—as they inevitably are in large events.

The concept of *resourcefulness* encompasses a wide variety of capacities and processes, including the ability to mobilize resources in response to disasters, restore resources that are lost as a consequence of disasters, and learn and apply knowledge across the hazard cycle. Preparing for, responding to, and recovering from disasters necessarily entails the use of a wide variety of tangible and intangible resources, ranging from materials, supplies, and financial resources to specialized technical knowledge and expertise and to cultural resources such as collective memory and narrative. Resourcefulness also includes the ability to apply creativity and to improvise in the face of disaster-induced disruption.

Rapidity is important for any resilience formulation because time is a critical element in key disaster-relevant activities such as saving lives and rebuilding and recovering following disasters. In addition to being thought of as a dimension of resilience, rapidity can be conceptualized as an outcome of the other three resilience capacities: systems that are highly robust, redundant, and resourceful can be expected to experience less disaster-induced disruption and to restore themselves more rapidly than less resilient ones. In some respects, however, rapidity can be a double-edged sword, in that an undue emphasis on the timeliness of recovery from disruption can potentially undermine longer-term adaptability and sustainability. Disaster researchers have long noted that tensions exist between efforts to "build back" as quickly as possible after disasters and efforts to "build better" in order to improve community quality of life and reduce losses from future disasters.

Researchers also consider how resilience is manifested in different domains or systems. The MCEER framework distinguished among technical, organizational, social, and economic resilience domains (Bruneau et al. 2003). Longstaff and colleagues (2010) identify five community subsystems to which resilience concepts can be applied: ecological, economic, physical infrastructure, civil society, and governance subsystems. Cutter and colleagues (2008) distinguish among six constituent domains of resilience: ecological, social, economic, institutional, and infrastructure resilience, along with community competence. A truly resilient community or society is one that achieves high levels of resilience across multiple domains.

Resilience domains do not exist independently of one another, but rather are interrelated in the sense that strengths and weaknesses in one domain spill over into others. Capabilities in the institutional area, for example, can help to ensure that ecological and infrastructure resilience goals are achieved, and resilient local economies can enhance social resilience in the aftermath of disaster. Alternatively, a lack of infrastructure resilience that is manifested in widespread building damage and utility system disruption when disaster strikes represents a significant threat to postdisaster resilience in other domains. These interdependencies are crucial, but to date research has done little to systematically address them. Rather, nascent efforts to quantitatively assess resilience tend either to be domain-specific or to treat different domains as contributing in an additive fashion to global resilience measures.

Resilience exists at different levels of analysis and different spatial and timescales. Within the economic domain, for example, resilience can be an attribute of an individual firm or a local, regional, or national economy. Within the social domain, individuals, households, social groupings and networks, neighborhoods, communities, and entire societies can exhibit differing degrees of resilience. These differences matter. For example, while Hurricane Katrina was absolutely devastating to the economy of New Orleans, its impact was not as great within the context of the Gulf region as a whole and even more muted within the entire U.S. economy, where the hurricane's impact on GDP growth was felt only during the last quarter of 2005. At the same time, units of analysis are interrelated. A major disaster that destroys numerous businesses and results in extensive business interruption may have broader ramifications for the resilience of local and regional economies. Similarly, a disaster that causes extensive household relocation will have ramifications for resilience at neighborhood and community levels.

Spatial scale is an important consideration in studies of resilience, in part because entities within some geographic areas in disaster-affected regions respond more resiliently than they do in others following disasters. For example, research on both the 1995 Kobe earthquake and Hurricane Katrina has documented differential patterns of postdisaster recovery across neighborhoods (Chang 2010; Finch, Emrich, and Cutter 2010). Studies suggest that such patterns can be the result of various factors, including the severity of disaster damage in different geographic locations, preexisting physical and population vulnerabilities, and the manner in which postdisaster assistance and recovery programs are implemented in different locales. Importantly, uneven spatial patterns of recovery are also indicative of resilience-related differences—distinctions that are often blurred when recovery data are aggregated over large geographic areas.

Finally, time is an important consideration in efforts to understand and assess resilience. It is difficult to compare disasters, but if we can imagine two communities of roughly the same size that experienced roughly the same types and severity of disaster impacts but showed different rates of recovery and outcomes over time, we might attribute at least some of those differences to differing resilience capabilities—although we would again have to keep in mind that in disaster recovery faster is not necessarily better. Of course, expectations regarding the ability of communities to bounce back after experiencing disasters must also take into account the size of the blow. As we continue to see with genuinely catastrophic disasters such as Hurricane Katrina and the Haiti and Tohoku earthquakes, event severity profoundly influences restoration and recovery times. Even so, we see significant differences across societies that have experienced catastrophic disaster events that are indicative of differences in resilience capability.

FORMS OF DISASTER RESILIENCE

In their efforts to understand and measure resilience in the face of hazards and disasters, researchers typically distinguish between properties of social units and systems that exist prior to disasters which render them better able to absorb the forces unleashed by those events without experiencing serious disruption, and the "bounce-back" properties and behaviors associated with postimpact coping, reorganization, and adaptation. As with other concepts in the resilience arena, researchers do not always agree on what to call these two forms of resilience; but following general conventions in the field, I will refer to them as *inherent* and *adaptive* resilience. The concept of inherent resilience refers to conditions, characteristics, and properties of analytic units that are associated with absorptive capacity and that can potentially be mobilized to enhance coping capacity when disasters occur. Adaptive resilience involves the activation of that potential in actual disaster situations, or strategies that overcome disaster-induced problems as they manifest themselves. At the risk of oversimplifying, we can view inherent resilience as associated with the properties of resistance, robustness, and existing redundancies within systems, while adaptive resilience relates mainly to resourcefulness and to how social units respond when they are excessively stressed—including efforts to reconstitute inherent forms of resilience. Here again, as with the general concept of resilience, these concepts can be applied across units of analysis and across different resilience domains. With respect to inherent resilience, households may possess assets such as savings that can aid them in weathering economic hard times, and neighborhoods may contain diverse community-based organizations, social networks, and institutions on which residents can rely during normal times and during disasters. Individual businesses may possess the size and financial assets that enable them to sustain themselves during economic downturns and other adverse events. Similarly, some local and regional economies may be more inherently resilient than others owing to the sheer volume of economic activity they generate, their degree of diversification, and particularly in the case of hazards, the spatial dispersion or deconcentration of economic activities. Economic entities that lack inherent resilience can find themselves overly exposed to broader negative economic forces and to disasters.

SOURCES OF INHERENT RESILIENCE

Inherent disaster resilience includes the buffering properties of natural, infrastructure, and social systems. Natural and ecological systems that are healthy and that provide ecosystem services are an important source of inherent disaster resilience. For example, the damage resulting from the 2004 Indian Ocean tsunami was substantially smaller in communities where mangrove forests had been maintained than in those that had lost those natural protective systems (Chang et al. 2006). When natural protective systems are compromised, the result is often a loss of resilience and higher disaster vulnerability. Worldwide, deforestation and land degradation are associated with flood severity and damage, as well as with slope instabilities, landslides, and debris flows. Activities that compromise forests, wetlands, grasslands, barrier islands, and other natural protections have a negative effect on inherent disaster resilience.

Similarly, built environments manifest varying levels of inherent resilience. With respect to buildings, as discussed earlier, well-designed and well-built structures that conform to state-of-the-art building codes can be expected to resist and absorb disaster forces significantly better than their lower-quality counterparts. However, such structures constitute only a tiny proportion of the building inventories in communities worldwide and a small proportion of those in the United States, for a variety of reasons. Broadly speaking, inventories can be divided into two categories: "engineered" structures, in which engineering design and code criteria have been used, and "nonengineered" ones. Most buildings around the world, including residential buildings but also many other types of structures, fall into the "nonengineered" category, and in many parts of the world large proportions of building inventories have been constructed by persons with no training in disaster-resistant design and construction methods. One typical example is Bam, Iran, which I visited after a devastating magnitude 6.6 earthquake struck in December 2003, killing 26,000 people and leaving over 100,000 homeless in Bam and surrounding villages and destroying or severely damaging about 80 percent of the structures in the city, including homes, businesses, and medical facilities. Most of the buildings in Bam were of mud-brick construction, and houses were built by homeowners themselves. For men, building one's own home is a matter of pride; a typical practice is to add on stories or rooms as families grow. Both construction materials and building practices rendered Bam's building inventory highly vulnerable to earthquakes, and when the 6.6 temblor struck during the early morning hours on December 26, most homes in Bam simply collapsed outright, killing those inside. Iran has had a seismic building code since 1989, but most structures in Bam were already in existence when the code was adopted, and the code was not widely enforced; in any case it was unlikely to have an influence on building practices because it did not take into account cultural norms and practices related to the ways residential structures are built.

"Engineered" structures constitute a minority of structures in building inventories worldwide. Such structures can be further subdivided according to criteria such as what, if any, hazard-resistance codes were in place at the time they were built, the competencies of the individuals and groups that were responsible for their design and construction, the quality of code enforcement at the time of construction, and what kinds

of programs, if any, had been implemented to remedy existing vulnerabilities, and to what effect.

The upshot is that communities throughout the United States and
around the world are currently living with legacy building inventories
that show considerable variability in their inherent capacity to absorb
disaster-induced forces. As we have already seen, adding to these vulnerabilities are organized efforts—usually led by development interests—to
oppose the application of hazard-resistance codes and standards. For
example, for decades such conflicts have erupted periodically in Memphis and Shelby County, Tennessee, over seismic codes. Given this location in the New Madrid Seismic Zone and the city's large inventory of
older, collapse-hazard buildings, strengthening earthquake codes and
enforcement would seem to be a straightforward matter; yet those advo-
cating for more earthquake-aware construction have had difficulty getting codes adopted even for new buildings, much less for existing ones.
Opponents continue to argue that stricter codes and better enforcement
will raise the cost of construction and make the area a less desirable
place in which to build. These kinds of struggles are common and are
part of the context that helps determine the inherent resilience of the
built environment.

Comparable variations in critical infrastructure systems have a direct
bearing on their inherent resilience. Worldwide, many infrastructure systems, such as roads and systems associated with irrigation, sewerage, and
flood control, have been constructed using traditional techniques without
any engineering input. For engineered infrastructure systems, because
hazard-resistant design and construction practices have improved over
time, age matters, as does the attention that has been paid to the maintenance and upgrading of systems and to overall system management.

Other properties that influence the inherent resilience of infrastructure
systems are related to their coupling and interdependencies. The notion
of "tightly coupled" systems was introduced in Chapter 5 and is reprised
here because of its relevance for inherent system resilience. The electric
power grid is tightly coupled, which makes it vulnerable to disruption
both on an everyday basis as a consequence of demand surges and system accidents, and on the basis of disasters. The power outages that took

place in India on July 30 and 31, 2012, which were the largest electrical power failures in history, are good illustrations of these vulnerabilities.

Infrastructure systems are also interdependent; for example, many utility and other critical systems depend upon the functioning of the electrical grid. The fact that electrical power is both vulnerable and fundamental to the operation of the entire critical infrastructure is one reason why so much emphasis is placed on ensuring the physical robustness of electrical systems and on creating redundancies in the form of alternative power supplies that can be activated when those systems fail. Requirements that organizations keep generators on hand for use during power outages are common in codes and standards for disaster preparedness and business continuity, such as standards promulgated by the Joint Commission for hospitals and other health-care facilities and business continuity standards such as the National Fire Protection Association's Standard 1600.

Just as a chain is only as strong as its weakest link, the inherent disaster resilience of infrastructure systems is typically determined by their weakest elements. Researchers who study such systems and professionals charged with maintaining them recognize that disasters invariably find and exploit system vulnerabilities. The most glaring recent example of the significance of weak links for overall system performance was the failure of the levee systems in New Orleans during Hurricane Katrina. As various reports have emphasized, the fifty levee breaches that caused the city to flood so catastrophically were caused by fundamental weaknesses in a system of flood control that had been developed in an uncoordinated fashion over time—vulnerabilities that were themselves the result of what one report called the "chaotic" and "dysfunctional" approach to protecting the city from hurricanes taken by the U.S. Army Corps of Engineers and the numerous boards that had jurisdiction over different levees (American Society of Civil Engineers 2007). That same report called the New Orleans hurricane protection system "a system in name only" and went on to say that

[i]n reality, it [the collection of flood protection systems around New Orleans] is a disjointed agglomeration of many individual projects that were conceived and constructed in a piecemeal fashion. Parts were then joined together in

"make-do" arrangements . . . there are hundreds of penetrations for roadways, rail lines, and pipelines throughout the levee system. Many of these penetrations have gates that are supposed to be moved into place under flood conditions either automatically or by hand operation. It was found, however, that many of the closure systems were either missing or inoperable, and offered little resistance to floodwaters. (American Society of Civil Engineers 2007: 63)

For New Orleans, it mattered little that many levees remained resistant to the forces unleashed by Katrina, because it was the weakest links that determined the overall inherent resilience of the so-called system. Examples abound of the significance of weak links for overall system performance in disasters and of the cascading effects they produce. In a water utility example, in the 1993 Midwest floods, the Des Moines, Iowa, water works treatment facility was flooded and left unable to function when the Raccoon River burst its banks. As a result, 250,000 Des Moines residents were without water for eleven days. Just over 40 percent of businesses in Des Moines were forced to close, and two-thirds of those businesses shut down because of the lack of availability of water, not because of flooding (Tierney 1997).

At the facility level, meltdowns occurred at the Fukushima Daiichi plant following the March 2011 Tohoku earthquake and tsunami because the plant lost its main source of electrical power for cooling but also because emergency generators, which were supposed to provide redundancy, were rendered unusable because they were in vulnerable locations. In another incident, the Texas Medical Center (TMC) in Houston was devastated by Tropical Storm Allison in 2001. When Allison struck, numerous buildings in the TMC complex were flooded to the extent that they became nonoperational. Within the complex, the basement of Memorial Hermann Hospital was flooded to a depth of nearly forty feet, and the consequences were devastating because systems that were essential for hospital operations, including electrical, plumbing, heating, ventilation, air conditioning (HVAC), and fire-protection systems, as well as laboratories and other important units, were located on the lower levels of the facility. In rapid succession, the hospital lost electricity, HVAC systems, elevators, telephone systems, and other essential services and was forced to evacuate 540 patients without the use of elevators and escalators. Losses to the hospital complex alone were estimated at $433 million, and full recovery took eighteen months, all because of the failure to protect critical system components from flooding, a source of vulnerability that should have been well understood (Risk Management Solutions 2001). Evidently other hospitals learned little from this experience, because almost identical problems occurred in Hurricane Katrina and Superstorm Sandy.

INHERENT FEATURES OF SOCIAL RESILIENCE

The foregoing discussions have offered a high-level look at disaster resilience that is horizontal—that is, we have looked "across" different domains. In contrast, this section will focus in a "vertical" fashion on social resilience at different levels of analysis, emphasizing inherent properties of social units that are associated with strength and absorptive capacity. Other things being equal, inherent resilience capacities protect social units from experiencing loss and disruption, enabling them to endure the challenges presented by disasters more effectively and fully than their less resilient counterparts. Looking across domains, I have argued that resilience domains are interdependent. Similarly, when focusing vertically on social resilience, the notion of interdependence also applies: social units such as families, neighborhoods, and communities are nested within larger social aggregations or contexts whose resilience capabilities affect their own. This is the case both for inherent resilience and for adaptive resilience, which is addressed in the chapter that follows.

CURRENT APPROACHES TO ASSESSING RESILIENCE

The growing interest in disaster resilience has been accompanied by multiple efforts to develop measurement and assessment methodologies that capture key dimensions of the concept, so that researchers, policy makers, and other decision makers have some idea of where things currently stand with respect to resilience, and also have some basis for determining how resilience-related variables are changing over time. The best of these assessment efforts blend theory-derived insights with careful analyses and interpretations of empirical data.

One such strategy for measuring resilience, which has been pioneered by geographer Susan Cutter and her colleagues (Cutter, Burton, and Emrich 2010) for application at the community level, employs a "social indicators" approach and identifies variables from nationally available secondary data sources, such as the U.S. Census and other readily available archival data, which can be combined in the construction of indices that serve as benchmark indicators of resilience. The resilience index is divided into five subcomponents of overall community resilience, termed social, economic, institutional, and infrastructure resilience, along with a subcomponent called "community capital." Social resilience indicators include such factors as population educational levels; the percentage of a community's population that is nonelderly and nondisabled; the extent of health coverage within the community; English-language competency within the population; and the percentage of the population that has access to a vehicle. Economic resilience measures include variables related to home ownership, income equality, female labor-force participation, and the presence of multiple employment sectors within the community. Institutional resilience is measured through information on such factors as community hazard mitigation planning, the proportion of housing units that are covered by disaster loss reduction programs such as the National Flood Insurance and Storm Ready programs, community expenditures on public safety programs, and other related variables, such as the extent to which members of a community's population participate in Citizen Corps, a Department of Homeland Security program designed to train community residents to respond to disasters. Infrastructure resilience indicators attempt to take into account the ability of the built environment to resist disaster-related damage—for example, by using proxies such as the age of housing units and the presence of mobile homes, which are vulnerable to life-threatening disaster damage—as well as factors that could affect community disaster response capabilities in areas such as evacuation and sheltering. Community capital indicators seek to capture information on community connectedness or cohesiveness through the use of data on such factors as community attachment, political participation, and community involvement in churches and civic associations.

The developers of this measurement approach, known as "baseline resilience indicators for communities," or BRIC, argue that these kinds of indicators provide a broad-brush picture of communities' inherent strengths and vulnerabilities, both in a general sense and with respect to hazards and disasters. This approach to assessing resilience has several advantages. Much of the data required for conducting these kinds of assessments can be collected economically and with relatively little effort, and they allow for comparisons across jurisdictions such as counties and metropolitan statistical areas. At the same time, the social indicators strategy is problematic along several lines. Reliance on census data, which are collected every ten years, means that some data will inevitably be outdated. Generic indicators that are summarized at large levels of aggregation are incapable of taking into account distinctive community features that contribute to resilience and local variations in resilience-related conditions, which can be large. A global measure of the resilience of Orleans Parish tells us something about the status of the parish vis-à-vis other parishes and counties across the nation but can mask significant differences in inherent resilience that exist between, say, the Lower Ninth Ward and the Garden District of New Orleans. The BRIC approach treats indicators as additive, but it is likely that some factors make more important contributions than others to community resilience, and that the importance of different indicators will vary across communities and disaster events. Even with these drawbacks, the BRIC measures represent an important effort to empirically ground an often vague and elusive concept.

Norris and colleagues (2008) take a different approach to resilience measurement, which is based on the idea that resilience emerges from sets of what they term "networked adaptive capacities." The logic behind this measurement strategy is that while resistance and absorptive capacity in the face of disaster—what was termed robustness in earlier discussions—is a highly desirable goal, disasters typically result in levels of disruption that render individuals, groups, and communities unable to function normally for some time and that therefore pressure them to adapt. For an individual who has experienced a disaster, adaptation has occurred when he or she returns to a state of psychological wellness, as indicated by a lack of psychological distress and the ability to function well in family, work-related, and other roles. Similarly, the concept of wellness and successful adaptation following the shock of disaster can be applied to populations and communities. Put simply, then, resilient individuals and communities can absorb losses and stresses caused by disasters and also cope in ways that avoid protracted disruption and dysfunctionality and enable them to adapt to the post-disaster "new normal."

This reasoning leads logically to the question of which building blocks contribute to the resilience-adaptation process. For Norris and her collaborators, those factors consist of various kinds of networked resources. They reason that because disasters result in resource losses of various kinds, resilience is predicated on the ability both to reduce the potential for loss and to protect remaining resources from further deterioration and apply them in ways that promote positive adaptation. The model of community resilience developed by the Norris group consists of four sets of networked capacities that are linked and mutually reinforcing: economic development, information and communication, community competence, and social capital. Resources and capacities in the area of economic development include resource levels such as household income and socioeconomic status and the financial well-being of firms and economic sectors; equitable distribution of economic resources; and the diversity of economic resources. Information and communication capacities are a reflection of factors such as the presence of trusted sources of information and systems for providing needed information to the public, and also on what Norris and colleagues (2008: 140) refer to as "communal narratives" that enable community members to collectively interpret and draw meaning from their disaster experiences in ways that foster successful postdisaster adaptation.

The concept of community competence refers to the capacity for collective problem identification, decision making, and problem solving, as well as the ability to engage in collective action. Other capacities associated with this concept include collective efficacy, empowerment, the capacity for successful conflict resolution, and the ability to exercise agency. Social capital, the fourth element in the "networked capacities" model, encompasses factors such as the amount of social support members of a community expect and receive; the social "embeddedness" that is fostered by informal relationships among community members; cooperative and collaborative ties among organizations; and residents' participation in community activities and their sense of attachment. Norris and colleagues stress that these building blocks of resilience are interrelated in complex ways, that they are continually subject to change as a consequence of broader societal forces, and, drawing on elements of the MCEER resilience framework, that they foster resilience "to the extent they are robust, redundant, or rapidly accessible" (2008: 142).

The "networked capacities" paradigm draws upon extensive literatures on factors that contribute to community well-being during non-disaster times and in disasters. The framework is especially sensitive to the importance of interpersonal and interorganizational networks, culture, and community empowerment in fostering adaptive capabilities. However, a potential drawback to this approach is that populating the model with data on a community-by-community basis is highly labor intensive and thus expensive.

As a way of addressing the difficulties inherent in collecting the data needed for this type of resilience measurement while also devising strategies that can help communities become more resilient, Norris and her colleagues developed a standardized method called the Community Assessment of Resilience Tool, which was further elaborated in a more comprehensive Communities Advancing Resilience Toolkit (both known as CART), that can be used in community-based participatory resilience assessments. The most sophisticated CART tools use social indicator data and data obtained through surveys and key informant interviews in ways that enable communities to evaluate their resilience on dimensions identified in the "networked capacities" framework and to decide on what actions to take (if any) to address deficiencies. Unlike BRIC assessment tools, CART tools are not intended for making cross-community comparisons. Rather, their primary objective is to provide resilience-related decision support for community leaders and groups (for details on CART methodologies, see Pfefferbaum, Pfefferbaum, and Van Horn 2011).

Other resilience assessment tools that are intended to support local decision making include the National Oceanic and Atmospheric Administration's Coastal Resilience Index and the Community and Regional Resilience Institute's Community Resilience System. Additionally, spurred by the massive loss of life in the 2004 Indian Ocean tsunami, The U.S. Agency for International Development, NOAA, the Nature Conservancy, and other agencies have collaborated on a set of guidelines for coastal resilience assessment called *How Resilient Is Your Coastal Community?* which places special emphasis on tsunami hazards (U.S. Indian Ocean Tsunami Warning System Program 2007).

"CAPITALS" AND DISASTER RESILIENCE

As the foregoing examples show, ways of defining and operationalizing disaster resilience vary, but theory and research in the area appear to be converging on the role of various forms of "capital," and in particular social capital, in enhancing resilience. An emphasis on different forms of capital provides the basis for recent resilience indicator development for coastal areas, which was undertaken by a team led by the Hazard Reduction and Recovery Center at Texas A&M University. That study emphasizes the significance of four forms of capital—social, economic, physical, and human—across the four phases of the "hazard cycle": mitigation, preparedness, response, and recovery (Peacock 2010). Other recent efforts to better understand social resilience have been modeled on the more comprehensive Community Capitals Framework (CCF), which was originally developed by Cornelia and Jan Flora to identify conditions that foster community entrepreneurship, economic development, and sustainability (Flora and Flora 2003, 2005). The CCF identifies seven types of capital—natural, cultural, human, political, financial, "built," and social capital—that endow communities with the capacity to achieve such goals as healthy ecosystems, social equity, political empowerment, economic well-being, and diversity (Flora et al. 2005). Natural capital assets include natural resources such as fisheries, forests, and mineral resources, but also include air and water quality, biodiversity, and other conditions that indicate a concern with long-term sustainability. Communities that are high in natural capital are able to reap benefits from natural resources, while at the same time they avoid excessively exploiting and depleting those resources and creating adverse environmental impacts; they seek to employ natural resources such as forests, lakes, and coastal ecosystems in ways that contribute to community well-being. Cultural capital includes shared values, customs, worldviews, valued places, and other elements of culture that contribute to collective identities and a sense of place. Investments in human capital include commitments in the areas of education and training, the capacity to provide opportunities for meaningful work and entrepreneurial and creative activity, as well as a commitment to fostering leadership capabilities within a group or population. The concept of political capital refers to the extent to which diverse groups and community sectors are able to mobilize politically—not just the extent to which small groups consisting of elite community members can influence decision making. Political capital also includes the capacity of neighborhoods, business districts, and communities to influence decisions and obtain resources from outside sources. Financial capital is related to such factors as levels of savings and other financial resources, income levels, and the capacity to increase financial resources through loans, philanthropic donations, taxes, grants, and other mechanisms. "Built" capital relates to the quality and adequacy of infrastructure and the built environment.

Social Capital: A Lynchpin of Disaster Resilience

While these various forms of capital are all seen as important for community well-being, many formulations accord primacy of place to social capital. The concept of social capital has a long and complex history in the social sciences, which will not be reprised here. As Aldrich (2012) observes in his book on social capital and disaster resilience, an emphasis on the significance of social capital across numerous dimensions of social life can be seen in work as diverse as the following: Alexis de Tocqueville, in the nineteenth century, on the prominence and value of social participation and civic associations in U.S. society; sociologist Mark Granovetter, on the role of social ties and "embeddedness" in economic and social life (1973, 1985); Pierre Bourdieu, whose work on social capital (1986) has had a major influence on sociological theory; and Robert Putnam, who brought the concept to the attention of nonacademic audiences through publications like *Bowling Alone* (2000). There are various schools of thought in the study of social capital, but the term is generally used to refer to "the ability of actors to secure benefits by virtue of membership in social networks or other social structures" (Portes 1998: 6). Common indicators of the concept include the extensiveness of different forms of social network ties, the density of civic associations and community institutions, and indicators of social participation such as voting and volunteering. Within the CCF, the concept is defined in similar ways and linked to evidence of norms of reciprocity that create a sense of obligation among individuals and groups; feelings of mutual trust and trust in institutions; cooperative relationships within and among groups; the capacity for conflict resolution; the ability to develop and maintain a common vision of community life; social participation and community engagement; and the nature and extent of social network relationships.

Many formulations, including the CCF, distinguish three forms of social capital: bonding social capital, or networks that exist within groups; bridging social capital, or ties that link different groups to one another; and linking social capital, or external relationships that extend beyond groups and communities to, for example, higher levels of government or national organizations that can provide resources to their local counterparts.

Forms of capital are generally viewed as interrelated and synergistic. Social capital can be thought of as a precondition for the development and maintenance of other forms of capital, such as political and cultural capital. At the same time, social capital can accrue as a result of the functioning of other forms of capital, such as financial, political, and cultural capital.

There are clear connections between "capitals-based" frameworks, especially social capital, and the study of disaster resilience. As earlier discussions have suggested, methodologies for measuring community disaster resilience such as the BRIC and "networked capacities" approaches reflect a concern with various forms of capital, and particularly with social capital. These linkages are currently being explored extensively by disaster sociologists Liesel Ritchie and Duane Gill (Ritchie and Gill 2011; Ritchie and Gill forthcoming) and by political scientist Daniel Aldrich (2012). Reviewing the literature on social capital and disasters, Ritchie (forthcoming) finds extensive evidence in both U.S. and international contexts of the role of social capital in buffering disaster-related stress and promoting postdisaster recovery. The logic connecting the concepts of social capital and other community capitals to resilience is straightforward: just as these capitals endow individuals, groups, and communities with the capacity to weather everyday stressors and achieve goals and objectives, they can also enhance resilience in the face of disasters. Conversely, deficits in social and other community capitals can reduce resilience in the face of environmental extremes.

The importance of social capital and its contributions to inherent and adaptive disaster resilience are illustrated in Eric Klinenberg's research (2002) on the 1995 Chicago heat wave, which resulted in nearly 750 excess deaths during the week in which it occurred. Klinenberg's careful "social autopsy" into who died, how, and why found that parts of the city with high death rates tended to have high percentages of African American residents and that death rates were high for elderly people living alone, but especially for elderly men, because they are less likely than women to maintain social contacts as they age. Klinenberg also conducted an in-depth study of two residential areas that were roughly similar socioeconomically, that were minority communities, and that experienced similar high temperatures, but that had significantly different rates of heat-related deaths. Klinenberg showed that these differences were related to social-structural characteristics of the two neighborhoods that are linked in turn to attributes of social capital. A basic finding from the comparative study was that the two neighborhoods differed starkly in what Klinenberg called their "ecology of support"—the existence of a social infrastructure that could serve as a safety net both during normal times and during times of crisis. The high-mortality neighborhood, North Lawndale, whose residents were predominantly African American, was characterized by a paucity of business and commercial activity, an abundance of abandoned buildings and structures that were in poor repair, and few amenities such as public spaces where people could gather and mingle. Residents who were financially able to leave the area had already done so, and their departure had disrupted kinship and other support networks. While some parts of the neighborhood were stable in terms of residential tenure, others had high numbers of transient residents. Importantly, high rates of crime and drug dealing and use made residents reluctant to venture into the streets, and in any case there wasn't much point in doing so because there was little to see, do, or purchase within the neighborhood. Residents generally drove or were driven to other parts of the city or to the suburbs to obtain needed goods and services. Many residents, particularly elderly ones, organized their lives around the fear of crime, staying inside with doors locked and windows closed. Community organizations such as churches and block clubs did exist, but their resources were insufficient to address community needs or reach out to all those who were vulnerable; despite the best efforts of committed members of the community, it was difficult to encourage social engagement and participation when so many people were afraid to venture out of their homes.

In contrast, while the low-mortality neighborhood, Little Village, resembled its high-mortality counterpart in poverty rates and the number of poor elderly persons and elderly persons living alone, it differed significantly along many dimensions related to social capital. It was a bustling neighborhood with many functioning businesses, a vibrant street life, high population density, and patterns of extended family ties within the neighborhood that brought older and younger family members into contact with one another on a regular basis. Unlike North Lawndale, which had been losing population, Little Village, which was populated mainly by Latinos, had been experiencing rapid population growth fueled largely by immigrants from Mexico and Central America, who contributed to the economic vitality of the neighborhood. Its violent crime rate was three times lower than that of the high-mortality neighborhood and twice as low as Chicago's as a whole. Elderly residents were not afraid to leave their homes, and because the neighborhood offered a wide variety of stores, services, and other amenities, they were able to bank, shop, receive medical care, worship, and attend social functions with relative ease. The same locations they frequented on a regular basis became places where they felt comfortable seeking relief during the heat wave. Churches, which were mainly Catholic and tended to be large and well integrated into Chicago's Catholic diocese, served as hubs for many community activities on a day-to-day basis and were converted to cooling centers during the heat wave.

Life was by no means idyllic in Little Village. Poverty and residential overcrowding presented significant problems, and multigenerational ties were showing signs of breaking down as geographic mobility increased. Nonetheless a combination of community vitality, strong social ties, and functioning social institutions helped to protect vulnerable community residents during the life-threatening heat wave, while the frayed social fabric of North Lawndale offered too few protections.

Overcoming Vulnerability Through Building Social Capital: The People of Grand Bayou

There is an automatic tendency to think of vulnerability and resilience as opposing concepts; those who are vulnerable are assumed to lack resilience, and in turn, deficits in resilience contribute to vulnerability. While these connections hold true for many vulnerable populations and groups, as the Little Village example illustrates, there are also many instances in which otherwise vulnerable groups are resilient in the face of disasters and other environmental stressors. The small community of Grand Bayou, Louisiana, is an example. Grand Bayou is located in Plaquemines Parish, in the "Bird's Foot Delta" that extends south from New Orleans to the Gulf of Mexico. Accessible only by water, Grand Bayou is a subsistence or natural resource community whose small population consists mainly of Atakapa-Ishak Native American peoples (a Native community not recognized as a tribe by the U.S. government), who over time have sustained themselves through shrimping, fishing, trapping, and growing fruits and vegetables. The community is rich in kinship and social ties and is also held together by strong religious faith. Those connections are reinforced by the community's proximity to ancestral burial mounds. Members have a long tradition of living off the land and enjoying abundant marine resources, and their connections to the bayou's natural environment are deeply organic in ways that are almost inconceivable to outsiders.

At the same time, Grand Bayou is a community that is vulnerable in many ways. Encroachment by the oil and gas industry and sea-level rise have resulted in coastal erosion, land subsidence, damage to marine ecosystems, and wetlands loss, which are in turn threatening natural capital and community livelihoods. Maintaining a traditional way of life and a largely subsistence-based economy is also difficult in the face of pressures to culturally assimilate and integrate with the region's cash economy. Historically the community has been marginalized politically, and efforts to press for a greater voice in local affairs and for government services have proved ineffective.

Grand Bayou is also vulnerable to hurricanes and other disasters. In the recent past, Tropical Storm Isadore and Hurricane Lili did significant damage in the community in 2002, but interestingly those two events also helped set in motion processes of change that would increase the resilience of Grand Bayou. The turnaround began through a participatory action research (PAR) project that was initiated with the community after those two disasters in 2002 by anthropologist and minister Kristina Peterson, who tapped several disaster researchers and practitioners to work with the community. The Center for Hazards Assessment, Response, and Technology at the University of New Orleans (UNO-CHART) and Shirley Laska, its director, became core supporters of a community organization called Grand Bayou Families United. Grand Bayou already possessed an abundance of cultural capital and bonding social capital, but the PAR project created potential for the development of extensive bridging, linking, and political capital that significantly enhanced community resilience capabilities. The project, initially supported by the Presbyterian Church (USA), obtained additional support from the National Science Foundation and other funding sources. These efforts helped to forge ties among the community, researchers from the University of New Orleans and other universities, and entities such as the American Planning Association; the U.S. Department of Agriculture's Extension Disaster Education Network and the same agency's Natural Resources Conservation Services; the NOAA Sea Grant Program; the U.S.

Army Corps of Engineers; and the Social Enterprise Alliance. External funding also enabled Grand Bayou community representatives to travel to workshops held by groups such as the Housing Assistance Council, which advocates for housing on behalf of rural people of color, and to other scientific and advocacy-oriented conferences. Long-term connections were also made with researchers who could assist the community with scientific assessments of its vulnerability to various hazards, and who in turn benefited from having access to community residents' local environmental knowledge.

When Hurricanes Katrina and Rita struck in 2005, the community was physically devastated. However, no lives were lost, and many fishing boats were saved when community members banded together, moved their boats, sought shelter from the storm, and received boat repair support from the Heifer Project. The community faced massive challenges in recovering, but by 2009 about a dozen families were able to return to the bayou and rebuild after a major struggle to receive small amounts of government aid, but more importantly through support they received from churches, foundations, and volunteers, which was in part a function of ongoing advocacy carried out in conjunction with CHART, the community's growing national visibility, and its ability to tap into diverse external support networks.

Life in Grand Bayou was beginning to settle into a post-Katrina "new normal" when the community was forced to deal with the impacts of the 2010 BP *Deepwater Horizon* oil spill, which posed a direct threat to its entire way of life. Through their extensive network of contacts, the Grand Bayou families were able to draw national attention to their desperate situation. The spill's impacts on the community were highlighted in stories in *National Geographic*, the *Huffington Post*, the radio and television program *Democracy Now!* and numerous other publications and web postings. The president of the Natural Resources Defense Council (NRDC) was filmed taking a tour of the Grand Bayou area with local community leaders, and Grand Bayou became a focus for a joint project by the NRDC, StoryCorps, and the sustainability-oriented storytelling group Bridge the Gulf, which was designed to document the experiences of local communities affected by the spill. In a remarkable example of grassroots solidarity, fisher folk and representatives of Alaskan Native communities that had been affected by the *Exxon Valdez* oil spill traveled to Grand Bayou to meet with local leaders, so that the community could learn what to expect in dealing with spill impacts and what the future might have in store with respect to negotiations with BP.

In a seemingly endless series of travails for this vulnerable population, Grand Bayou was once again struck by Hurricane Isaac in 2012. Although the flooding was extensive, only one house was severely damaged, because the homes in Grand Bayou had been rebuilt with raised foundations after Katrina. That house, which belongs to community activist Ruby Ancar, was subsequently restored.

The future remains uncertain for the people of Grand Bayou, who struggle daily to maintain their culture and way of life. Yet the community has shown itself to be remarkably resilient in the face of environmental degradation and a series of major disaster events, in part as a result of the external networks of support it has succeeded in developing over time. In addition to its efforts to recover from recent disasters, Grand Bayou has subsequently offered itself as a teaching community for researchers and students from around the world. For example, the community has embarked on participatory projects with university-based researchers that will incorporate indigenous environmental knowledge into efforts to map the effects of disaster events and climate change, and to provide decision support for coastal restoration projects. The accomplishments of the Grand Bayou community illustrate how efforts to enhance community resilience through strengthening different forms of social capital can have positive impacts for at-risk populations. Already internally cohesive before its recent disaster experiences, the community has developed extensive bridging and linking ties that have multiplied and diversified its external sources of support and increased its political influence.

Community Activism and Inherent Resilience: The Tulsa Case

Many other communities have engaged in conscious efforts to increase their inherent disaster resilience through collective action. The city of Tulsa, Oklahoma, is one such community. Situated on the Arkansas River in the Mingo Creek watershed, Tulsa has had a long history of flooding, including major flood events in 1923, 1970, 1974, and 1976, followed by a damaging flood in 1984 that resulted in fourteen fatalities. One reason why flood losses were so severe in Tulsa is that the city had a history of relying on levees and dams for flood protection while permitting intensive development in its floodplain.

After the 1974 flood, the city began the Mingo Creek Improvement Project, which protected approximately seven hundred homes from future flooding. Following the 1976 flood, the city received federal funding to begin buying up land in the floodplain and passed a moratorium to halt floodplain development. Following the flooding in 1984, the city relocated three hundred homes and a mobile-home park, began a detainment basin project with the Army Corps of Engineers, established a city department of storm water management, and initiated a storm water utility fee. Over time, Tulsa acquired one thousand flood-prone properties, preserved one quarter of its floodplain as open space, and adopted strict flood-resistant building codes. Once the nation's leader in federal disaster declarations, Tulsa now receives a rating of 2 on the Community Rating Scale for flood risk reduction, in which 1 is the highest rating (Patton 1994; Meo, Ziebro, and Patton 2004).

Tulsa is also a national leader in preparedness for tornadoes and other disasters. During the 1990s the city received federal funding under FEMA's short-lived Project Impact Program, which encouraged loss reduction planning projects, community education, and the development of public-private disaster preparedness partnerships. When that program was abruptly ended under the first George W. Bush administration, Tulsa formed a spin-off organization called Tulsa Partners to continue its resilience-enhancing activities. The city also became active in Citizen Corps, a Department of Homeland Security program to engage community volunteers in disaster preparedness and response activities. In 2006, Tulsa Partners joined with the insurance industry-supported Institute of Business and Home Safety to establish a Disaster Resistant Business Council. More recently, in collaboration with the Tulsa Zoo, Tulsa Partners launched the Millennium Center for Green and Safe Living to provide environmental education and disaster loss reduction programs for community residents. Tulsa also participates in the Mayors' Climate Protection Agreement, a project of the U.S. Conference of Mayors. The Tulsa case illustrates how with sufficient political will communities are able to access resources and build social and other forms of capital, such as financial capital, toward the goal of increasing their inherent resilience in the face of disasters and other perils, including climate change.

Disasters and Damage to Capitals

One reason why disasters are so devastating is that they damage or destroy the various forms of capital, including social capital, that enable communities to function. This point was brought home decades ago in Kai Erikson's study of the 1972 Buffalo Creek, West Virginia, disaster, *Everything in Its Path: Destruction of Community in the Buffalo Creek Flood* (1976). Caused by the failure of a retention dam owned by the Pittston Coal Company, the area's major employer, Buffalo Creek was a horrific event that literally washed communities away, killing 125 people, injuring more than 1,000, and leaving 4,000 people homeless out of a population of about 5,000. Erikson chronicled how the flood disrupted community social networks and caused a subsequent decline in the emotional well-being of residents of the small West Virginia communities that were most affected. In Erikson's telling, it was the "collective trauma," "loss of communality," and loss of trust in the coal company and government institutions experienced by already vulnerable groups that resulted in protracted mental health problems for victims. Erikson later amplified these themes in *A New Species of Trouble: Explorations in Disaster, Trauma, and Community* (1994), which dealt with the ways social ties are frayed by threats associated with toxic contamination and other environmental hazards.

More recently, Liesel Ritchie has studied how disasters can deplete social and other forms of capital, and the consequences of those losses. In addition to destroying resources that are important for the social life of a community, disasters weaken family, neighborhood, and workplace ties, and they can also engender community conflict and resentment of entities that caused the disruption or did little to help victims overcome it. For example, conducting research in Cordova, Alaska, nearly fifteen years after the *Exxon Valdez* oil spill, Ritchie found that the spill itself, the protracted litigation that followed, and ongoing uncertainty about the future were continuing to erode social capital, as evidenced by their negative effects on trust, social relationships, and other social capital indicators (Ritchie 2012). This long-term damage to social capital was a continued source of the still significant levels of stress community residents were reporting so many years after the *Exxon* disaster. Communities that experience sustained periods in which social networks and other forms of capital are weakened find disaster recovery difficult and may be more vulnerable to subsequent disaster events.

Cautions Regarding Social Capital

As the foregoing discussions have shown, social capital-based frameworks offer a powerful set of tools for theorizing about and measuring disaster resilience, but some caveats are also in order. Alejandro Portes (1998), who conducted pioneering research on social capital, observes that social capital is neither a particularly new concept nor a panacea for the problems societies face. Portes also notes that while social capital is often portrayed as an unalloyed good, there are also many examples of "negative social capital," such as situations in which closely knit groups use their solidarity to exclude others or exert so much influence on members that they drain their resources or pressure members toward conformity. Gangs, factions engaged in civil wars, and racist groups may rank high on social capital, but that is not considered a good thing. Political scientist Daniel Aldrich, whose research is discussed in the following chapter (see Aldrich 2012), also calls attention to the "Janus-faced" nature of social capital, arguing like Portes that strong in-group solidarity can result in the exclusion of out-group members and even violent social conflict.

Forms of social capital also matter: marginalized groups may possess high levels of bonding social capital but still remain vulnerable owing to a lack of bridging and linking ties. In contrast with the residents of Grand Bayou, internally cohesive groups that lack or have weak external connections have difficulty making their needs known and obtaining resources, both during normal times and in disaster situations. Researchers also caution that social capital which is mobilized in some domains of community life, such as community economic development, may not necessarily transfer to other domains, such as environmental sustainability and disaster loss reduction (Bridger and Luloff 2001).

Many disaster resilience formulations assume that social capital increases resilience, without also acknowledging that social network ties can be mobilized to oppose resilience-enhancing activities or, as we have seen in cases like New Orleans and Natomas, to foster rent-seeking activities that can increase disaster vulnerability. Cohesive and well-connected elites—groups that are high in social capital—can use their influence to impose risks on more vulnerable groups that lack power and influence; this pattern is seen in situations involving environmental inequalities like those, discussed earlier, in the city of Phoenix. Tea Party and property-rights advocates employ their social capital to block efforts to make communities more sustainable. It would thus be incorrect to focus on the resilience-enhancing properties of social capital without also considering its downside.

This chapter has provided an overview of inherent qualities of social units and systems that exist prior to and independent of the occurrence of a disaster and that act as a cushion against extensive damage and disruption. In contrast, adaptive resilience, which is discussed in the next chapter, is activated when a disaster event actually occurs. Under such circumstances, a lot depends on ingenuity, flexibility, and adaptability as communities, groups, and individuals face the inevitable surprises disasters bring forth.

CHAPTER 8

Adaptive Resilience in the Face of Disasters

THE PREVIOUS CHAPTER CONDENSED current thinking on the concept of resilience, with an emphasis on inherent resilience. In this chapter, we consider adaptive resilience, consisting of actions that are carried out during and after disasters that permit social entities to cope and bounce back in response to loss and disruption. This form of resilience involves both the mobilization of inherent resilience capabilities and novel and emergent forms of behavior and social organization that develop in response to disaster-related demands. We begin with forms of resilience that manifest themselves immediately after disaster strikes and later consider resilience in the context of postdisaster recovery.

An overarching theme here is that adaptive resilience represents a blending of novel and preplanned activities, or what researcher John Harrald (2006) has referred to as "agility and discipline." Disasters inevitably disrupt social life, and they always contain elements of surprise; that is their very nature. Events that do not surprise are not disasters by definition. Surprise in turn evokes the need for agility: workarounds to deal with system outages; new strategies for meeting unanticipated needs; new ways of organizing people, resources, and information; learning on the fly; trying different approaches and keeping those that work. Social organization does not disappear during disasters, but it does take new forms. Prior planning remains important, but so does deviating from plans and creating new ones. Bureaucracies do many things well, but coping with disasters is not one of them. Fortunately, even as people face death, destruction, and dire conditions, they are able to be resilient—although in a society and world marked by glaring inequalities, some are more resilient than others.

Resilience is also evident in collective efforts to make sense of what is happening during and after disaster impact. Disaster conditions can resemble the "fog of war," and as we saw in earlier discussions of failures of sensemaking during Hurricane Katrina, the inability to assess, with some degree of veracity, conditions as they exist on the ground and to determine what is needed in extreme situations can seriously hamper response efforts.

CONTRIBUTORS TO ADAPTIVE RESILIENCE: POSTDISASTER MOBILIZATION PATTERNS

Although the concept of disaster resilience itself is relatively new, disaster scholars have been studying processes that contribute to adaptive resilience for more than sixty years. When the organized social scientific study of disasters began in the late 1940s, it was closely aligned with planning for nuclear war. Faced with the reality that the Soviet Union had atomic weapons, federal government entities wanted answers to questions about how members of the general public would respond in the event of a nuclear attack on U.S. soil. Although there was extensive evidence of how populations in Germany, England, and Japan behaved when subjected to firebombing and to attacks using nuclear weapons during World War II, our political and military elites believed that research was needed that would focus specifically on U.S. communities. According to pioneering researcher E. L. Quarantelli (1987), who took an active role in early Cold War disaster research, as well as historical research on the emergence of the field of disaster studies (Knowles 2011), funders were concerned about whether members of the public would panic under a nuclear assault, whether they would become so despairing and demoralized that they would be unable to function after an attack, whether mental illness would become widespread, whether looting and lawlessness would prevail following a nuclear exchange, and whether critical emergency personnel would continue working under wartime conditions or abandon their posts to see to the needs of their own families. Disasters were thought of as proxies for wartime situations in many of their impacts, so social scientists began receiving funding to conduct field research on quick response following major disasters. Early research was carried out from 1950 to 1954 by the National Opinion Research Center at the University of Chicago and the Psychiatric Institute at the University of Maryland with support from the Army

Chemical Center. Other studies were conducted around the same time by sociologists at the University of Oklahoma and by the Committee on Disaster Studies (1951–1957) and later by the Disaster Research Group (1957–1962) at the National Academy of Sciences (Quarantelli 1987). Funding for early disaster research was provided by military agencies, the Federal Civil Defense Administration, the Office of Civil and Defense Mobilization, the National Institute of Mental Health, and the Ford Foundation. Many different types of disaster events were studied in the early days, including airline crashes, tornadoes, fires, hurricanes, explosions, and contamination episodes. The Disaster Research Center (DRC), under the directorship of sociologists E. L. Quarantelli, Russell Dynes, and J. Eugene Haas, was subsequently established at the Ohio State University in 1963 with initial funding from the Office of Civil Defense and the Air Force Office of Scientific Research, again with a focus on what could be learned about wartime conditions through the study of disaster events. DRC, which moved to its current home at the University of Delaware in 1985, has conducted hundreds of studies on disasters over its fifty-year history.

PRO-SOCIAL NORMS, CONVERGENCE, ORGANIZATIONAL ADAPTATION, AND GROUP EMERGENCE

As evidence began to accumulate from early field studies, the picture of disaster-related social behavior that developed was very different from what the military research sponsors presumably expected. In the earliest studies conducted on disaster responses, researchers identified three predominant processes: the emergence of pro-social or altruistic norms; postdisaster convergence; and adaptation at the organization level, including the emergence of forms of social organization that did not exist prior to disaster impact. Panic, looting, and lawlessness were found to be rare. Rather than presenting a doomsday scenario, early research emphasized processes such as the emergence of widespread pro-social behavior and the formation of "therapeutic communities" in the wake of disaster (Fritz 1961). Studies showed that rather than being dazed and in shock, residents of disaster-stricken communities moved into action almost immediately to assist one another. While inarguably stressful, disasters only rarely resulted in severe or long-term emotional problems. Upon examination, it turned out that community and group morale actually rose when people were confronted with disaster situations and that they were more willing to help one another in those situations than during normal, nondisaster times.

In contrast with images of victims fleeing in panic after disaster impact, researchers noted an entirely different pattern: helpers from within and outside stricken communities converged on disaster scenes, as did supplies, equipment, and other resources, whether requested or not. In fact, convergence was found to be difficult to manage in the aftermath of disasters as volunteers and donations poured into communities (Fritz and Mathewson 1957; Neal 1994). One sociologist used the term "mass assault" to describe patterns of large-scale convergence that were documented in disasters of all types (Barton 1969).

In painting such a positive picture of the ways communities respond when disasters strike, early research glossed over the fact that social inequities and conflicts remain and manifest themselves during disasters. As I discuss in more detail elsewhere (Tierney 2007), the so-called good-news perspective on public responses that was advanced in early studies downplayed the fact that members of minority and marginalized communities have been treated harshly and even violently in past disasters and that such treatment can exist alongside intensified feelings of social solidarity. There is no reason to expect that social inequalities vanish during disasters or that pro-social behavior entirely eclipses social injustice. Indeed, fellow victims were wantonly murdered in disasters such as the 1923 Great Kanto (Tokyo) earthquake in Japan and Hurricane Katrina. However, such occurrences do not belie the fact that most social behavior in disasters is adaptive and socially beneficial.

Classical disaster research also called attention to the ways in which organizations and groups adapt when faced with disaster-related challenges. One often-cited typology identified four common patterns of adaptation, referred to as existing, expanding, extending, and emergent forms of social organization (Brouillette and Quarantelli 1971). Some organizations in affected communities undergo little change during disasters.

Others expand in size while carrying out the same kinds of tasks they performed prior to the disaster. Examples of this pattern of expansion include fire and police departments that add personnel from neighboring and even far-off communities, and agencies like the Red Cross that take on volunteers in order to better serve disaster victims. Still other organizations, called extending organizations, suspend their ordinary activities and begin to perform disaster-related tasks, even though such tasks may be unfamiliar. Among many examples of extending organizations are the automobile dealerships and neighborhood schools in Kobe, Japan, that served as emergency shelters after the 1995 earthquake. More recent examples of organizational extension in Superstorm Sandy in 2012 include Occupy Sandy, a group that formed through a repurposing of Occupy Wall Street groupings in New York City, and the Red Hook Initiative, a community-based organization devoted to youth empowerment, which shifted gears rapidly to provide disaster relief in New York's Red Hook community after the storm.

Finally, entirely new groups emerge in disaster situations, beginning first with residents of affected areas who are often joined later by converging volunteers. Typically starting out as loosely organized collections of community residents, emergent groups perform a wide variety of tasks in disasters, from sandbagging to prevent flooding, to searching for and rescuing disaster victims, removing debris, and addressing a host of victim needs. Such groups include entities like the Common Ground Collective, which emerged in the Algiers neighborhood in the aftermath of Hurricane Katrina to provide food, medical assistance, and shelter to victims, and which is still in existence. Acting as focal points for converging helpers, groups like Common Ground form both because of the strength of altruistic norms that develop in disasters and because of collective definitions that the needs of victims are not being met through official channels, or not being met quickly enough. Most emergent groups are short-lived, but during the time they function they often provide critical forms of aid. For example, a long-standing research finding is that most lifesaving activity in disasters is undertaken not by official uniformed responders such as public safety officers, but rather by loosely organized groups of community residents. In a discussion on search and rescue activities following earthquakes, for example, disaster physician Eric Noji has observed that

[i]n Southern Italy in 1980, 90% of the survivors of an earthquake were extricated by untrained, uninjured survivors who used their bare hands and simple tools such as shovels and axes. . . . Following the 1976 Tangshan earthquake, about 200,000 to 300,000 entrapped people crawled out of the debris on their own and went on to rescue others. . . . They became the backbone of the rescue teams, and it was to their credit that more than 80% of those buried under the debris were rescued. (1997: 162)

After a major earthquake struck Mexico City in 1985, the governmental response was sluggish, but civil society responded rapidly as residents of damaged areas organized themselves into search and rescue groups and saved numerous lives. Post-earthquake surveys found that in the three weeks following the earthquake approximately 10 percent of Mexico City's population, or about two million people, were involved in one way or another in emergency response and supportive activities (Wenger and James 1994). In the aftermath of the 1995 Kobe earthquake, an estimated 1.3 million people took part in a massive spontaneous volunteer effort that took both Japanese officials and the public by surprise (Atsumi et al. 1996; Tierney and Goltz 1997). With no equivalent term in Japanese, the loan word "borantia" (volunteer) was incorporated into the language to describe this spontaneous form of organized aid provision. The year 1995 was subsequently dubbed the "first year of the volunteer" in Japan, and the earthquake led to changes in legislation governing the nonprofit sector in Japan and in cultural perceptions of volunteer behavior (Schwartz 2002).

In that same year in Tokyo, the Aum Shinrikyu cult released sarin gas in the Tokyo subway. Individuals interviewed by writer Haruki Murakami in *Underground* (2000), his book on the subway attack, describe in detail how they assisted others, often putting themselves in great danger. These accounts show that it was fellow subway riders and subway line attendants, rather than public safety personnel, who were the first responders in that attack. Some of those who were interviewed had been so committed to helping their fellow passengers that they did not recognize the extent of their own exposure to the sarin fumes until later.

When Hurricane Katrina struck, two emergent groups of private citizens joined together to form the "Cajun Navy," a flotilla of between three and five hundred boats that traveled into St. Bernard, Orleans, and other parishes to rescue victims who were trapped by the floodwaters. The navy is credited with saving thousands of people, including residents of senior citizen facilities and hospice patients. In addition to its extensive search and rescue work, the navy set up an improvised base known as "Camp Katrina" to provide support for those who were rescued, and it began stockpiling and transporting supplies and equipment well in advance of official response agencies (Hennessy 2007).

In her beautifully written tribute to civil society's effervescence in disasters, *A Paradise Built in Hell: The Extraordinary Communities That Arise in Disaster* (2009), Rebecca Solnit provides numerous accounts of emergent collective action in disasters ranging from the 1906 San Francisco earthquake to the London Blitz, the 1985 Mexico City earthquake, the terrorist attacks of September 11, 2001, and Hurricane Katrina. In Solnit's telling, disasters, by disrupting the social order, free people to be creative and resourceful and to feel, more so than during nondisaster times, that the help they are able to give really matters. Bureaucratic organizations and command-and-control hierarchies don't work nearly as well in disaster situations as decentralized decision making and action by those who understand their own communities and are sensitive to local problems and needs. Solnit notes that disasters give people a feeling of connection to their communities and a sense of purpose that is often lacking in day-to-day life and that is deeply gratifying:

The joy in disaster comes, when it comes, from that purposefulness, the immersion in service and survival, and from an affection that is not private and personal but civic: the love of strangers for each other, of a citizen for his or her city, of belonging to a greater whole, of doing the work that matters. (2009: 306)

This outpouring of feeling for fellow sufferers and a willingness to act on their behalf is a fundamental source of adaptive resilience.

EMERGENT NETWORKS AND DISASTER RESILIENCE

Crisis-related collective action also includes the formation of emergent networks of organizations that coordinate their activities during and after disasters. Emergent multiorganizational networks (EMONs) are the manifestation of new organizational interconnections that reflect collective efforts to manage crisis events. EMONs are heterogeneous, consisting of existing organizations with predesignated crisis management responsibilities, other organizations that may not have been included in prior planning but that become involved in crisis response activities because their leaders and members believe they have some contribution to make, and emergent groups. As crisis conditions change, EMON structures evolve; new organizations link into networks, and new relationships form.

Like emergent groups, EMONs develop because of the surprises disasters generate; problems inevitably emerge that were not envisioned in prior planning, so new organizational actors join networks to address those issues. Emergent pro-social norms and the need to become involved in aiding victims compel organizational entities that may have had no prior connection with formal emergency management agencies to mobilize their resources. Organizations that constitute nodes in emergent networks also attract converging personnel, volunteers, and supplies and equipment. What is sometimes described as the chaotic response to disasters is more appropriately seen as network emergence, as both existing and emergent organizations, formally designated response organizations, and other entities that define themselves as having a role to play, begin to coordinate, collaborate, and work out strategies for action in response to needs that develop in rapidly shifting disaster environments.

EMONs have been studied with varying degrees of sophistication for more than thirty years (see Drabek et al. 1981; Topper and Carley 1999; Drabek 2003), but it was not until the terrorist attacks of September 11, 2001, that researchers began to study them on a large scale using advanced network analytic techniques (Tierney and Trainor 2004; Comfort and Kapucu 2006; Kapucu, Arslan, and Collins 2010; Schweinberger, Petrescu-Prahova, and Vu 2012). Sociologist Christine Bevc (2010) conducted extensive analyses of the World Trade Center disaster EMON. Using data sources ranging from agency situation reports to newspaper accounts and interviews with agency personnel, she documented and mapped over 6,600 interactions and collaborations among over seven hundred governmental, private, and nonprofit organizations and emergent groups over the twelve-day emergency period following the terrorist attacks. EMON activities were organized around no fewer than forty-two different tasks, ranging from standard response activities such as firefighting, injury treatment, and law enforcement to tasks that were more directly associated with the distinctive impacts of the attacks themselves, such as remains identification and forensic investigations. Other researchers working with the same data showed that while some key actors in the EMON, such as the Federal Emergency Management Agency, were formally designated response coordinators and thus would be expected to be central to the response, other organizations, such as Verizon and the Health Care Financing Administration, took on major coordinating roles on an emergent basis (Schweinberger, Petrescu-Prahova, and Vu 2012). In an almost entrepreneurial way, some organizations moved rapidly to establish central positions in the Trade Center EMON. For example, on the day of the attacks and in the absence of any predisaster authority, New York City's Department of Design and Construction defined for itself a major role in the management of site stabilization and debris removal activities at Ground Zero (Langewiesche 2002). Additionally, a wide array of organizations and groups, including providers of remote-sensing technologies, spatial analysts and mappers from New York City universities, vendors of geographic information system (GIS) products, and information technology service providers converged on an unplanned basis to assist with the response (Tierney and Trainor 2004).

Studies on other disasters provide additional information on the size, scale, and complexity of network emergence in disasters. For example, Carter Butts, Ryan Acton, and Christopher Marcum (2012) studied EMONs in the warning period and aftermath of Hurricane Katrina. Using about 4,500 documents, including situation reports, press releases, and maps, they identified 187 networks that were active in the states affected by Katrina, and they also explored how those networks changed, formed into distinct clusters, and became more closely interrelated over time. Like those who studied the World Trade Center EMON, these researchers note that Katrina EMON leadership displayed both institutionalized and emergent properties, observing that "coordination roles in the inner core of the Katrina EMON appear to be filled by a combination of organizations with a standing mandate to bridge diverse groups and organizations whose centrality emerges from task and resource considerations that are peculiar to the specific event" (Butts, Acton, and Marcum 2012: 25).

Studies like those discussed here rely on official and published accounts of organizational activities and interactions during crises, and thus the network relationships on which they focus undoubtedly constitute only the tip of the iceberg with respect to network emergence. Large-scale disasters serve as magnets for organizations and groups that sense they have some role to play in dealing with impacts and aiding victims, and draw new organizational actors onto the scene whose relationships with one another are emergent and fluid.

EMONs constitute a significant source of adaptive disaster resilience for several reasons. Although the management of disasters is often characterized in command-and-control terms, in which a single organizational entity or group of entities is in charge of disaster operations, the reality of disaster response is that no organization can command all responding entities; as opposed to control, collaboration is the norm among myriad organizations that play a role in responding to disaster. Research on network forms of organization indicates that networks are superior to hierarchies in a number of ways: they provide the agility and responsiveness that hierarchies too often lack, enhance organizational learning, and facilitate the diffusion of innovations (Polodny and Page 1998), and compared with hierarchical organizational forms they have a greater ability to adapt in turbulent environments such as disaster situations. Networks offer access to diverse sources of information and resource pools, and multiple network ties also introduce redundancy, creating additional paths along which information can travel. As researchers who studied how financial firms responded in the wake of the September 11 attacks observed:

[i]n situations of radical uncertainty, diversity of ties and diversity of means increase the likelihood that interaction will yield unpredictable solutions through "creative abrasions" and "generative friction." (Buenza and Stark 2003: 153)

Networks thus constitute the locus for the rapid information gathering, resource mobilization, and learning that must take place under conditions of ambiguity, uncertainty, and surprise. Political scientist Louise Comfort, who has conducted extensive multinational research on social system responses to earthquakes, argues that the most effective responses are those that are "self-organizing": "high on organizational flexibility and high on cultural openness to new information and new methods of action" (1999: 73). Because of their decentralization and capacity for accommodating new organizational members, networks provide this kind of flexibility and openness.

EMERGENCE AND SOCIAL CAPITAL

As longtime disaster researcher Russell Dynes (2005) notes, emergent activity in the aftermath of disasters both builds on preexisting social capital resources and creates and enhances new forms of social capital. For example, emergent group activities typically grow out of existing social relationships, such as family, workplace, and neighborhood ties; these activities are informed by local knowledge developed on the basis of social interaction. For example, Aguirre and colleagues (1995), who conducted research on a gas explosion that leveled the neighborhood of Analco in Guadalajara, Mexico, in 1992, found that preexisting peer group, family, church, and neighborhood relationships formed the basis for groupings that emerged to carry out search and rescue activities. Social ties also helped determine the difference between life and death for victims; as Aguirre and coauthors observe, "the chances of people surviving the blast were in direct proportion to the presence among searchers of a person or persons who cared for the victim and who knew the victim's likely location at the time of the blast" (1995: 81).

Organizational expansion, extension, and emergence, as well as EMON formation and evolution, can thus be reframed as processes that reinforce existing stocks of social capital and lead to the creation of new ones. Such processes increase the size of entities that are responding to disasters, transform existing social relationships for disaster-related purposes, and lead to the formation of new groups and heterogeneous interorganizational networks. Developing out of localized and event-specific situation assessments, these novel forms of social capital are well suited to address the distinctive challenges different disasters pose.

WHAT'S JAZZ GOT TO DO WITH IT?
IMPROVISATION, CREATIVITY,
AND ADAPTIVE RESILIENCE

Disasters do not follow preordained scripts. Even in situations where there is extensive disaster experience, those seeking to respond invariably confront unforeseen situations. One counterproductive way of dealing with the unexpected is to adhere to plans and procedures even when they are ineffective or offer no guidance in the face of unfamiliar challenges. Another response is to experience paralysis and take no action at all. A third approach, and one that is typically seen in disaster situations, is to adapt—to develop new courses of action, bring to bear new resources, or combine actions and resources in new ways.

Researcher Adam Rose, who studies the resilience of economic entities and systems in disasters, defines adaptive resilience as the "ability in crisis situations to maintain function on the basis of ingenuity or extra effort" (2009: 10). For example, businesses that have been damaged or disrupted as a consequence of a disaster can develop ways of recapturing lost production, substitute inputs for those that have been lost (for example, using a generator for electric power when the power grid is down), relocate, take steps to make their business processes more flexible, or engage in a variety of other activities in order to stay afloat during difficult postdisaster conditions.

Predisaster planning is one way of enhancing adaptive capacity and achieving postdisaster resilience. Within the economic domain, the objective of business continuity planning is to enable businesses to reduce and cope with postdisaster disruptions. More broadly, the goal of various planning activities, such as developing disaster plans and collaborative agreements, training personnel, stockpiling supplies and equipment, engaging in disaster drills and exercises and "what if?" scenarios, and undertaking predisaster planning for postdisaster recovery, is to improve adaptive disaster resilience. Planning is designed to help social actors—individuals, households, businesses, communities—anticipate the challenges disasters will bring and adjust accordingly. Plans and planning activities are therefore a key source of postdisaster resilience. At the same time, in disasters plans often turn out to be inadequate in light of the effort that responding requires; resources that were counted on are destroyed by the disaster itself or fail to materialize; new and unexpected dangers emerge. Even in cases where planning activities have been sound and extensive, surprises emerge that call for improvisation and creativity.

Sociologist Tricia Wachtendorf and geographer and policy scientist James Kendra have made extensive inquiries into processes of postdisaster improvisation, focusing in particular on responses to the September 11 attacks on the World Trade Center (Kendra and Wachtendorf 2003; Wachtendorf 2004; Kendra and Wachtendorf 2006; Wachtendorf and Kendra 2006). Unexpected events reached traumatic proportions on that day. Two massive skyscrapers were attacked by planes and totally collapsed within hours. Debris from those collapses set fire to another skyscraper, World Trade Center 7, which housed New York City's Mayor's Office of Emergency Management and its state-of-the art Emergency Operations Center (EOC), a facility that was intended to be the city's nerve center in the event of a disaster. That building collapsed on the afternoon of September 11, and in a stunning example of the problems posed by a lack of redundancy, there was no operational backup EOC. With the collapse of World Trade Center 7, the city lost, among other things, a well-resourced space in which to convene representatives of responding agencies, its advanced information technologies, and its crisis mapping and communications capabilities. On September 11, city officials and those charged with managing the response to the attacks were literally out on the street in the midst of an unprecedented disaster. It was initially unknown how many people had lost their lives, how many were trapped in the debris, and how many needed medical assistance. With much of the transportation and communications systems lost in Lower Manhattan, hundreds of thousands of Trade Center evacuees, tourists, and commuters struggled to make their way to safety, even as responding personnel and volunteers surged into the affected area. New York City was forced to cope with an event that was simultaneously a disaster, an act of terrorism, and a national security emergency, but without adequate facilities to do so.

Wachtendorf (2004) has documented and analyzed several examples of improvisational activity that were associated with the response to the September 11 attacks. After emergency personnel gathered in two locations that turned out to be unsuitable, the city was able to begin to reconstitute its EOC about three days after the attacks in a pier facility on the Hudson River that was normally used for entertainment cruises—a structure the city had reserved, ironically, for a disaster drill that was to have taken place on September 12. Computing equipment, agency representatives, mapping experts, and all manner of supplies began to flow into the facility, which was much larger than the original EOC. At first, handwritten signs designated different functional areas within the improvised EOC; later, makeshift offices were set up and eventually enclosed with cloth partitions. Areas were established for dining and sleeping, and personal-care items such as toothpaste, deodorant, and soap, along with items of clothing, began appearing in order to meet the needs of the hundreds of workers that staffed the EOC around the clock. The U.S. Navy hospital ship *Comfort* pulled up next to the pier, to act as a shield against possible attacks and to provide beds and services to the emergency workers. When federal agencies arrived to begin providing assistance, they established their own headquarters at an adjacent pier. Golf carts were brought in to carry personnel between the two locations.

As Wachtendorf (2004) explains, a number of important disaster-related tasks also had to be improvised. With so many converging personnel, including outside search and rescue teams, public safety personnel, and contractors responsible for removing debris at Ground Zero, a credentialing system for the thousands who were involved in responding to the attacks had to be developed on the fly. In addition to being a disaster site, Ground Zero was also a crime scene, so protocols had to be formulated for sorting through and separating massive amounts of debris and searching for, labeling, and tracking human remains and potential evidence. Volunteers and donations were flowing into the city, and they had to be put somewhere, so the Jacob Javits Center was designated as a staging area for converging resources. Families were desperate to locate their missing loved ones, and so the Armory, at Twenty-sixth and Lexington, was initially identified as a place where they could receive assistance, counseling, and bereavement services; those activities were later moved to another pier on the Hudson near the EOC, so that various elements of the response could be better coordinated.

In another extraordinary example of improvisation, on the day of the attacks all manner of maritime vessels, including ferries, entertainment boats, tugboats, and other watercraft, organized themselves to evacuate people who were stranded in Lower Manhattan and take them to New Jersey, Staten Island, and other destinations. Many mariners responded spontaneously shortly after the attacks took place, while others acted after hearing a call from the Coast Guard directing "all available boats" to assist with the waterborne evacuation. Important for this discussion, although the Coast Guard issued the call, it did not command or control the activities of the emergent fleet; while there were mariners who heard and acted on the call, many others collaborated to make their own arrangements for loading and transporting evacuees, and still others took part in the waterborne evacuation but were unaware that the Coast Guard had asked them to mobilize. Somewhere between 300,000 and 500,000 people were evacuated by the improvised flotilla, which also transported supplies and emergency workers (for details, see Kendra, Wachtendorf, and Quarantelli 2002; Kendra and Wachtendorf 2006; Wachtendorf and Kendra 2006).

Many social scientists who have sought to understand how improvisational activities emerge and are organized have looked for clues to the world of jazz, and to a lesser degree to the world of improvisational acting. Organizational theorist Karl Weick (1998) relied heavily on Paul Berliner's study *Thinking in Jazz: The Infinite Art of Improvisation* (1994) for insights into how organizations improvise. In defining improvisational activity, Weick quotes from Berliner, who argues that in jazz "[i]mprovisation involves reworking precomposed material and designs in relation to unanticipated ideas conceived, shaped, and transformed under the special conditions of performance" (Weick 1998: 544), and he also relies on Berliner to clarify aspects of improvisation that are often misunderstood. For example, while improvisation is commonly thought of as spontaneous and intuitive, studies of jazz indicate that improvisation is actually based on players' experience and disciplined application of a broad stock of musical knowledge. Weick emphasizes that in viewing improvisation as music created wholly in the moment, "we overlook the major investment in practice, listening, and study that precedes a stunning performance" (544). He also notes that improvisation involves a continuum that ranges from making slight changes in a composition to highly creative and innovative performances. In other words, some improvisational activity adheres closely to the original musical score, while other forms of improvisation take more liberties. This notion of a continuum is clearly applicable to behavior under crisis conditions. As Wachtendorf (2004) has shown, during the 9/11 disaster some activities, such as collective efforts to reconstitute New York City's EOC, attempted to keep response configurations on track as originally designed. Others, like the waterborne evacuation, retained many aspects of pre-event activities (moving boats on water, boarding passengers), but performed them in new ways, for new purposes, in new organizational arrangements. At the far end of the continuum are highly novel collaborations developed in the face of deep uncertainty for which plans offer little or no guidance. This was the case for the World Trade Center debris sorting and remains identification that was carried out at the Fresh Kills landfill sight.

David Mendonca and William Wallace (2007) have studied what jazz improvisation reveals about how organizations align themselves as they respond to disasters. For example, both jazz combos and response organizations have predesignated roles and operate under conditions where there are time constraints and circumstances that have not been planned for. Both must work with the resources they have on hand, and both must have the flexibility to decide when and how they will depart from plans—prespecified disaster plans and musical scores—and begin to improvise. In jazz, musicians base their playing on referents, or rough musical blueprints from which different improvisational performances emerge. Similarly, in disaster response, organizations often base their activities on plans and guidelines that indicate what needs to be done but not exactly how it should be done. Under conditions of surprise, the plan may become the referent upon which improvisational strategies and tactics are devised. Alternatively, when plans prove useless, some other sort of referent will have to be found.

These and other students of improvisation are careful to point out that the most adept improvisers are those with the deepest knowledge of musical and theatrical traditions, who can coordinate their actions with those of other ensemble members and understand, from knowledge and experience, where their joint performances are leading. Those who study improvisation in both jazz and disaster response often quote jazz great Charles Mingus, who referred to the importance of such knowledge when he said that "you can't improvise on nothing, man. You gotta improvise on something." Comparing disaster workers to performers, Wachtendorf and Kendra (2006) observe that

[a] great jazz musician or improv actor, after all, must do more than simply make "something out of nothing." Spontaneous composition of music and performance depends on the ability to draw upon a repertoire of training, experience, and a shared vision with fellow performers. Performers must be skilled in reading their cues and making sense of the performance's direction. Similarly, an emergency responder—whether a formal or informal responder—must be able to draw upon a repertoire of training or education, experience, knowledge of the community, and a shared vision with other organizations. These repertoires are what help responders make sense of an emerging disaster environment and are what facilitate effective improvisation.

Thus, in disasters, the ability to adhere to plans and the ability to knowledgeably deviate from them are important sources of adaptive resilience.

In a similar vein, research on high-reliability organizations has documented sources of resilience for organizations operating in both non-crisis and crisis times. That research points to the importance of such factors as extensive prior knowledge, diverse competencies and experiences, effective communication, and mindfulness in enhancing resilience (Weick, Sutcliffe, and Obstfeld 1999; Sutcliffe and Vogus 2003).

In an interesting formulation that resonates with my earlier discussions on resourcefulness, redundancy, and the necessity for mixing discipline and agility, Schulman has highlighted the importance of three types of "slack" as contributors to resilience. Resource slack consists of funds, personnel, and other resources that are possessed by an organization but not committed to ongoing projects and thus have the potential for being readily available when they are needed—for example, in a crisis. Control slack refers to the extent to which the actions of organizational members are "unconstrained by formal structures of coordination or command" (Schulman 1993: 54), allowing for flexibility and latitude in decision making. Conceptual slack refers to a diversity in perspectives within an organization that permits members to question assumptions and explore alternative courses of action—a type of antidote to group-think and unthinking adherence to rules and procedures. Schulman's point is that while conventional theories of organizations and manage-ment tend to view slack as an indication of inefficiency or organizational dysfunction, slack can confer significant benefits in the form of increased resilience, especially during turbulent times.

Borrowing a concept from anthropologist Claude Lévi-Strauss (1966), organizational scholars such as Weick (1993b, 1998) and disaster research-ers Kendra and Wachtendorf (2003) point to processes of bricolage as enablers of improvisational ability and adaptive resilience under crisis conditions. A bricoleur is a person who is able to use materials that are at hand to carry out projects, rather than seeking out materials on a project-by-project basis. The successful bricoleur is someone who has been collecting objects over time, thinking that they might prove useful in some future situation, even if it is not exactly clear how. Transferring this concept to disaster situations and broadening it to include knowledge and repertoires of action as well as material objects, bricolage in disasters is a form of improvisation that combines elements that are available to responders in new ways to deal with problems at hand.

If we focus again on the September 11 terrorist attacks in New York, in addition to completely destroying buildings in the World Trade Center complex, the attacks damaged numerous buildings and other structures around the Ground Zero area, many of them severely, creating a need for rapid structural damage assessments to determine which buildings were safe to reoccupy and which should be made off-limits and possibly slated for demolition. Searching for a way of carrying out this task, some members of an emergent group of volunteer engineer building inspectors knew that a building inspection protocol, including a field manual, forms for documenting damage, and guidelines for tagging buildings to indicate their level of danger, had been developed by engineers in California for post-earthquake safety assessments. In an example of bricolage, that protocol, called ATC-20,[1] was appropriated for use in inspections conducted on approximately four hundred buildings.

A key issue in the study of resilience centers on factors that enable improvisation and bricolage to occur; conditions must exist that allow for the emergence of adaptive improvisational activity. As Schulman's concept of control slack indicates, organizational and interorganizational structures must not be too centralized or control-oriented, because centralization and control stifle resilience. Weick, Sutcliffe, and Obstfeld (2005) note that in order to encourage mindful and resilient responses, organizational structures should be "underspecified" and perhaps even anarchic, giving those closest to emerging problems the authority to discover solutions and enabling collective deliberations on new courses of action. Structures must also encourage independent decision making and action.

On this last point, following Hurricane Katrina, while FEMA and the Department of Homeland Security were scathingly criticized, the U.S. Coast Guard was widely praised for its effective response efforts, which saved many lives. That success was attributed to several factors, but perhaps key among them was what a Government Accountability Office (2006) report singled out as a distinctive Coast Guard operating procedure: the "principle of on-scene initiative," which "involves Coast Guard personnel being given latitude to act quickly and decisively within the scope of their authority, without waiting for direction from higher levels in the chain of command" (2006:11). As *Time* magazine reporter Amanda Ripley observed after Katrina (2005), even though the Coast Guard is chronically underfunded and poorly equipped, it performs well during crises because it "trusts itself"; lower-level personnel are empowered to act on the basis of their own situation assessments and do not have to seek clearance from superior officials, making for a decentralized, rapid, and flexible response. She points out that respecting the initiative of close-to-the-action Coast Guard personnel is a long-standing part of the organization's culture, as indicated by stories like this one:

One of the Coast Guard's most celebrated rescues was of the crew of the doomed oil tanker the Pendleton in 1952 off Massachusetts. In 60-ft. seas, during a snow-storm, Coast Guard officers managed to pile all 32 survivors into a 36-ft. wooden lifeboat moments before the tanker capsized. But when the coxswain radioed his superiors for further direction, his commanders argued over the radio waves about what to do next. Instead of wasting precious time, the coxswain switched off the radio and made up his mind to head to shore. Everyone survived, and the Coast Guard crew received gold lifesaving medals. (Ripley 2005)

With the Coast Guard example we see that devolving authority and not only permitting but rewarding the exercise of agency are key sources of adaptive resilience in crisis.

Along these same lines, while highlighting the importance of bricolage as an adaptive resource within organizations, Duymedjian and Rüling (2010) caution that organizations can thwart efforts at bricolage. Organizations that place a high value on professional identities, maintain a strict division of labor, and stress the importance of specialists' staying within their designated area of expertise are loath to grant legitimacy to bricoleurs. Here again we see that an overemphasis on structure—on discipline as opposed to agility—places constraints on adaptive resilience. A similar point was made by Karl Weick in his now-classic study of the death of firefighters in the 1949 Mann Gulch disaster (Weick 1993a), as recounted by Norman Maclean in his 1972 award-winning book *Young Men and Fire*. In that crisis, firefighters were killed in part because their commitment to group structure and their firefighting roles left them unable to improvise in the face of a collapse in structure and of role-related expectations that were inappropriate for the situation. When structure began to be lost as a result of unfolding events, meaning was also lost, spiraling downward into a further deterioration of structure, further confusion and unwillingness to improvise, and ultimately to the deaths of all but a few members of the firefighting team.

RESILIENT DISASTER RECOVERY

After disaster, individuals, families, and communities are immediately confronted with the need to recover. Once seen by researchers as physical reconstruction or a stage-like process in which those affected return over time to levels of predisaster functioning, recovery is now seen as a series of processes, taking place at different scales, that can lead to successful adaptation to a "new normal" following disasters, or conversely, to continued dysfunction and poor recovery outcomes (Tierney and Oliver-Smith 2012). In line with current thinking, Smith and Wenger (2006) define postdisaster recovery as "the *differential* process of restoring, rebuilding, and reshaping the physical, social, economic, and natural environment" (237, emphasis added), in order to convey the idea that disaster victims and places affected by disaster do not experience recovery uniformly along similar paths, but rather experience a range of recovery trajectories and fates. This definition encapsulates the idea that for some, recovery may be relatively rapid and unproblematic, while for others disaster effects may linger or even worsen over time.

One source of these disparities is differences in levels of inherent and adaptive resilience. At one end of the recovery continuum, and holding constant the severity of disaster impacts, more rapid disaster recovery and more satisfactory recovery outcomes for various social entities (households, businesses, neighborhoods, communities) are associated with low levels of predisaster vulnerability, high inherent resilience, and postdisaster coping capacities and adaptation. At the other end of the continuum and again taking into account disaster severity, recovery can be expected to be most difficult and problematic in circumstances where vulnerability levels are high, inherent resilience is low, and there is low capacity for adaptive resilience. For example, in my research on recovery outcomes for businesses affected by disasters, I found clear connections between predisaster vulnerability factors, postdisaster challenges, and recovery. Small businesses and those in the retail and service sectors—the types of businesses that tend to have high failure rates during nondisaster times—were more likely to be worse off following disasters, as were businesses that were located in areas where there were significant amounts of residential damage and thus the potential for loss of customers. Poor recovery outcomes were also associated with a variety of postdisaster business operational problems, such as difficulty with getting employees to come to work, declines in customer demand, and disrupted transportation routes and supply chains, which were beyond the coping capacity of business owners. There is also evidence that existing sources of postdisaster aid for businesses are insufficient in helping businesses to recover and that in some cases aid may be associated with poorer outcomes, suggesting that after disasters some business recovery needs exceed available resources (Dahlhamer and Tierney 1998; Webb, Tierney, and Dahlhamer 2000, 2003).

Other researchers have taken a more fine-grained look at business recovery following disasters. Daniel Alesch and his colleagues conducted extensive in-person interviews with owners of small businesses and nonprofits that had experienced significant damage and disruption in disasters. They found three factors that were associated with postdisaster business recovery. Being in poor financial condition prior to the disaster and the length of time the business was unable to operate after the disaster were both associated with an inability to recover fully. The third factor, on which the researchers placed the most emphasis, was the business owner's ability to understand the postdisaster environment and adapt accordingly—in other words, the capacity for adaptive resilience. Put simply, to be successful in the postdisaster environment, owners had to recognize how that environment had changed and had to be able to adjust accordingly. Businesses that were most at risk of not recovering were those that remained inflexible in the face of the "new normal." In the words of Alesch and his collaborators,

[e]verywhere, we saw businesses and not-for-profit organizations struggle to achieve viability by doing the same thing after the event that they were doing before. . . . Doing business as usual was fine as long as the relevant environment was unaltered. Doing business as usual when the customers had no discretionary money or moved away was disastrous. The firms that survived and attained viability . . . were those where the owner/operator adapted. (2001: 21)

In discussing businesses that failed to recover, the researchers called attention to a pattern they referred to as the "dead business walking": a business going steadily downhill and draining the owner's resources because the owner, who insists on running the business in the same way as before the disaster, is unwilling or unable to see that the economic environment has changed. These researchers concluded that

[p]erhaps the most important variable in the survival equation is the extent to which the owner or operator recognizes and adapts to the post-event situation. Communities never return to what they were before the event. The post-event environment is always different. Those who perceive the changes and respond appropriately have an excellent chance of surviving and becoming viable again. Those who continue to do business under the old paradigm, assuming that the community will return to pre-existing conditions, have all the cards stacked against their long-term survival. (Alesch et al. 2001: 3)

Depending on postdisaster economic conditions, it may be necessary to change product lines, business processes, or locations for successful recovery. For some business owners, such as those who were close to retirement prior to the disaster, the most prudent thing may have been to close the business. Rather than being seen as business failures, strategic closures may be beneficial under some circumstances, particularly if the outlook is poor for continued business viability.

Like businesses, disaster-stricken communities must also adjust in the aftermath of disasters in order to recover. Resourcefulness is one component of adaptive disaster resilience; some communities are more resourceful than others when facing recovery challenges. Focusing on governmental resources, for example, comparative research on disaster-stricken communities conducted in the 1970s and early 1980s highlighted the importance of three factors in community recovery: knowledge of what to do in order to facilitate recovery, based on emergency management capabilities and on prior experience; political, administrative, and community leadership; and the capacity to take appropriate action, which is based in turn on administrative capabilities, technical knowledge, and financial resources that are sufficient to support recovery activities. Additionally, recovery studies highlighted the quality of intergovernmental relations—that is, local, state, and federal linkages and collaboration—as critical for recovery, because achieving recovery goals is based in part on the ability to obtain resources from supralocal governmental sources (Rubin, Saperstein, and Barbee 1985; see also Rubin 2009). Communities that possess these kinds of assets are likely to fare better after disasters than their less-resourced and less-connected counterparts.

Low levels of vulnerability and high inherent resilience can serve as a cushion against disaster-induced damage and disruption, but the ability to adapt in the aftermath of disasters is just as important. Generally speaking, for households higher socioeconomic status is associated with both inherent and adaptive resilience. Inherent resilience has been discussed elsewhere, so here I emphasize adaptive resilience capacities. Those who are better off are more likely to be homeowners and thus more likely to have insurance coverage, which speeds the recovery process. They also have financial resources that enable them to cope with recovery-related challenges such as residential dislocation, decreased income streams, and increased caregiving burdens, whereas those lower on the status ladder may be overwhelmed by such challenges. Well-off and well-educated people are in a better position to understand with relative ease where to seek and how to qualify for different types of assistance, including government assistance and private sources of recovery aid, such as loans, and are also in a better position to invest time in obtaining those resources. Having savings and wealth in reserve increases recovery options, and the ability to exercise options is a major factor in adaptive resilience (Tierney 2005).

Recently, researchers have begun to focus on social capital as a key source of postdisaster resilience and a critical force in disaster recovery. Political scientist Daniel Aldrich (2012) has conducted a series of studies that highlight the role of social capital in generating positive recovery outcomes. Focusing on two earthquakes in Japan—the 1923 Great Kanto (Tokyo) and 1995 Kobe earthquakes—as well as the 2004 Indian Ocean tsunami, and Hurricane Katrina, Aldrich marshals evidence showing that irrespective of such factors as preexisting socioeconomic conditions and the severity of disaster impacts, social capital indicators are predictive of positive postdisaster recovery outcomes at the neighborhood and community levels. In his telling, social capital aids recovery in several ways. It functions as a form of "informal insurance," enabling friends and neighbors to share physical, financial, and informational resources. By overcoming barriers to collective action, it facilitates community mobilization around response and recovery needs and enables disaster survivors to wield political power to their own benefit. By enhancing community cohesiveness in the aftermath of disasters, social capital increases the likelihood that affected residents will remain and make a commitment to recover, as opposed to leaving the community. Compared with communities that rank high in social capital assets, those that are low in social capital are disadvantaged during the recovery process owing to their relative inability to access and share information and other resources and to articulate their needs.

Although he defines recovery somewhat narrowly in these different cases—for example, as the repopulation of disaster-devastated neighborhoods, or as the amount of assistance received by households—Aldrich does succeed in showing that the foundations of postdisaster recovery capabilities can be found in predisaster social relationships and community activism, as well as in the ability to bring into being new organizational forms in the aftermath of disaster. Aldrich's analytic reach is vast, encompassing both qualitative and quantitative research, but for our purposes a few illustrative examples of the link between social capital and adaptive resilience may suffice. In the Kobe earthquake and the conflagration that followed, two geographically proximate neighborhoods, the wards of Mano and Mikura, which were demographically similar and had comparable levels of devastation, experienced different postdisaster recovery outcomes, owing mainly to differences in social capital. Mano ward had a thirty-year history of community mobilization and civic participation; when the earthquake occurred, residents immediately organized themselves into firefighting brigades and were successful in containing earthquake-induced fires. In Mikura, residents were unable to organize an effective response and instead simply watched as fire engulfed their neighborhood. In the earthquake's aftermath, Mano residents formed a number of community-based organizations that were successful in articulating their needs to government officials, including the need for housing for the elderly, cooperative housing programs, and a day-care center; while the Mikura neighborhood was less successful in developing community-based groups and consequently less successful in lobbying for recovery-related programs. In a postdisaster environment in which recovery needs were extensive, resources flowed into the two wards on the basis of their capacity for collective action. Owing to both preexisting community ties and new social relationships that emerged following the earthquake, Mano was better positioned to pressure for and participate in recovery programs than its less-organized counterpart.

Focusing on recovery processes and outcomes among six villages in India's southeastern state of Tamil Nadu in the aftermath of the Indian Ocean tsunami, Aldrich found evidence of the importance of both bonding and linking social capital for community recovery. Most significant in this case were village-level councils based on occupational specialization—in this case, fishing—and on caste, kinship, and religion. Four villages had such councils prior to the tsunami, and two did not, and these conditions shaped differential recovery outcomes. Where councils existed, they could provide a contact point for the Indian government and for international nongovernmental organizations and could act as distributors of recovery aid. In addition to being a source of bonding or in-group social capital, village councils provided a vehicle for linking social capital, or ties that gave access to resources controlled by nonlocal entities. Here again, forms of solidarity that organized social activities prior to the tsunami were activated to assist victims in the aftermath of the catastrophe.

As Aldrich points out, social capital can help compensate for social and economic disadvantage and ensure that groups that might ordinarily be ignored and marginalized have a place at the table. For example, after the 1989 Loma Prieta earthquake, when low-income Chicano farmworkers in Santa Cruz County organized to pressure government agencies to recognize their distinctive recovery-related needs, that mobilization grew directly out of pre-earthquake labor struggles (Bolin and Stanford 1990). The Mary Queen of Vietnam Catholic Church was a center of community life for Vietnamese Americans in the Village de L'Est and Versailles communities in New Orleans, and when Hurricane

Katrina struck, church-based networks helped to keep residents together as they evacuated, facilitated their early return to their neighborhoods, and provided a platform for articulating the community's needs within the city's political system. Among other things, the community set up its own redevelopment corporation and formulated a recovery plan and later was successful in attracting a charter school and funding for housing units for the elderly. Residents remained politically active, and in the year after the hurricane local groups again mobilized to prevent the city from siting a landfill in the community. The Vietnamese community also experienced disruption and losses as a result of the 2010 BP oil spill and was effective in calling attention to the plight of its fisher folk. As discussed in the previous chapter, subsistence minority communities like Grand Bayou, which was also severely affected by both Katrina and the BP spill, would normally not be considered significant political actors either during normal times or in the context of disasters, but bonding and in particular linking social capital can empower such communities.

Earlier discussions have emphasized the importance of diversity and heterogeneity as sources of resilience. Community- and neighborhood-based forms of social capital can provide communication channels for diverse interests and voices during postdisaster recovery. Where diverse community groups are able to mobilize and have an influence on recovery decision making, they can serve as a counterweight for elite-focused forms of decision making that too often dominate the recovery process.

The case of the city of Santa Cruz following the 1989 Loma Prieta earthquake is an example of an inclusive approach to recovery that generated positive outcomes. The earthquake, which took place on October 17, caused severe damage throughout Santa Cruz County and concentrated damage in the downtown business district of Santa Cruz, where approximately half of the businesses that were operating before the quake were destroyed. Many downtown structures had to be completely demolished, and the city faced the prospect of the loss of its business center, which had been declining before the earthquake. However, government officials and business proprietors, with the help of volunteers, improvised a strategy to keep businesses and shoppers in the downtown area by providing large tents to house businesses so that they could be back in operation in time for the Christmas shopping season and so they would not be tempted to leave the downtown area. Some businesses operated out of tents for more than three years.

In January 1990, a group called Vision Santa Cruz, consisting of thirty-six business owners, government officials, and community leaders, was formed and charged with guiding the recovery process. Additionally, in November 1990, voters in the city and county of Santa Cruz approved a quarter-cent sales tax increase whose proceeds would be used to help finance downtown recovery. Over several years, Vision Santa Cruz, which came to be known as the "gang of 36," held numerous meetings, many of which were contentious because of the divergent interests of participants. Business leaders were confronted by community activists who had their own ideas about how they wanted the city to recover, and activists in turn had to adjust some of their expectations in the interest of downtown recovery. Wisely opting for careful deliberations over time that took into account the post-earthquake "new normal," rather than rapid restoration of the downtown as it had existed before the earthquake, Santa Cruz ultimately created an attractive downtown which is now significantly larger and more profitable than it was before the quake and which includes a mixture of retail space, offices, and residential rental units, along with restaurants, theaters, and other entertainment venues that attract visitors during the evening hours.

THE CRITICAL CIVIC INFRASTRUCTURE: COMMUNITY-BASED ORGANIZATIONS AND GROUPS AND DISASTER RESILIENCE

Many emergency management and homeland security programs focus on critical infrastructure protection and resilience, largely framed as efforts to ensure that the electrical power grid, other utilities, and transportation and banking systems remain operational when disasters or terrorist attacks take place. Significantly less emphasis is placed on enhancing the resilience of our critical *civic* infrastructure, the community-, faith-, and culturally based institutions and groupings that provide connection and support for community residents on a day-to-day basis and to which vulnerable populations turn during times of crisis. As previous discussions have shown, preexisting affiliations and centers of social activity offer a critical social safety net when disasters strike. Catholic churches during the Chicago heat wave and Hurricane Katrina served as focal points for mobilizing endangered communities and saving lives. When the Kobe earthquake struck, prior social organization and community engagement enabled one ward to protect itself and to recover successfully, while its less-organized neighbor could not launch effective response and recovery efforts. Community organizations established for other purposes can redirect their efforts to address disaster-related challenges, as seen in the Red Hook community following Superstorm Sandy. Disasters themselves can serve as a catalyst for greater community participation and civic engagement. Hurricane Katrina sparked more intensive community engagement in New Orleans and gave rise to a number of new organizations and coalitions that were able to influence the recovery process (Weil 2011).

Community- and faith-based organizations that provide services for vulnerable and special needs populations, such as homeless people, immigrants, and those suffering from mental illness, offer ongoing daily support and must also be able to continue offering services when disasters strike. These kinds of organizations constitute a reservoir of adaptive resilience capabilities, but unfortunately they are frequently overwhelmed by day-to-day demands, and what little research has been done suggests that they are not well prepared for disasters. My own research on community- and faith-based organizations in the city and county of San Francisco found that organizational leaders are struggling under the demands of large caseloads and the need to maintain funding, and they often lack the expertise needed to plan for disasters. Many community-based San Francisco organizations are located in structures that could collapse in a major earthquake, and their leaders understand that earthquake-related damage and disruption could compromise their ability to serve clients. At the same time, with their personnel already pressed to provide services in the face of burgeoning needs, they cannot devote time to planning activities for their facilities or to establish linkages with community-wide preparedness networks (Ritchie, Tierney, and Gilbert 2010). A study conducted by the Urban Institute following Hurricane Katrina (De Vita et al. 2008) found that faith-based and secular community organizations provided extensive services to disaster victims, including emergency aid, case management, direct human services, and housing assistance, particularly in the immediate postimpact period. However, it also found that those organizations were generally unconnected to the emergency management system and had not engaged in disaster planning prior to the hurricane. Like many organizations facing disaster, these community-based organizations improvised their response.

Helping community-based organizations become better prepared for disasters would be a major contribution to community resilience. The critical civic infrastructure represents a reservoir of untapped potential that can increase communities' adaptive resilience, as well as the resilience of neighborhoods, households, and businesses. The Federal Emergency Management Agency apparently recognized this recently when it articulated a policy it calls the "whole community" approach to disaster risk reduction, which emphasizes the need to engage a broad range of community institutions in managing hazards and disasters. The "whole community" philosophy represents a shift from post–September 11 programs that emphasized the role of "first responders" and security-related agencies in responding to terrorism and other threats. For some time after 9/11, homeland security agencies seemed to regard civil society groups and community residents negatively—as potential sources of terrorism, on the one hand, or as panicky victims that first responders would need to assist and control, on the other. Homeland security discourses elevated the importance of experts who could detect, thwart, or respond to terrorist attacks, as opposed to members of the general public who could offer assistance (Tierney 2003). The recent emphasis on the "whole community" as a source of disaster resilience acknowledges that managing hazards and disasters requires the participation of nongovernmental entities and non-experts, including businesses and entities in the nonprofit sector. The extent to which this new policy initiative will take hold at the community level remains to be seen.

CHAPTER 9

Looking Ahead

A Move Toward Safety, or More of the Same?

REVISITING EARLIER INSIGHTS

In the preceding chapters we have examined the societal factors and processes that contribute to the expansion of risk as well as the social dimensions of resilience. A key principle that has guided discussions of both concepts is the idea that risk and resilience are ineluctably linked to the social fabric of contemporary societies. Both so-called natural and technological disasters can be traced to a common set of sociocultural, sociopolitical, and socioeconomic factors. Unlike earlier theories of disasters that saw such events as emerging out of the natural world or technology and disturbing the social order, the approach advanced here sees disaster as arising out of the social order itself: cultural beliefs and routine practices; micro-, meso-, and macro-features of social organization, such as the manner in which risks are regulated or allowed to expand within organizations, interorganizational fields, and the broader world system; and the operation of political-economic forces at different scales. Risk is ever present in contemporary societies, a latent feature of social structure at multiple interacting levels—that is, until it reveals itself in the form of disaster.

Like risk, resilience also has its origins in the social order. In addition to facing more substantial risks than their better-off counterparts, poor and marginalized groups lack options for protecting themselves against natural and technological threats. In many respects the ability to be resilient in the face of hazards is associated with economic prosperity and the protections it buys. Social networks and social capital form the basis for resilient response and recovery following disasters, but those advantages are often in short supply within vulnerable populations. When disaster strikes, resilient responses reflect the capacity for creativity and innovation, but that capacity can be thwarted when groups lack resources or are unable to act.

227

We have seen how culture permits and even encourages practices that contribute to risk buildup, sometimes inadvertently but often intentionally. At the broadest level, cultural constructs that enable risk to expand include viewing the natural world primarily as a source of resources that can be exploited in ever more-intensive efforts to generate growth and produce profits, and seeing nature as a sink into which the hazardous by-products and wastes of industrial society can be wantonly dumped. The value placed on growth and the profits it yields for elites also drives societal practices that push the envelope of safety, such as intensified building in hazardous areas behind weak levees and in floodplains; corner cutting during the construction process, as seen in Florida in the period preceding Hurricane Andrew; and projects like the Mississippi River Gulf Outlet in Louisiana, which was promoted by local growth boosters but generated a host of negative externalities throughout its existence and contributed to the devastation caused by Hurricane Katrina. Within the economic sector, late-twentieth-century constructs like the idea that wealthy societies had crossed the threshold into a "new economy" provided license to ignore basic economic fundamentals, encouraged speculative bubbles, and courted financial risk on a scale never paralleled in human history. Faith in the ability of financial engineering to tame risk is a reflection of a more pervasive cultural belief that technology and ingenuity provide answers to the dilemmas that societies face, even when technology overreaches and fails us.

We have also seen how culturally sanctioned routines within institutions and organizations can encourage the drift toward increasingly risky practices while creating blinders that make it impossible to recognize the potential for worst-case events. Culture provides ways of not seeing as well as ways of seeing. The operators of the Fukushima nuclear facility in Japan knew that massive earthquakes and tsunamis had occurred in the past, but they chose not to focus their risk reduction efforts on that possibility, concentrating instead on ameliorating threats from more likely events. Institutions and organizations also have ways of forgetting the lessons of disaster, even when those lessons are relatively recent. As we saw earlier, investigations of the *Challenger* accident uncovered numerous regulatory, organizational, and procedural flaws that set the stage for that disaster, but those findings did not prevent NASA from continuing with practices that ultimately led to the *Columbia* accident. BP refused to act on signals that its cost-saving practices were courting risk and even failed to learn from multifatality accidents it had caused, right up until the catastrophic *Deepwater Horizon* blowout.

Organizations and institutions are not immune to the influence of fads and fashions, forms of collective behavior that create bandwagon effects like those which held sway during the craze that developed around mortgage-backed securities and exotic financial instruments, such as credit default swaps and collateralized debt obligations. Greed and the desire for ever-larger paydays were important psychological drivers that led to the financial crash of 2008, and cognitive heuristics like myopia and the optimistic bias clearly played a role; but to understand how the crash took place it is also necessary to attend to the broader meso- and macro-level cultural constructs that encouraged irrational exuberance and compelled mass participation in the bubble. These same kinds of speculative influences play out, albeit in a less feverish way, in local land-use and industrial practices that zero in on upside outcomes such as profits while ignoring the potential for future disaster losses. As we have also seen, upside thinking works for speculators because they typically do not have to deal with downside losses, which are offloaded to others, including those who reside in unsafe places as well as future generations.

Both established and more ephemeral aspects of culture are important for understanding risk buildup, but so are the structural features of organizations, multiorganizational networks, and economies from local to global scales. The search for greater efficiency, bigger market share, and larger profits leads industries to consolidate their operations, meaning that when things go wrong in hazardous facilities, major disasters can occur. As sociologist Charles Perrow tells us, features of contemporary societies also include ever-larger agglomerations of people residing in hazardous areas and concentrated power that resists transparency and regulation. Reflecting these features of the present-day political economy, both the massiveness of the financial sector and its ability to function with impunity are implicated in the catastrophic deleveraging spiral that began in the mid-2000s and that continues to unfold. In the realm of so-called natural hazards, owing to the meteoric growth of urban centers around the world, hundreds of millions of people, many of them poor, become more vulnerable to death and destruction from earthquakes, tropical cyclones, and other disaster agents as they flock to teeming informal settlements, creating environmental problems and further expanding their own vulnerability in their struggle to survive.

As Perrow observed three decades ago (1984), the potential for disaster resides in physical and organizational system properties such as tight coupling and interactivity, which when systems are stressed can produce unexpected, cascading failures. That is what happened in the Three Mile Island nuclear disaster, and that is also what happened in the financial meltdown of 2008, as the tightly coupled elements of the global financial system fell like dominoes. The rise of global supply chains, in which there may be only one supplier for critical inputs in a manufacturing process, makes contemporary commerce uniquely vulnerable to system perturbations caused by disasters. The devastating impacts of the 2011 Japan earthquake on the production of semiconductors and materials required for automobile production, and the effects on major corporations such as Apple and General Motors, brought this concern to the fore. Later that same year, massive flooding in Thailand disrupted the supply chains of Apple, Honda, Toyota, and other companies. These linkages across space mean that disasters are no longer strictly local or regional; in many cases they are global, and attention to the design and configuration of multiorganizational networks that serve as the circulatory systems for economies at national and global scales is an important consideration for disaster risk analysis.

The scale on which organizational operations now take place and the complexity of both organizational structures and interorganizational relationships make it difficult to identify risks, much less manage them. For intraorganizational checks on risk to function effectively, entities charged with managing risks must have the requisite authority and resources. Yet research documents numerous instances in which internal regulators are improperly placed within organizations, underresourced, given insufficient authority, or ignored. Within multiorganizational fields, regulatory capture and the drift toward deviance it inevitably spurs help ensure that risky practices are not brought to light or eliminated, paving the way for larger losses when triggering conditions are present. In the absence of countervailing forces, entities whose activities endanger others will continue to see how little they can do to manage risks while averting disaster, until they cut one too many corners and invite ruin.

Scale and complexity stand in the way of routine efforts to manage risk and effective responses when disaster strikes. Earlier, for example, we saw how the vast homeland security apparatus that developed in the aftermath of 9/11 was incapable of detecting and interpreting signals of impending catastrophe when Hurricane Katrina threatened the Gulf Coast. Mounting an effective response to disaster requires on-the-fly sensemaking and accurate situation assessment, which are difficult to achieve in highly complex multiorganizational environments. The Katrina example demonstrates that even state-of-the-art communications technologies and improved crisis management strategies cannot compensate for the handicaps created by the enormous size and byzantine forms of organization that are characteristic of institutions which presumably exist to protect us. Sources of risk are also difficult to discern when complex economic interrelationships are spatially distributed, as they increasingly are in our globalized economy. For example, at a conference in Washington, D.C., in early 2013, a high-ranking Toyota executive noted that his company, which clearly had a vested interest in knowing such things, had not understood the vulnerabilities inherent in its own automobile supply chains until the 2011 triple disaster exposed those vulnerabilities.[1]

Within both private- and public-sector organizations, subtle and not-so-subtle production pressures result in the buildup of risk. Safety and productivity are in tension with one another; pursuing one often means neglecting the other. When unreasonable production standards and deadlines are advanced, when organizational leaders signal that it is acceptable to avoid regulatory requirements, when staffing is insufficient for both production activities and risk management, and when those who champion sound safety practices are held up for ridicule, disaster can be expected to follow. However, here again, organizational drift toward ever-riskier practices cannot take place without an enabling environment—an interorganizational ecology that allows risk to flourish. The poster child for such arrangements is, of course, the U.S. financial sector in the early twenty-first century.

Political and economic forces have a profound influence on risk at local, national, and global scales. Research in the United States highlights how local growth machine coalitions exert political power in ways that often result in opposition to risk-aware land-use planning and the growth of vulnerability in hazardous places. Local governments are often willing partners in rent seeking and speculative development, offering incentives and subsidies for reckless development schemes. To enable development to proceed in flood-prone areas, levees are touted as offering protection from flooding, even in places like Greater New Orleans and the Northern California Delta, where levees offer minimal protections at best. Rent seeking is an inevitable feature of a political economy of place that is organized around generating profits for proponents while transferring future losses to homeowners, businesses, insurance and reinsurance companies, and ultimately taxpayers. When developers succeed in creating real estate booms, construction typically outpaces the ability of local governments to ensure construction quality—for example, through thorough building inspections—and in the face of production pressures, builders cut corners. Thus it happened that many hastily constructed South Florida residential developments sustained severe damage in Hurricane Andrew and subsequent hurricane disasters.

Processes that shape development in urban areas in the United States combine with patterns of social inequality to create differential vulnerability. Poor people, members of minority and ethnic groups, female-headed households, and other vulnerable populations often lack the means to take protective action in the face of hazards and disasters yet are also disproportionately exposed to those risks. Significantly more than their better-off counterparts, members of vulnerable groups have no choice but to live in hazardous dwellings such as mobile homes and older structures in poor repair, or in urban areas that are adjacent to hazardous facilities. Although not commonly recognized as such, the exposure of these groups to hazards can be seen as a form of environmental injustice, as exemplified by the extent to which minority group members and the poor in Phoenix are exposed to extreme heat, the most deadly natural hazard, as a consequence of historical practices of residential discrimination. Because poor people also tend to be renters, there is little they can do to address structural hazards in their residences or insure their property against damage.

Viewed on a global scale, poverty, powerlessness, and disaster death tolls are closely correlated. There is a close association between disaster vulnerability and a nation's position in the core, periphery, or semiperiphery of the global political economy. Economic losses from disasters are higher in core nations—because there is more to lose—but proportional losses, death tolls, and injuries are higher in less-developed countries. These losses are driven by demographic pressures such as rapid urbanization, the growth of slums in hazardous areas, and the environmental degradation that inevitably accompanies these trends. Megacities continue to proliferate and expand, and a substantial amount of this growth is taking place in vulnerable areas such as the megacity of Dhaka, Bangladesh, and urban areas in the Philippines, where ever-larger populations are at risk owing to the interaction of climate change impacts and extreme events.

Contributing further to risks in nations outside the core of the world system are deficiencies in governance that include outright state failure, lack of state capacity to manage risks, and pervasive corruption. It is unreasonable to expect states to protect their populations from disaster when they are incapable of delivering even basic protections and services. Research indicates that independent of other factors, such as levels of poverty, societal corruption is a predictor of disaster death tolls. Beyond corruption, poor nations are often seriously deficient in areas such as professional expertise and training, knowledge of state-of-the-art measures for addressing disaster vulnerabilities, and sheer capacity to carry out disaster risk reduction projects. Shortcomings like these combine to produce catastrophes like the 2010 Haiti earthquake.

At the same time, the problems experienced by nations outside the core of the world system are often not of their own making; structural readjustment programs, economic sanctions, wars, and the accidents of geographic location are also major contributors. With all the political will in the world, nations like the Philippines, Bangladesh, and many island nations in the Caribbean remain exposed to more hazards on a regular basis than other countries. As researcher Greg Bankoff (2003) notes, the Philippine archipelago is so disaster-prone that disasters have become a normal feature of everyday life, resulting in a national "culture of disaster." Haiti exhibits this same pattern. Although the 2010 earthquake was indeed devastating, Haiti is continually buffeted by hurricanes and subject to intense flooding, and when United Nations troops were sent to the island after the earthquake, they brought with them cholera, causing an epidemic that killed thousands. Global institutions like the United Nations and the World Bank purport to be fielding programs that will reverse environmental degradation and reduce future disaster losses in highly vulnerable places around the world, but the ultimate outcomes of those efforts have yet to be seen, and any positive outcomes may well be canceled out by future risks created by those same entities. I will return later to the question of the feasibility of reducing disaster-related death and destruction within the framework of today's global political economy.

Of course, corruption as a risk-generating problem is not exclusive to poor and poorly governed nations. The epicenter of the 2008 global financial meltdown was the U.S. financial services system, and even today it is difficult to truly appreciate the scale on which corruption was allowed to flourish during the housing boom with the collusion of so many parties, including rating agencies, regulators, and congressional bodies charged with overseeing the financial services sector, all of which should have been alert to the growth of systemic risk but instead were its enablers. Willing participants in the corrupt practices that caused the crash included some of the most widely lauded financial leaders on the planet, who as a consequence of virtually complete regulatory capture were able to act with impunity and who even now have not been held accountable for the economic wreckage they helped cause. This lack of accountability is one reason why many believe that more financial collapses are in the offing.

The idea that improving resilience is the key to reducing disaster risks achieved prominence in the aftermath of the terrorist attacks of September

11, 2001, supplanting earlier ideas about the importance of effective disaster responses and resistance or robustness in the face of disaster forces. According to new resilience-focused formulations, which draw upon insights in multiple fields of study, systems of all kinds, including social systems at multiple scales, fare better when they are able to both absorb the damaging forces and stresses created by extreme events and bounce back, adjust, and adapt following disaster impact. When disasters strike, resilience requires both adherence to predisaster plans and the capacity to depart from plans when they no longer apply and to improvise and innovate. During disasters, resilience is achieved when novel behaviors, groups, and networks emerge that are responsive to disaster conditions. The capacity for resilient responses is undercut by overly rule-bound social and organizational practices, as well as by practices that reduce the slack that is necessary for rapid resource mobilization. Lean organizations and just-in-time work processes achieve efficiency during normal times, but they do so at the expense of effectiveness during crises.

The network forms of organization that emerge during disasters enhance resilience by virtue of their ability to add new entities and establish new interconnections in response to evolving disaster conditions. There is often redundancy in such networks, and redundancy increases resilience. Emergent networks are also diverse, consisting of a mix of official response organizations, other entities without experience in disaster preparedness and response activities, and newly formed groups. Like redundancy, network diversity contributes to resilience.

Networks are also important for the resilience of families and individuals. Network embeddedness contributes to social capital, which is important during normal times and in disasters. Social capital facilitates the flow of information and resources and provides a foundation for the kinds of collective action that are often needed by disaster victims and disrupted communities during and after disasters: the provision of mutual aid and the ability to exert political pressure in order to have needs addressed. Where diverse forms of social capital—bonding, bridging, and linking—are "invested" in disaster response and recovery, network participants have a better chance of successfully coping with and overcoming disaster-related challenges.

It follows, then, that conditions and practices that have a negative effect on social capital undermine disaster resilience capabilities. These negative influences include high residential turnover and high vacancy rates in neighborhoods; an absence of places and spaces where people can come together for recreation and entertainment; weak and under-resourced community institutions; high crime rates that create fear and discourage community participation; and low wages that force community residents to work multiple jobs, leaving little time for community involvement. Instituting austerity measures and shrinking government are framed by some political interests as ways of coping with financial strains, but such measures are quite likely to have a detrimental effect on the ability to manage risks and launch resilient responses when disaster strikes. Where such conditions intersect with high levels of physical and social vulnerability, those affected will have a difficult time responding effectively and recovering when disaster hits.

Hazards and disasters can themselves create conditions that erode social capital and reduce resilience. Chronic toxic hazards can create ongoing psychological and social stressors and often give rise to conflict within affected communities, as some residents downplay hazards and are eager to "move on" following contamination episodes, while others remain concerned. Disasters can result in short- and longer-term residential displacement, which disrupts livelihoods and occupationally based social networks. Disasters can also result in collective demoralization when they destroy valued community symbols, institutions, and relationships with nature.

Official responses to disasters tend to overlook the need to protect and restore social capital. For example, postdisaster housing assistance is frequently provided in ways that sever social network ties, and housing and other assistance programs typically focus on monetary compensation for disaster losses at the level of individual households and businesses, as opposed to more holistic forms of assistance that would help to restore the social fabric of affected communities. An alternative approach would place a priority on reconstructing entire neighborhoods, rebuilding churches, revitalizing community-based organizations, reestablishing parks and playgrounds, and getting major employers up and running after disasters. However, that is not the way postdisaster recovery activities are undertaken in the United States and around the world. Rather, recovery takes place in a disjointed, haphazard fashion, dependent on diverse funding streams, with little attention to the need to restore social capital and community vitality. As the Haiti example shows, after disasters poor nations are dependent for aid on international nongovernmental organizations (NGOs) whose rules often render them unable to provide needed assistance over the long term. And indeed many disaster assistance organizations are more attentive to how their programs are perceived by donors than to their impact on the survivors they claim to serve. Government by NGO is a poor substitute for effective, accountable, transparent governance, and the same can be said for disaster recovery by NGO. Yet in the United States and around the world, institutions pursue uncoordinated recovery efforts rather than strategies that would strengthen inherent and adaptive resilience.

RESILIENCE AND TRANSFORMATION

So far, resilience in the face of threats has been framed only in positive terms, as a quality that all elements of social systems should seek to acquire and enhance. Yet the idea of resilience presents a double paradox. First, those seeking to decrease risks and cope with disaster need to be resilient, but the systemic forces that maintain the status quo and allow risks to proliferate are also resilient. The patterns and processes that are characteristic of our contemporary political economy are themselves both resistant to change and adaptable in the face of external pressures. When developers are opposed, they find ways of neutralizing that opposition. When new checks on the untrammeled power of U.S. financial institutions are proposed, the financial sector mobilizes. When efforts are made to promote risk-reducing regulations, industry fights back. When communities seek to take action to adapt to climate-related hazards, property rights activists are there to block those actions. Systems of domination are nothing if not flexible and adaptable; that is how domination is maintained. To achieve a safer and more sustainable future, strategies must be employed that undercut that dominance, but that is a difficult task.

Second, while we have seen many examples of resilience as a positive force, it is also important to keep in mind that adaptation to hazards in the short term may actually stand in the way of the kinds of transformational changes that are needed for the long term. The societies that are dominant within the contemporary world system are resilient in the sense that they resist change and adapt when sufficient pressure is brought to bear, but that very quality insulates them against more fundamental changes that are imperative for averting future crises rooted in widespread unsustainable practices (Handmer and Dovers 1996).

We have reached the point at which adapting and maintaining business as usual is simply not enough. The United States is a wealthy country—so wealthy that even large-scale disasters like Hurricane Katrina are mere perturbations when viewed in the context of the highly resilient national economy. However, we are now beginning to see that Katrina, although an outlier, was indicative of future trends. In 2011, there were fourteen weather-related events that each caused more than a billion dollars in damage. In 2012, Superstorm Sandy caused more than $60 billion in damage. As climate change advances, losses from droughts and wildfires will increase, and so will damages from major winter storms like the one that struck New England in February 2013. Because efforts to reduce greenhouse gases have been insufficient, extremely costly adaptation measures must be undertaken, and soon, before losses from slow-onset processes, such as sea-level rise, and from rapid-onset extreme events become unsustainable.

Megadisasters are the new normal. We owe a debt to nature, and she has come to collect it from us, in the form of ever-larger losses and disaster assistance packages, paid for by American taxpayers, along with ever-larger insurance payouts. Within the financial sector, similar processes are playing out, as institutions that were deemed too big to fail in 2008 are even larger now due to post-meltdown mergers. Our modest efforts to reform the financial sector seem doomed to fail eventually, meaning that taxpayers can look forward to more expensive bailouts in the future, although next time it may be student loan debt that leads to collapse rather than mortgage-backed securities.

Even for prosperous societies like the United States, this is clearly an unsustainable course. Funds that are expended on disaster assistance and financial bailouts could more profitably be used elsewhere—for example, in infrastructure improvements, education, research, and prudent forms of development. When disasters happen and aid flows into communities, that aid may offer a temporary boost to affected economies, for example by providing employment for contractors and craftspeople, but it does not create value in the long term. Yet our societal approach to disasters and resilience seldom takes into account tradeoffs between outlays for disaster response and recovery and investments that produce real value and taxpayer savings—including vigorous efforts to act in advance to reduce disaster losses and to grapple with the challenges of climate change.

The problem is that current attempts to reduce disaster-related risks are incremental rather than transformational. One major shortcoming of mainstream approaches is that advocates for disaster risk reduction typically focus on bringing about reforms of the kind that fall within the purview of institutions with specific disaster-related responsibilities. However, risk buildup is driven by other more powerful institutions that unless checked will continue to cause risks to proliferate. Disaster-related legislation is a case in point. Predisaster mitigation measures are designed to increase inherent disaster resilience and reduce future losses, and with those goals in mind the Disaster Mitigation Act of 2000 (DMA2K) requires the development and updating of hazard mitigation plans. According to FEMA records, as of April 2012 plans had been completed by fifty states, the District of Columbia, five territories, approximately 20,000 local communities, and 105 tribal governments. Champions of enhanced disaster resilience consider this a victory, and in a way it is. However, more than a decade after the passage of DMA2K, no large-scale assessments of the quality of the planning efforts the legislation stimulated have been undertaken, much less analyses of the extent to which plans are being actualized on the ground, and to what effect. Research that has been carried out, primarily on plans involving coastal hazards, suggests that planning is deficient in crucial respects, such as the quality of the vulnerability assessments and risk analyses that serve as the basis for planning. Significant gaps have also been found in the designation of agencies that are responsible for carrying out planned activities and timelines for implementation (Kang, Peacock, and Husein 2010; Lyles,

Berke, and Smith 2012)—a shortcoming that does not bode well for see-ing action on the ground. It appears that when mandated by federal law to produce plans, governmental jurisdictions comply but without much attention to specifying actions they will take to carry out those plans, or to actually undertaking such actions. If past patterns are any indica-tion, serious efforts to do so, for example by curtailing development in hazardous areas or requiring stricter building codes and code enforce-ment, will be vigorously opposed by growth machine boosters. Equally important, disaster-specific laws and plans have little impact on social vulnerabilities, which are the product of broader societal forces such as income inequality and patterns of racial discrimination that generate environmental injustices.

REPRISE: RISK AND POWER

A main thread that runs through this volume is that risk and power are connected. Powerful political and economic interests acting at multiple scales contribute to risk buildup and set the parameters for how risk will be managed—or ignored. Those same interests preside over a social order in which glaring inequities render large numbers of people vulnerable to disaster. Following Lukes (1974, 2005), this power operates in three ways. In the first and most obvious case, power is reflected in the ability to prevail in political conflicts. In the case of hazards and risks, this means being able to influence regulatory practices in areas as diverse as land use, industrial safety standards, financial transactions, and the emission of greenhouse gases from fossil fuels. It also means, among other things, being able to marginalize critics, silence potential whistle-blowers, and off-load the consequences of risky behavior onto others.

A second manifestation of power is the ability to keep issues that are troubling to elites off political agendas entirely. In the case of Japan, for example, once national elites adopted an energy policy for which nuclear power was the centerpiece and then sold a reluctant nation on that policy, the need for nuclear power went largely unquestioned within Japan's political economy, until Fukushima. It was simply taken for granted that Japan could not survive as a highly developed, prosperous nation with-out nuclear power, just as it is taken for granted that the United States and China must be able to continue to operate coal-fired power plants and emit greenhouse gases in ever-larger volumes. Power means being able to ensure that certain measures, such as slowing the rate of growth in at-risk coastal areas or ending subsidies to hazard insurance ratepayers, are "off the table" for serious political discussion.

At an even more subtle level, power rests in the ability of dominant groups to shape elements of culture and institutions in ways that make the existing social order and its practices seem natural and immutable, so that they are accepted almost without question. Using this third dimension of power, sometimes called cultural hegemony (Gramsci 1971), powerful interests mobilize the consent of the less powerful through cultural means.

In this volume, we have touched on various manifestations of Lukes's third form of power, from the taken-for-granted acceptance of societies' appetite for super-tall buildings to the taken-for-granted idea that development in hazard-prone areas is a rising tide that lifts all boats. To the delight of developers and bankers, U.S. communities evidently see no road to prosperity other than through more-intensive land use, and to the delight of rent seekers, community residents are perfectly willing to believe that there is only an upside to the development projects they finance with their taxes. As demonstrated by the growing number of disasters and the catastrophic financial crash, which were paid for with taxpayers' money, those same taxpayers have drifted into accepting the idea that while profits are privatized, risks and losses are frequently socialized.

The idea that regulation results in higher costs for consumers and stifles economic creativity is also an article of faith, even though risk expands as regulation decreases. Rather than being seen as a potential danger, lax regulation is framed as beneficial for the public, because otherwise the putative costs of regulation would have to be passed on to the consumer in the form of higher prices. In the boom period that preceded the financial crash of 2008, regulatory controls over the financial sector were systematically weakened through measures justified in part by narratives stressing the value of widening opportunities for home ownership. Those narratives, which were championed by Fannie

Mae, governmental and financial institutions, and both political parties, and which drew on long-standing criticisms of the industry regarding racial discrimination in lending, masked the wildly avaricious motives of financial institutions that eventually resorted to making "liar loans" to low-income homebuyers who had no hope of being able to make their payments. Those who suffered most directly as a consequence of lax lending practices and the financial meltdown they fueled were members of racial and ethnic minorities—the very people the banking industry claimed were the beneficiaries of relaxed lending standards—while the real beneficiaries were lending institutions and their executives (Morgenson and Rosner 2011).

Former chief executive officer of General Motors and former secretary of defense Charles Wilson has been misquoted as saying that "what's good for General Motors is good for the country, and vice versa" (what he actually said is that for years he believed that was the case). That statement sounds archaic, especially in light of that corporation's aggressive forays into subprime lending, but during the bubble years there was evidently a widespread belief that what was good for Goldman Sachs, Countrywide, Fannie Mae, and other financial institutions was also good for the country. In the wake of the crash that belief remains unexamined, criticisms of the banking industry notwithstanding. And just as Japan accepted as natural the *amakudari* tradition through which regulatory controls on its nuclear industry were eroded, Americans accept the revolving door tradition that allows banking executives to move back and forth between financial institutions, federal reserve banks, regulatory agencies, and the Department of the Treasury. These are the kinds of practices that need to change if risks are to be kept in check.

Elite actors and institutions employ hegemonic power to shape the ways in which risks, their consequences, and their management are framed. Prior to the rise of the tobacco control movement, cigarette manufacturers succeeded in suppressing information on the links between smoking, cancer, and other illnesses while characterizing tobacco use as glamorous, sophisticated, and linked to American values like independence. Movie stars smoked cigarettes on-screen, and the Marlboro Man embodied rugged individualism and life on the frontier. Today interests associated with the fossil fuel industry and conservative politics have channeled large amounts of money into the climate change denial industry, which in the face of overwhelming scientific evidence is still able to sell to many segments of the public the idea that climate change either is not happening or is a matter of scientific controversy (McCright and Dunlap 2000, 2010; Dunlap and McCright 2011). Through its sponsored research, web sites, blogs, and other means of communication, the denial industry characterizes climate change research as biased, contradictory, and agenda-driven. Elements of the denial narrative also draw on a broader strand of American culture that frames events and trends in terms of conspiracies, which in the case of climate change involves the assertion that there is a vast conspiracy among scientists to obtain more funding for their work.

Hegemonic narratives regarding climate change emphasize that the current carbon-based economy is a major source of employment and that efforts to mitigate greenhouse gas emissions will kill jobs. While arguing that climate change is not a problem, those narratives also hold that even if it is, human beings are endlessly adaptable and inventive enough to develop technological solutions to the problem, such as geoengineering projects, making it unnecessary to worry about climate change. At the same time, the interests of the fossil fuel industry are promoted by the media and political figures who praise the industry for helping the nation achieve independence through natural gas drilling and hydraulic fracturing, which contribute significantly to greenhouse gas emissions.

The point is clear: hegemonic political and economic power carries with it the ability to create risks with impunity, influence risk-related decisions and practices in ways that favor elites, and control policy discourses related to risk. Because this is the case, it follows that addressing the problem of super-sized risks and losses necessitates confronting and curtailing that power. One obvious route to that goal is through improving the operation of existing mechanisms for keeping powerful risk-generating institutions in check. There are many examples of prior successes in other risk domains, from seat-belt legislation and air bags to smoking bans, as well as in the area of hazards and disasters. The Oil Pollution Act of 1990, which was passed in direct response to the

Exxon Valdez oil spill, has reduced the frequency of oil spills (Homan and Steiner 2008), even though the law is by no means perfect and did nothing to prevent the *Deepwater Horizon* disaster. Title 3 of the Superfund Amendments and Reauthorization Act (SARA), known as the Emergency Planning and Community Right-to-Know Act, stripped from hazardous materials producers and handlers their ability to keep secret from community residents the kinds and quantities of dangerous chemicals to which they were exposed. That law, passed in 1986, was in part a response to the devastating Bhopal tragedy, which had occurred two years earlier in a plant owned by Union Carbide, and to a major hazardous chemical release from a Union Carbide plant in Institute, West Virginia, in August 1985. SARA Title 3 represented significant progress in the management of hazardous materials, even though it has still done little to help the beleaguered residents of communities like Richmond, California, an environmental justice community that is home to multiple hazardous waste sites, chemical factories, and California's largest refinery, which is operated by Chevron. The refinery is a major polluter that has caused a number of toxic fires and hazardous releases; in August 2012 a major incident sent 15,000 residents to area hospitals. Thanks to legislation, Richmond residents have the right to know about the dangers in their midst, but like many other victims of environmental injustice they still have only a limited ability to do something about them.

Richmond's plight and the behavior of corporations like Massey Energy, which was responsible for the 2010 Upper Big Branch mine disaster in West Virginia, remind us that to have an impact, the sanctions associated with laws and regulations must have teeth, and those responsible for causing disasters must be held accountable. Massey had a long history of impunity in violating safety regulations, falsifying and destroying documents, lying to investigators, and conspiring to receive advanced warning of safety inspections, but even after the Big Branch disaster, which killed twenty-nine miners, there have been few criminal prosecutions.[2] As discussed in Chapter 5, BP had a history of cutting corners and causing major accidents at its facilities long before the *Deepwater Horizon* blowout. However, penalties levied against the company did little to change its behavior. Perhaps the size of the payouts

BP will be forced to make as a result of that disaster will finally lead the company to change its safety culture, but criminal prosecution of BP executives would likely have been more effective. To date, key actors in the financial services sector have also escaped serious sanctions for what by any standard constituted unethical and in some cases outright criminal behavior. Evidently, being too big to fail also means being too big to jail. Why should financial institutions change their behavior when continuing to function as they have brings such large rewards and so few sanctions? We cannot expect to see significant progress in reducing risk if those who produce it are not held accountable, but accountability is lacking within current institutional arrangements.

Causing economic pain is an important strategy for getting the attention of industries that produce risk. That is the logic behind campaigns to divest from fossil fuel companies, which are being led by 350.org, Fossil Free, Green Grandparents, and other organizations seeking to reduce greenhouse gas emissions and global climate change. Students are demanding that their university endowments divest, and mayors like Mike McGinn in Seattle are requesting that their pension funds also do so.

Forcing entities responsible for risk buildup to suffer reputational damage is another strategy that may in some cases alter their behavior. "Name and shame" campaigns have proliferated in areas as diverse as drunk driving, tax dodging, and sweatshop manufacturing, and there are also examples of subtle and not-so-subtle "name and shame" measures in the disaster loss reduction area as well. The application of standards and rating systems constitutes a mild form of naming and shaming. The International Organization for Standardization (ISO) provides a number of standards that can be used as indicators of community commitment to reducing disaster losses, such as the Building Code Effectiveness Grading Schedule, which provides information on codes that are in force in municipalities around the country, and on the quality of their code enforcement. The National Flood Insurance Program uses the Community Rating System to indicate which communities are doing a better (or worse) job of managing flood hazards—that is, among communities that choose to be rated. The American Society of Civil Engineers, which is well known for its report card on the quality of the nation's infrastructure systems, is also showing an interest in developing a resilience report card, and we can expect to see a variety of report cards dealing with climate change being developed in the near future. A less subtle approach can be seen in efforts to exert pressure on building owners to reduce the number of collapse-hazard buildings in California. The state's government code, section 8875.8, requires owners of unretrofitted unreinforced masonry buildings in the highest-hazard areas (seismic zone 4), which are subject to collapse due to earthquake-induced ground motions, to post signs on their buildings that state "Earthquake warning. This is an unreinforced masonry building. You may not be safe inside or near unreinforced masonry buildings during an earthquake." The hope is that such postings will motivate members of the public to demand higher levels of building safety.

Through their organizing and advocacy activities, social movements can play a significant role in challenging hegemonic power. The U.S. antismoking and environmental movements have been responsible for many successes in controlling health and environmental risks. Although the Occupy movement has not succeeded in changing the behavior of the "one percent" it argues is responsible for the worldwide recession, it has succeeded in keeping the fallout from financial institutions' risk-creating activities on the public agenda. Disaster loss reduction has been characterized as a "policy without a public" (May 1990), meaning that the general public is not actively engaged in the policy process surrounding disaster risk and few interest groups have developed around the issue. Nonetheless, elite and professional movements, consisting, for example, of scientists, engineers, and political leaders concerned about disaster losses, are active within the loss reduction arena. At a more grassroots level, environmental justice movement organizations are pressing for the reduction of the environmental injustices that put poor people and people of color at risk from environmental hazards.

Policy entrepreneurship focusing on disaster risks, which can be thought of as movement activity that arises from within policy systems, is also common within the disaster domain. Examples of policy entrepreneurs concerned with lessening the impacts of disasters in the United States include the California Seismic Safety Commission, the

Cascadia Regional Earthquake Work Group, the Central U.S. Earthquake Consortium, the Natural Hazards Mitigation Association, the Federal Alliance for Safe Homes, the Institute for Business and Home Safety, the Applied Technology Council, the Public Entity Risk Institute, the Pacific Risk Management Ohana, the Disasters Roundtable of the National Academy of Sciences, and the Congressional Hazards Caucus. Largely unknown to the public, groups like these work on an everyday basis to keep disaster loss reduction on the public agenda and attempt to take advantage of policy windows (Kingdon 2002) that can open briefly when major disasters occur. Many of these interest groups have close ties through membership and funding streams with governmental agencies whose missions include the reduction of disaster losses, such as the Federal Emergency Management Agency, the U.S. Geological Survey, and the National Oceanic and Atmospheric Administration, as well as with research centers, individual researchers, think tanks, professional associations, and locally based loss reduction champions. Without pressure by these and related groups, the nation would be even more vulnerable to disasters.

But here again the efforts of most advocacy groups seek reform within the disaster policy system, when threats to safety actually originate outside it. Transformational change of the risk landscape will only come about when the fundamental assumptions on which the current system of risk production is based are challenged and replaced. This is a radical position but one that acknowledges the linkage that exists between contemporary political-economic forces, disaster vulnerability, and disaster impacts. Current practices are unsustainable, and sustainability and safety will not be achieved without a radical rethinking of the cultural assumptions, social arrangements, and institutional practices focused on in previous discussions.

This book must end on a pessimistic note, however, because there is little indication that the power to produce risk with impunity is being effectively checked. Perhaps advances in reducing risk must inevitably be piecemeal and incremental, reformist rather than revolutionary, arising in response to disasters that temporarily hold the power of elite political and economic actors in abeyance. That has been our history to date and may well be our future. Moreover, because of the savage inequalities that characterize U.S. society and many societies around the world, vulnerability is increasing even more rapidly, and efforts to significantly reduce vulnerability may well prove futile. With much of the developed world in the grip of recession and misguided austerity programs that are eroding even basic social provisions, and with many so-called emerging nations and less-developed countries already in a state of environmental crisis, risk may well be a wicked problem that in the end defies solution. If this is not the world we wish our children to inherit, we must be more ambitious and creative—and more radical—in addressing the problem of widening risk than we have been so far.

Reference Matter

Notes

CHAPTER 2

1. The Southern California Earthquake Center estimates that probability to be 67%.

2. It is important to note, however, that some people do suffer from anxiety disorders of various kinds in which it is difficult to find an experiential base for feelings of fear.

CHAPTER 3

1. Here again, Beck's characterization of risk wavers between realism and social constructionism. He speaks of natural disasters as being "attributed" to outside forces—an assertion that clearly refers to the perception or the social construction of risk—but still maintains a realist perspective on risk. In later work (2008) he argues, unconvincingly in my view, that realism and constructivism are not in conflict, except when they are used "naively."

CHAPTER 4

1. It is interesting, for example, that the new World Trade Center complex in lower Manhattan is being built at a time when office space is not in demand. The original World Trade Center had major difficulties attracting tenants, and it remains to be seen how the new complex will fare. Clearly, the need to build a super-tall building that is exactly the same height as the original 1WTC is a purely symbolic move. The Burj Khalifa was originally called the Burj Dubai. Its name was changed in recognition of the major contributions made by Sheik Khalifa of Abu Dhabi, who footed the bill for the project's completion. Does anyone believe that Dubai, or the world for that matter, actually needs a 160-story building? Millions make the annual pilgrimage to Mecca, but do they really need to find lodgings in a 95-story hotel?

2. In the United States, the Terrorism Risk Insurance Act (TRIA) effectively makes the U.S. government the insurer of last resort for large-scale terrorism losses. In return, insurers are required to offer terrorism insurance on commercial policies. The U.S. government charges no premiums for this form of insurance coverage. The TRIA has been extended twice, most recently in 2007. It will be in effect through December 31, 2014.

3. The building was originally called Freedom Tower, but the name was later changed. The height of the building, 1,776 feet, evokes the founding of the nation, and a light on the mast of the building is meant to evoke the torch of the Statue of Liberty. The building has many design features that were added specifically to thwart future attacks and prevent collapse.

CHAPTER 5

1. In contrast with the United States, the major public universities in Japan are more prestigious than private ones. Todai is the most prestigious, followed by Kyoto University. Public university retirees are of course not prevented from assuming positions at private universities, but many use retirement as an opportunity to move into industry.

2. The incident was graded as a "4" on the International Atomic Energy Agency's 7-point scale. In contrast, Chernobyl and Fukushima were assigned a rating of "7."

3. STA subsequently revoked JCO's license. It should be noted that the Japanese Nuclear and Industrial Safety Agency is the entity that is responsible for safety at nuclear plants, while STA has jurisdiction over processing facilities like the Tokaimura plant.

4. Plans for nuclear cooperation between Japan and Southeast Asian countries were not derailed by Fukushima. See Tabuchi 2011; Asianpower 2013.

5. While details cannot be provided here, the report contains extensive discussions on the numerous ways the oil industry successfully evaded efforts at regulation, as well as the ways the MMS became increasingly ill equipped to meet regulatory requirements in the context of industry-wide change and declines in its own resources, including resources to conduct appropriate safety inspections.

6. Procedures for launching such a response were outlined in the plan's Catastrophic Annex.

7. Unless otherwise noted, these times refer to Central Time.

8. The average salary for the airline's captains is $67,000. The first officer who lost her life in the crash was making $23,000 a year.

9. Those analyses were conducted by Science Applications International Corporation.

10. Los Angeles began a pre-earthquake planning for post-earthquake recovery program during the 1980s. Since that time, many other communities nationwide have begun to plan how they will organize the recovery process following disasters that they expect to occur.

CHAPTER 6

1. The 1928 Flood Control Act (FCA) does give immunity to the Army Corps from claims resulting from negligence in flood control activities. However, the court originally noted that MR-GO is not a flood control project and thus is not covered by the FCA. The levees that failed were flood control projects, but MR-GO, which acted on the levees in ways that caused them to fail, was not, and therefore the court found the corps liable for negligence in its maintenance of MR-GO. However, that judgment was later reversed.

2. Discussions that frame Bay Area planning initiatives as inspired by Agenda 21 socialism can be found on web sites such as www.freedomadvocates.org; www.theglobaltruth.net; www.agenda21news.com; and various other property rights sites.

CHAPTER 8

1. The inspection system is so named because it was developed by the Applied Technology Council (ATC), a California nonprofit engineering and design organization.

CHAPTER 9

1. Remarks by Yoshimi Inaba, Chairman, Toyota Motor Sales U.S.A., Inc., in a session entitled "Cascading Disasters" at the annual meeting of the National Council for Science and the Environment, January 15, 2013.

2. Moreover, even when such prosecutions have taken place, the penalties have been relatively mild. For example, Gary May, superintendent of the Upper Big Branch mine, who was complicit in numerous violations at the mine, was allowed to plead guilty to the charge of defrauding the federal government and received a sentence of twenty-one months in prison and a $20,000 fine.

References

Adger, W. Neil. 2000. "Social and Ecological Resilience: Are They Related?" *Progress in Human Geography* 24: 347–364.

Aguirre, Benigo E., Dennis Wenger, Thomas A. Glass, Marcelino Diaz-Murillo, and Gabriela Vigo. 1995. "The Social Organization of Search and Rescue: Evidence from the Guadalajara Gas Explosion." *International Journal of Mass Emergencies and Disasters* 3: 67–92.

Akarca, Ali T., and Aysit Tansel. 2008. *Impact of the 1999 Earthquakes on the Outcome of the 2002 Parliamentary Elections in Turkey.* IZA Discussion Papers, no. 3466.

Alaska Oil Spill Commission. 1990. *Spill: The Wreck of the Exxon Valdez.* Alaska Oil Spill Commission, Anchorage.

Aldrich, Daniel P. 2005. "Japan's Nuclear Power Plant Siting: Quelling Resistance." *The Asia-Pacific Journal: Japan Focus,* June 13.

———. 2008. *Site Fights: Divisive Facilities and Civil Society in Japan and the West.* Ithaca, NY: Cornell University Press.

———. 2012. *Building Resilience: Social Capital in Post-Disaster Recovery.* Chicago: University of Chicago Press.

Alesch, Daniel J., Lucy A. Arendt, and William J. Petak. 2005. *Seismic Safety in California Hospitals: Assessing an Attempt to Accelerate the Replacement or Seismic Retrofit of Older Hospital Facilities.* Multidisciplinary Center for Earthquake Engineering Research, State University of New York at Buffalo.

———, James N. Holly, Elliott Mittler, and Robert Nagy. 2001. *Organizations at Risk: What Happens When Small Businesses and Not-for-Profits Encounter Natural Disasters.* Public Entity Risk Institute, Fairfax, VA.

———, and William J. Petak. 1986. *The Politics and Economics of Earthquake Hazard Mitigation.* Institute of Behavioral Science, University of Colorado Boulder.

Alexander, Jeffrey C. 1996. "Critical Reflections on 'Reflexive Modernization.'" *Theory, Culture and Society* 13 (4): 133–138.

Ambraseys, Nicholas, and Roger Bilham. 2011. "Corruption Kills." *Nature* 469: 153–155.

American Society of Civil Engineers. 2007. *The New Orleans Hurricane Protection System: What Went Wrong and Why. A Report by the ASCE Hurricane Katrina External Review Board.* Reston, VA: American Society of Civil Engineers.

Ananda, Rady. 2011. "Midwest Floods: Both Nebraska Nuclear Power Stations Threatened." *Global Research,* June 16.

Ariyabandu, Madhavi M. 2006. "Gender Issues in Recovery from the December 2004 Indian Ocean Tsunami: The Case of Sri Lanka." *Earthquake Spectra* 22: 759–775.

Arnold, Margaret, Robert S. Chen, Uwe Deichmann, and Maxx Dilley. 2006. *Natural Disaster Hotspots: Case Studies.* Washington, DC: World Bank.

Asch, S. E. 1951. "Effects of Group Pressure on the Modification and Distortion of Judgments." In *Groups, Leadership and Men,* edited by Harold Guetzkow, 177–190. Pittsburgh, PA: Carnegie Press.

Asianpower. 2013. "Vietnam to Award Nuclear Plant Contract to Japan." *Asianpower*, July 8.

Atsumi, Tomo, Toshio Sugiman, Hisatoshi Mori, and Ichiro Yatsuduka. 1996. "Participant Observations on Volunteer Organizations Emerging After the Great Hanshin Earthquake: Case of the Nishinomiya Volunteer Network and the Local NGOs Co-Ordinating Team for the Great Hanshin Earthquake." In *Proceedings of the International Conference on Water Resources and Environmental Research*. Vol. 2, 455–462. Kyoto, Japan.

Bankoff, Greg. 2003. "Vulnerability and Flooding in Metro Manila." *IIAS Newsletter*, July.

———, George Frerks, and Dorothea Hilhorst. 2004. *Mapping Vulnerability: Disasters, Development, and People*. London: Earthscan.

Barry, John. 2005. *The Great Influenza: The Story of the Deadliest Pandemic in History*. Penguin.com.

———. 2007. *Rising Tide: The Great Mississippi Flood of 1927 and How It Changed America*. New York: Simon & Schuster.

Barton, Allen H. 1969. *Communities in Disaster: A Sociological Analysis of Collective Stress Situations*. New York: Doubleday.

Baxter, Lawrence G. 2011. "'Capture' in Financial Regulation: Can We Channel It Toward the Common Good?" *Cornell Journal of Law and Public Policy* 21: 175–200.

Beck, Ulrich. 1992a. "From Industrial Society to the Risk Society: Questions of Survival, Social Structure and Ecological Enlightenment." *Theory, Culture and Society* 9 (1): 97–123.

———. 1992b. *Risk Society: Toward a New Modernity*. London: Sage.

———. 1998. *World Risk Society*. Cambridge, UK: Polity Press.

———. 1999. "From Industrial Society to Risk Society." In *Modernity: Critical Concepts*. Vol. 4, edited by M. Walters, 17–39. London: Routledge.

———. 2008. *World at Risk*. Cambridge, UK: Polity Press.

———, Anthony Giddens, and Scott Lash. 1994. *Reflexive Modernization: Politics, Tradition and Aesthetics in the Modern Social Order*. Stanford, CA: Stanford University Press.

Berger, A., Carolyn Kousky, and Richard Zeckhauser. 2008. "Obstacles to Clear Thinking About Natural Disasters: Five Lessons for Policy." In *Risking House and Home: Disasters, Cities, Public Policy*, edited by J. M. Quigley and L. A. Rosenthal, 73–94. Berkeley, CA: Berkeley Public Policy Press.

Berger, Peter L., and Thomas Luckmann. 1966. *The Social Construction of Reality: A Treatise in the Sociology of Knowledge*. Anchor Books, Doubleday.

Berliner, Paul F. 1994. *Thinking in Jazz: The Infinite Art of Improvisation*. Chicago: University of Chicago Press.

Bernstein, Sharon. 2005. "How Risky Are Older Concrete Buildings?" *Los Angeles Times*, October 11.

Bevc, Christine. 2010. "Working on the Edge: Examining Covariates in Multi-Organizational Networks on September 11th Attacks on the World Trade Center." Doctoral dissertation, University of Colorado Boulder.

Birkland, Thomas A. 1997. *After Disaster: Agenda Setting, Public Policy, and Focusing Events*. Washington, DC: Georgetown University Press.

———. 2004. "Learning and Policy Improvement After Disaster: The Case of Aviation Security." *American Behavioral Scientist* 48 (3): 341–364.

———. 2006. *Lessons of Disaster: Policy Change After Catastrophic Events*. Washington, DC: Georgetown University Press.

———. 2009. "Disasters, Lessons Learned, and Fantasy Documents." *Journal of Contingencies and Crisis Management* 17 (3): 146–156.

Blaikie, Piers, Terry Cannon, Ian Davis, and Ben Wisner. 1994. *At Risk: Natural Hazards, People's Vulnerability and Disasters*. London: Routledge.

Bolin, Bob. 2006. "Race, Class, Ethnicity, and Disaster Vulnerability." In *Handbook of Disaster Research*, edited by Havidan Rodriguez, E. L. Quarantelli, and Russell R. Dynes, 113–129. New York: Springer.

———, Sara Grineski, and Timothy Collins. 2005. "The Geography of Despair: Environmental Racism and the Making of South Phoenix, Arizona, USA." *Human Ecology Review* 34: 317–339.

———, and Lois Stanford. 1990. "Shelter and Housing Issues in Santa Cruz County." In *The Loma Prieta Earthquake: Studies of Short-Term Impacts*, edited by Robert Bolin, 98–108. Natural Hazards Center, University of Colorado Boulder.

———, and Lois Stanford. 1998. *The Northridge Earthquake: Vulnerability and Disaster*. London: Routledge.

Bonanno, George A., Chris R. Brewin, Krzysztof Kaniasty, and Annette M. La Greca. 2010. "Weighing the Costs of Disaster: Consequences, Risks, and Resilience in Individuals, Families, and Communities." *Psychological Science in the Public Interest* 11: 1–49.

Booth, Edmund Dwight, and David E. Key. 2006. *Earthquake Design Practice for Buildings*. London: Thomas Telford.

Borden, Kevin A., and Susan L. Cutter. 2008. "Spatial Patterns of Natural Hazards Mortality in the United States." *International Journal of Health Geographics* 7: 64.

Bourdieu, Pierre. 1980. *The Logic of Practice*. Stanford, CA: Stanford University Press.

———. 1984. *Distinction: A Social Critique of the Judgment of Taste*. London: Routledge.

———. 1986. "The Forms of Capital." In *Handbook of Theory and Research for the Sociology of Capital*, edited by J. G. Richardson, 241–258. New York: Greenwood Press.

Bragg, Rick. 1999. "Storm over South Florida Building Codes." *New York Times*, May 27.

Brand, Fridolin Simon, and Kurt Jax. 2007. "Focusing the Meaning(s) of Resilience: Resilience as a Descriptive Concept and a Boundary Object." *Ecology and Society* 12: 23 [online].

Bridger, Jeffrey C., and A. E. Luloff. 2001. "Building the Sustainable Community: Is Social Capital the Answer?" *Sociological Inquiry* 71 (4): 458–472.

Brouillette, John R., and Enrico L. Quarantelli. 1971. "Types of Patterned Variation in Bureaucratic Adaptations to Organizational Stress." *Sociological Inquiry* 41 (1): 39–46.

Brown, Phil, Rachel Morello-Frosch, and Stephen Zavestoski. 2011. *Contested Illnesses: Citizens, Science, and Health Social Movements*. Berkeley: University of California Press.

Browne, Mark J., and Robert Hoyt. 2000. "The Demand for Flood Insurance: Empirical Evidence. *Journal of Risk and Uncertainty* 20: 291–306.

Bruneau, Michel, Stephanie E. Chang, Ronald T. Eguchi, George C. Lee, Thomas D. O'Rourke, Andrei M. Reinhorn, Masanobu Shinozuka, Kathleen Tierney, William A. Wallace, and Detlof von Winterfeldt. 2003. "A Framework to Quantitatively Assess and Enhance the Seismic Resilience of Communities." *Earthquake Spectra* 19 (4): 733–752.

Brunkard, Joan, Gonza Namulanda, and Raoult Ratard. 2008. "Hurricane Katrina Deaths, Louisiana, 2005." *Disaster Medicine and Public Health Preparedness* 2 (4): 215–223.

Buenza, Daniel, and David Stark. 2003. "The Organization of Responsiveness: Innovation and Recovery in the Trading Rooms of Lower Manhattan." *Socio-Economic Review*: 135–164.

Bullard, Robert Doyle. 1990. *Dumping in Dixie: Race, Class, and Environmental Quality.* Boulder, CO: Westview Press.

Burby, Raymond J. 2006. "Hurricane Katrina and the Paradoxes of Government Disaster Policy: Bringing About Wise Governmental Decisions for Hazardous Areas." *Annals of the American Academy of Political and Social Science* 604: 171–191.

Burton, Christopher G., and Susan L. Cutter. 2008. "Levee Failures and Social Vulnerability in the Sacramento-San Joaquin Delta Area, California." *Natural Hazards Review* 9: 136–149.

Butts, Carter T., Ryan M. Acton, and Christopher Steven Marcum. 2012. "Interorganizational Collaboration in the Hurricane Katrina Response." *Journal of Social Structure* 13: 1–37.

Carter, Nicole T., and Charles V. Stern. 2006. *Mississippi River Gulf Outlet (MRGO): Issues for Congress.* Washington, DC: US Congressional Research Service.

Central Disaster Management Council. 2005. *Report of the 15th Special Committee on the Earthquake Just Beneath the Tokyo Metropolis.* Tokyo: Cabinet Office, Government of Japan.

Cerulo, Karen A. 2008. *Never Saw It Coming: Cultural Challenges to Envisioning the Worst.* Chicago: University of Chicago Press.

Chandler, Carla C., Leilani Greening, Leslie J. Robison, and Laura Stoppelbein. 1999. "It Can't Happen to Me ... Or Can It? Base Rates Affect Subjective Probability Judgments." *Journal of Experimental Psychology: Applied* 5: 361–378.

Chang, Stephanie E. 2010. "Urban Disaster Recovery: A Framework and Its Application to the 1995 Kobe Earthquake." *Disasters* 34: 303–327.

———, Beverley J. Adams, Jacqueline Alder, Philip R. Berke, Ratana Chuenpagdee, Shubharoop Ghosh, and Colette Wabnitz. 2006. "Coastal Ecosystems and Tsunami Protection After the December 2004 Indian Ocean Tsunami." *Earthquake Spectra* 22 (Suppl. 3): 863–887.

Chemical Safety Board. 2007. "U.S. Chemical Safety Board Concludes Organizational and Safety Deficiencies at All Levels of the BP Corporation." Press Release. Washington, DC: Chemical Safety Board.

Clarke, Lee. 1989. "Capitalism Is Richer, Democracy Is Safer." *Society* 27 (1): 17–18.

———. 1999. *Mission Improbable: Using Fantasy Documents to Tame Disaster.* Chicago: University of Chicago Press.

———. 2006a. *Worst Cases: Terror and Catastrophe in the Popular Imagination.* Chicago: University of Chicago Press.

———. 2006b. "Worst Case Katrina." www.forums.ssrc.org/understandingkatrina/author/clarke.

———. 2008. "Possibilistic Thinking: A New Conceptual Tool for Thinking About Extreme Events." *Social Research: An International Quarterly* 75 (3): 669–690.

Cohen, Michael D., James G. March, and Johan P. Olsen. 1972. "A Garbage Can Model of Organizational Choice." *Administrative Science Quarterly* 17: 1–25.

Colignon, Richard A., and Chikako Usui. 2001. "The Resilience of Japan's Iron Triangle—Amakudari." *Asian Survey* 41: 865–895.

———, and Chikako Usui. 2003. *Amakudari: The Hidden Fabric of Japan's Economy.* Ithaca, NY: Cornell University Press.

Comfort, Louise K. 1999. *Shared Risk: Complex Systems in Seismic Response.* Oxford, UK: Pergamon.

———, and Naim Kapucu. 2006. "Inter-Organizational Coordination in Extreme Events: The World Trade Center Attack, September 11, 2001." *Natural Hazards* 39: 309–327.

Cooper, Christopher, and Robert Block. 2006. *Disaster: Hurricane Katrina and the Failure of Homeland Security.* New York: Macmillan.

Cuny, Frederick C. 1983. *Disasters and Development.* Oxford, UK: Oxford University Press.

Cutter, Susan L. 1996. "Vulnerability to Environmental Hazards." *Progress in Human Geography* 20: 529–539.

———. 2001. *American Hazardscapes: The Regionalization of Hazards and Disasters.* Washington, DC: Joseph Henry Press.

———, Lindsey Barnes, Melissa Berry, Christopher G. Burton, Elijah Evans, Eric Tate, and Jennifer Webb. 2008. "A Place-Based Model for Understanding Community Resilience to Natural Disasters." *Global Environmental Change: Human and Policy Dimensions* 18: 598–606.

———, Bryan J. Boruff, and W. Lynn Shirley. 2003. "Social Vulnerability to Environmental Hazards." *Social Science Quarterly* 84: 242–261.

———, Christopher G. Burton, and Christopher T. Emrich. 2010. "Disaster Resilience Indicators for Benchmarking Baseline Conditions." *Journal of Homeland Security and Emergency Management* 7: 1–22.

Dade County Grand Jury. 1989. "A Critique of Construction Regulation." Grand Jury Report, Dade County, FL.

Dahlhamer, James M., and Kathleen J. Tierney. 1998. "Rebounding from Disruptive Events: Business Recovery Following the Northridge Earthquake." *Sociological Spectrum* 18 (2): 121–141.

Damasio, Antonio. 1996. "The Somatic Marker Hypothesis and the Possible Functions of the Prefrontal Cortex [and Discussion]." *Philosophical Transactions of the Royal Society of London. Series B: Biological Sciences* 351: 1413–1420.

David, Emmanuel, and Elaine Enarson. 2012. *The Women of Katrina: How Gender, Race and Class Matter in an American Disaster.* Nashville, TN: Vanderbilt University Press.

Davis, Mike. 2006. *Planet of Slums.* Brooklyn, NY: Verso.

De Vita, Carol J., Fredrica D. Kramer, Lauren Eyster, Samuel Hall, Petya Kehayova, and Timothy Triplett. 2008. *The Role of Faith-Based and Community Organizations in Post-Hurricane Human Service Relief Efforts.* Washington, DC: Urban Institute.

de Young, Mary. 2004. *The Day Care Ritual Abuse Moral Panic.* Jefferson, NC: McFarland.

Dhawan, Rajeev, and Karsten Jeske. 2006. *How Resilient Is the Modern Economy to Economic Price Shocks?* Atlanta: Federal Reserve Bank of Atlanta.

Dillon, Robin L., and Catherine H. Tinsley. 2008. "How Near-Misses Influence Decision Making Under Risk: A Missed Opportunity for Learning." *Management Science* 54 (8): 1425–1440.

———, Catherine H. Tinsley, and Matthew Cronin. 2011. "Why Near-Miss Events Can Decrease an Individual's Protective Response to Hurricanes." *Risk Analysis* 31 (3): 440–449.

DiMaggio, Paul J., and Walter W. Powell. 1983. "The Iron Cage Revisited: Institutional Isomorphism and Collective Rationality in Organizational Fields." *American Sociological Review* 48: 147–160.

Dingwall, Robert. 1999. "'Risk Society': The Cult of Theory and the Millennium?" *Social Policy and Administration* 33: 474–491.

Douglas, Mary, and Aaron B. Wildavsky. 1983. *Risk and Culture: An Essay on the Selection of Technological and Environmental Dangers.* Berkeley: University of California Press.

Downey, Liam, and Marieke Van Willigen. 2005. "Environmental Stressors: The Mental Health Impacts of Living Near Industrial Activity." *Journal of Health and Social Behavior* 46 (3): 289–305.

Drabek, Thomas E. 2003. *Strategies for Coordinating Disaster Responses.* Institute of Behavior Sciences, Boulder, CO.

————, Harriet L. Tamminga, Thomas S. Kilijanek, and Christopher R. Adams. 1981. *Managing Multiorganizational Emergency Responses: Emergent Search and Rescue Networks in Natural Disaster and Remote Area Settings.* Natural Hazards Center, University of Colorado Boulder.

Dunlap, Riley E., Michael E. Kraft, and Eugene A. Rosa (eds.). 1993. *Public Reactions to Nuclear Waste.* Durham, NC: Duke University Press.

————, and Aaron M. McCright. 2011. "Climate Change Denial: Sources, Actors, and Strategies." In *Routledge Handbook of Climate Change and Society,* edited by Constance Lever-Tracy, 240. New York: Routledge International Handbooks.

Dunsinberre, Martin, and Daniel P. Aldrich. 2011. "Hatoko Comes Home: Civil Society and Nuclear Power in Japan." *Journal of Asian Studies* 70: 1–23.

Duymedjian, Raffi, and Charles-Clemens Rüling. 2010. "Towards a Foundation of Bricolage in Organization and Management Theory." *Organization Studies* 31 (2): 133–151.

Dynes, Russell. 2000. "The Dialogue Between Voltaire and Rousseau on the Lisbon Earthquake: The Emergence of a Social Science View." *International Journal of Mass Emergencies and Disasters* 18 (1): 97–115.

————. 2005. "Community Social Capital as the Primary Basis for Resilience." No. 344. Disaster Research Centre, University of Delaware, Newark.

Eden, Lynn. 2004. *Whole World on Fire: Organizations, Knowledge, and Nuclear Weapons Devastation.* Ithaca, NY: Cornell University Press.

Elliot, Anthony. 2002. "Beck's Sociology of Risk: A Critical Assessment." *Sociology* 36: 293–315.

Elliott, James R., and Jeremy Pais. 2006. "Race, Class, and Hurricane Katrina: Social Differences in Human Responses to Disaster." *Social Science Research* 35 (2): 295–321.

Elnashai, A. S., T. Jefferson, F. Fiedrich, and L. J. Cleveland. 2009. *Impact of New Madrid Seismic Zone Earthquakes on the Central USA. MAE Center Report no. 09-03.* Mid-America Earthquake Center, University of Illinois, Urbana.

Enarson, Elaine. 2007. "Identifying and Addressing Social Vulnerabilities." In *Emergency Management: Principles and Practice for Local Government.* 2nd ed., edited by William Waugh and Kathleen Tierney, 257–278. Washington, DC: International City and County Management Association.

————, and Betty H. Morrow (eds.). 1998. *The Gendered Terrain of Disaster: Through Women's Eyes.* Westport, CT: Greenwood.

Erikson, Kai T. 1976. *Everything in Its Path.* New York: Simon & Schuster.

————. 1994. *A New Species of Trouble.* New York: Norton.

Escaleras, Monica, Nejat Anbarci, and Charles A. Register. 2006. *Public Sector Corruption and Natural Disasters: A Potentially Deadly Interaction.* Working Paper 06005. Revised August 2006 edition. Department of Economics, College of Business, Florida Atlantic University, Boca Raton.

Fears, Darryl. 2011. "Virginia Residents Oppose Preparations for Climate-Related Sea Level Rise." *Washington Post,* December 17.

Finch, Christina, Christopher T. Emrich, and Susan L. Cutter. 2010. "Disaster Disparities and Differential Recovery in New Orleans." *Population and Environment* 31: 179–202.

Flora, Cornelia Butler, Mary Emery, Susan Fey, and Corry Bregendahl. 2005. "Community Capitals: A Tool for Evaluating Strategic Interventions and Projects." Available at www.Ag.Iastate.edu/centers/rdev/projects/commcap/7-Capitalshandout.pdf.

————, and Jan L. Flora. 2003. "Social Capital." In *Challenges for Rural America in the Twenty-First Century*, edited by David L. Brown, Louis E. Swanson, and Alan W. Barton, 214–227. University Park: Pennsylvania State University Press.

————, Jan L. Flora. 2005. "Creating Social Capital." In *The Earthscan Reader in Sustainable Agriculture*, edited by Jules Pretty, 39–63. London: Earthscan.

Flynn, James, Paul Slovic, and C. K. Mertz. 1994. "Gender, Race, and the Perception of Environmental Health Risk." *Risk Analysis* 14: 1101–1108.

Folke, Carl, Steve Carpenter, Thomas Elmqvist, Lance Gunderson, C. S. Holling, and Brian Walker. 2002. "Resilience and Sustainable Development: Building Adaptive Capacity in a World of Transformations." *Ambio* 31: 437–440.

Foreign Policy. 2012. "The Failed States Index 2011." July 7.

Fothergill, Alice. 2004. *Heads Above Water: Gender, Class, and Family in the Grand Forks Flood.* Albany, NY: SUNY Press.

Freudenburg, William R. 2003. "Institutional Failure and the Organizational Amplification of Risk: The Need for a Closer Look." In *The Social Amplification of Risk*, edited by Nick Pidgeon, Roger E. Kasperson, and Paul Slovic, 102–120. Cambridge, UK: Cambridge University Press.

————, Robert B. Gramling, Shirley Laska, and Kai Erikson. 2009. *Catastrophe in the Making: The Engineering of Katrina and the Disasters of Tomorrow.* Washington, DC: Island Press.

Fritz, Charles E. 1961. "Disaster." In *Contemporary Social Problems*, edited by Robert K. Merton and R. A. Nisbet, 651–694. New York: Harcourt.

————, and John H. Mathewson. 1957. *Convergence Behavior in Disasters: A Problem in Social Control: A Special Report Prepared for the Committee on Disaster Studies.* Washington, DC: National Academy of Sciences National Research Council.

Fussell, Elizabeth, Narayan Sastry, and Mark VanLandingham. 2010. "Race, Socioeconomic Status, and Return Migration to New Orleans After Hurricane Katrina." *Population and Environment* 31 (1–3): 20–42.

Galloway, Gerald E., John J. Boland, Raymond J. Burby, Christopher B. Groves, Susan Lein Longville, Lewis E. Link Jr., Jeffrey F. Mount, Jeff Opperman, Raymond B. Seed, George L. Sills, James J. Smyth, Ronald Stork, and Edward A. Thomas. 2007. *A California Challenge—Flooding in the Central Valley. A Report to the Department of Water Resources.* Sacramento, CA.

Garmezy, Norm. 1993. "Children in Poverty: Resilience Despite Risk." *Psychiatry* 56: 127–136.

Geis, Donald E. 2000. "By Design: The Disaster Resistant and Quality-of-Life Community." *Natural Hazards Review* 1 (3): 151–160.

Glassman, James K., and Kevin A. Hassett. 1999. *Dow 36,000.* New York: Crown.

Goffman, Erving. 1974. *Frame Analysis: An Essay on the Organization of Experience.* Cambridge, MA: Harvard University Press.

Government Accountability Office. 2006. *Coast Guard: Observations on the Preparation, Response, and Recovery Missions Related to Hurricane Katrina.* Washington, DC: Government Accountability Office.

Gramsci, Antonio. 1971. *Selections from the Prison Notebooks.* London: Lawrence and Wishart.

Granovetter, Mark S. 1973. "The Strength of Weak Ties." *American Journal of Sociology* 78: 1360–1380.

———. 1985. "The Problem of Embeddedness: Economic Action and Social Structure." *American Journal of Sociology* 91: 481–510.

Green, Penny. 2005. "Disaster by Design: Corruption, Construction and Catastrophe." *British Journal of Criminology* 45: 528–536.

Greene, Richard Allen. 2012. "Corps of Engineers Not Liable for Katrina Damage, Court Rules." *CNN*, September 25.

Greenwood, Royston, Christine Oliver, Kerstin Sahlin, and Roy Suddaby. 2008. "Introduction." In *The Sage Handbook of Organizational Institutionalism*, edited by Royston Greenwood, Christine Oliver, Roy Suddaby, and Kerstin Sahlin, 1–46. Thousand Oaks, CA: Sage.

Grineski, Sara, Bob Bolin, and Christopher Boone. 2007. "Criteria Air Pollution and Marginalized Populations: Environmental Inequity in Metropolitan Phoenix, Arizona." *Social Science Quarterly* 88: 535–554.

Grossi, Patricia, and Mary Lou Zoback. 2010. *1868 Hayward Earthquake: 140-Year Retrospective*. Menlo Park, CA: Risk Management Solutions.

Guillen, Mauro F., and Sandra L. Suarez. 2010. "The Global Crisis of 2007-2009: Markets, Politics, and Organizations." In *Markets on Trial: The Economic Sociology of the U.S. Financial Crisis: Part A*, edited by Michael Lounsbury and Paul M. Hirsch, 257–279. Bingley, UK: Emerald Group.

Handmer, John W., and Stephen R. Dovers. 1996. "A Typology of Resilience: Rethinking Institutions for Sustainable Development." *Organization and Environment* 9 (4): 482–511.

Hannigan, John. 1998. *Fantasy City: Pleasure and Profit in the Postmodern Metropolis*. London: Routledge.

Harlan, Sharon, Anthony J. Brazel, Lela Prashad, William L. Stefanov, and Larissa Larsen. 2006. "Neighborhood Microclimates and Vulnerability to Heat Stress." *Social Science and Medicine* 63 (11): 2847–2863.

Harrald, John R. 2006. "Agility and Discipline: Critical Success Factors in Disaster Response." *Annals of the American Academy of Political and Social Science* 604: 256–272.

Hennessy, Jefferson. 2007. "The Cajun Navy: Heroic Louisiana Volunteers Saved Thousands of Hurricane Katrina Evacuees." *Yahoo!*, September 5.

Hewitt, Kenneth. 1983. *Interpretations of Calamity: From the Viewpoint of Human Ecology*. New York: Unwin Hyman.

Hilgartner, Stephen. 1992. "The Social Construction of Risk Objects: Or, How to Pry Open Networks of Risk." In *Organizations, Uncertainties, and Risk*, edited by James F. Short and Lee Clarke, 39–53. Boulder, CO: Westview Press.

Holling, C. S. 1973. "Resilience and Stability of Ecological Systems." *Annual Review of Ecology and Systematics* 4: 1–23.

Hollnagel, Erik, David D. Woods, and Nancy Leveson. 2006. *Resilience Engineering (Ebk) Concepts and Precepts*. Brookfield, VT: Ashgate.

Homan, Anthony C., and Todd Steiner. 2008. "OPA 90's Impact at Reducing Oil Spills." *Marine Policy* 32 (4): 711–718.

Hopkins, A. 2010. "Why BP Ignored Close Calls at Texas City." *Risk and Regulation* (Special Issue on Close Calls, Near Misses and Early Warnings): 4–5.

Interagency Floodplain Management Review Committee. 1994. *A Blueprint for Change— Sharing the Challenge: Floodplain Management into the 21st Century*. Washington, DC: U.S. Government Printing Office.

Interagency Performance Evaluation Task Force. 2008. *Performance Evaluation of the New Orleans and Southeast Louisiana Hurricane Protection System: Final Report of the Interagency Performance Evaluation Task Force*. Washington, DC: U.S. Army Corps of Engineers.

Jaeger, Carlo C., Ortwin Renn, Eugene A. Rosa, and Thomas Webler. 2001. *Risk, Uncertainty, and Rational Action*. London: Earthscan.

Jalali, Rita. 2002. "Civil Society and the State: Turkey After the Earthquake." *Disasters* 26 (2): 120–139.

Janssen, Marco A., Michael L. Schoon, Weimao Ke, and Katy Börner. 2006. "Scholarly Networks on Resilience, Vulnerability and Adaptation Within the Human Dimensions of Global Environmental Change." *Global Environmental Change* 16 (3): 240–252.

Johnson, Corey G. 2011. "Under Pressure, State Redraws Quake Hazard Maps." *California Watch*, April 10.

Kahan, Dan M., and Paul Slovic. 2006. *Cultural Evaluations of Risk: "Values" or "Blunders"?* Public Law Working Paper No. 111. Yale Law School, New Haven, CT.

Kahn, Matthew E. 2005. "The Death Toll from Natural Disasters: The Role of Income, Geography, and Institutions." *Review of Economics and Statistics* 87 (2): 271–284.

Kahneman, Daniel, Paul Slovic, and Amos Tversky. 1982. *Judgment Under Uncertainty: Heuristics and Biases*. Cambridge, UK: Cambridge University Press.

Kang, J. E., W. G. Peacock, and R. Husein. 2010. "An Assessment of Coastal Zone Hazard Mitigation Plans in Texas." *Journal of Disaster Research* 5 (5): 520–528.

Kapucu, Naim. 2006. "Interagency Communication Networks During Emergency: Boundary Spanners in Multiagency Coordination." *American Review of Public Administration* 36: 207–225.

———, Tolga Arslan, and Matthew Lloyd Collins. 2010. "Examining Intergovernmental and Interorganizational Response to Catastrophic Disasters: Toward a Network-Centered Approach." *Administration and Society* 103: 222–247.

Kates, Robert William, Craig E. Colten, Shirley Laska, and Stephen P. Leatherman. 2006. "Reconstruction of New Orleans After Hurricane Katrina: A Research Perspective." *Proceedings of the National Academy of Sciences* 103 (40): 14653–14660.

Kaufman, Michael T., and Kate Zernike. 2012. "Activists Fight Green Projects, Seeing U.N. Plot." *New York Times*, February 3.

Kendra, James M., and Tricia Wachtendorf. 2003. "Elements of Resilience After the World Trade Center Disaster: Reconstituting New York City's Emergency Operations Centre." *Disasters* 27 (1): 37–53.

———, and Tricia Wachtendorf. 2006. "The Waterborne Evacuation of Lower Manhattan on September 11: A Case of Distributed Sensemaking." Preliminary Paper no. 355. Disaster Research Center, University of Delaware, Newark.

———, Tricia Wachtendorf, and E. L. Quarantelli. 2002. "Who Was in Charge of the Massive Evacuation of Lower Manhattan by Water Transport on September 11? No One Was, Yet It Was an Extremely Successful Operation. Implications?" *Securitas* 1.

Kingdon, John W. 2002. *Agendas, Alternatives, and Public Policies*. 2nd ed. London: Pearson.

Klinenberg, Eric. 2002. *Heat Wave: A Social Autopsy of Disaster in Chicago*. Chicago: University of Chicago Press.

Knowles, Scott Gabriel. 2011. *The Disaster Experts: Mastering Risk in Modern America* Philadelphia: University of Pennsylvania Press.

Koch, Wendy. 2011. "East Coast Earthquake: Twice What Nuclear Plant Designed to Withstand." *ABCNews.Go.com*, September 10.

Kousky, Carolyn, and Richard Zeckhauser. 2006. "Jarring Actions That Fuel the Floods." In *On Risk and Disaster: Lessons from Hurricane Katrina*, edited by Ronald J. Daniels, Donald F. Kettl, and Howard C. Kunreuther, 59–73. Philadelphia: University of Pennsylvania Press.

Krimsky, Sheldon, and Dominic Golding. 1992. *Social Theories of Risk*. Vol. 58. Westport, CT: Praeger.

Krueger, Anne O. 1974. "The Political Economy of the Rent-Seeking Society." *American Economic Review* 64 (3): 291–303.

Kunreuther, Howard C., and Erwann O. Michel-Kerjan. 2010. "Overcoming Myopia: Learning from the BP Oil Spill and Other Catastrophes." *Milken Institute Review* (4): 47–57.

Kurokawa, K. 2012. "The Official Report of the Fukushima Nuclear Accident Independent Investigation Commission." Tokyo: National Diet of Japan.

Langewiesche, William. 2002. *American Ground: Unbuilding the World Trade Center*. New York: North Point Press.

Laska, Shirley. 2004. "What If Hurricane Ivan Had Not Missed New Orleans? *Natural Hazards Observer* 29: 5–6.

Lévi-Strauss, Claude. 1966. *The Savage Mind*. Chicago: University of Chicago Press.

Lewis, Michael. 2010. *The Big Short: Inside the Doomsday Machine*. New York: Norton.

Lieberman, Dan. 2011. "Critics: New Pilot Fatigue Rules Not Enough." *ABC News*, December 21.

Loewenstein, George F., Elke U. Weber, Christopher K. Hsee, and Ned Welch. 2001. "Risk as Feelings." *Psychological Bulletin* 127 (2): 267.

Logan, John R. 2006. "The Impact of Katrina: Race and Class in Storm-Damaged Neighborhoods." Working Paper. Spatial Structures in the Social Sciences Initiative, Brown University, Providence, RI.

———, and Harvey Molotch. 1987. *Urban Fortunes: The Political Economy of Place*. Berkeley: University of California Press.

Longstaff, Patricia H., Nicholas J. Armstrong, Keli Perrin, Whitney May Parker, and Matthew Hidek. 2010. "Building Resilient Communities: A Preliminary Framework for Assessment." *Homeland Security Affairs* 6: 1–22.

Lukes, Steven. 1974. *Power: A Radical View*. London: Macmillan.

———. 2005. *Power: A Radical View*. 2nd ed. Basingstoke, UK: Palgrave Macmillan.

Lupton, Deborah. 1999. "Introduction: Risk and Sociocultural Theory." In *Risk and Sociocultural Theory: New Directions and Perspectives*, edited by Deborah Lupton, 1–11. Cambridge, UK: Cambridge University Press.

Luthar, Suniya S., Dante Cicchetti, and Bronwyn Becker. 2000. "The Construct of Resilience: A Critical Evaluation and Guidelines for Future Work." *Child Development* 71 (3): 543–562.

Lyles, Ward, Phillip Berke, and Gavin Smith. 2012. *Evaluation of Local Hazard Mitigation Plan Quality*. Institute for the Environment, Coastal Hazards Center, University of North Carolina, Chapel Hill.

Mackay, Charles. 2008 [1841]. *Extraordinary Popular Delusions and the Madness of Crowds*. Radford, VA: Wilder.

Mann, Leon, Trevor Nagel, and Peter Dowling. 1976. "A Study of Economic Panic: The 'Run' on the Hindmarsh Building Society." *Sociometry* 39: 223–235.

Masten, Ann S. 2001. "Ordinary Magic: Resilience Processes in Development." *American Psychologist* 56 (3): 227.

Mauss, Armand L. 1975. *Social Problems as Social Movements*. Philadelphia: Lippincott.

May, Peter J. 1990. "Reconsidering Policy Design: Policies and Publics." *Journal of Public Policy* 11: 187–206.

McCarthy, G. 2004. "The Price of Living in Urbanized Areas." *Unnatural Disasters*, special report by the *San Bernardino [CA] Sun*, June 29.

McCright, Aaron M., and Riley E. Dunlap. 2000. "Challenging Global Warming as a Social Problem: An Analysis of the Conservative Movement's Counter-Claims." *Social Problems* 47: 499.

———, and Riley E. Dunlap. 2010. "Anti-Reflexivity: The American Conservative Movement's Success in Undermining Climate Science and Policy." *Theory, Culture and Society* 27 (2–3): 100–133.

McLean, Bethany, and Joe Nocera. 2011. *All the Devils Are Here: The Hidden History of the Financial Crisis*. Penguin. com.

Mencimer, Stephanie. 2011. "We Don't Need None of That Smart-Growth Communism." *Mother Jones Magazine*, March/April.

Mendonca, David J., and William A. Wallace. 2007. "A Cognitive Model of Improvisation in Emergency Management." *Systems, Man and Cybernetics, Part A: Systems and Humans, IEEE Transactions on* 37 (4): 547–561.

Meo, Mark, Becky Ziebro, and Ann Patton. 2004. "Tulsa Turnaround: From Disaster to Sustainability." *Natural Hazards Review* 5 (1): 1–9.

Meyer, John W. 2008. "Reflections on Institutional Theories of Organizations." In *The Sage Handbook of Organizational Institutionalism*, edited by Royston Greenwood, Christine Oliver, Roy Suddaby, and Kerstin Sahlin, 788–809. Thousand Oaks, CA: Sage.

Michel-Kerjan, Erwann, and Howard Kunreuther. 2011. "Redesigning Flood Insurance." *Science* 333: 408–409.

———, Sabine Lemoyne de Forges, and Howard Kunreuther. 2012. "Policy Tenure Under the US National Flood Insurance Program (NFIP)." *Risk Analysis* 32 (4): 644–658.

Mileti, Dennis. 1999. *Disasters by Design: A Reassessment of Natural Hazards in the United States*. Washington, DC: National Academies Press.

Molotch, Harvey. 1976. "The City as a Growth Machine: Toward a Political Economy of Place." *American Journal of Sociology*: 309–332.

Morgenson, Gretchen, and Joshua Rosner. 2011. *Reckless Endangerment: How Outsized Ambition, Greed, and Corruption Led to Economic Armageddon*. London: Macmillan.

Murakami, Haruki. 2000. *Underground: The Tokyo Gas Attack and the Japanese Psyche*. London: Harvill Press.

Nathan, Debbie, and Michael Snedeker. 1995. *Satan's Silence: Ritual Abuse and the Making of a Modern American Witch Hunt*. New York: Basic Books.

National Commission on the BP Deepwater Horizon Spill and Offshore Drilling (US), Bob Graham, and William Kane Reilly. 2011. *Deep Water: The Gulf Oil Disaster and the Future of Offshore Drilling: Report to the President*. Washington, DC: U.S. Government Printing Office.

National Research Council. 2011. *Building Community Disaster Resilience Through Private-Public Collaboration*. Washington, DC: National Academies Press.

———. 2012. *Disaster Resilience: A National Imperative*. Washington, DC: National Academies Press.

National Transportation Safety Board. 1990. *Marine Accident Report: Grounding of the U.S. Tankship, Exxon Valdez on Bligh Reef, Prince William Sound Near Valdez,*

Alaska, March 24, 1989. Washington, DC: U.S. Department of Transportation, National Transportation Safety Board.

Neal, David M. 1994. "Consequences of Excessive Donations in Disasters: The Case of Hurricane Andrew." *Disaster Management* 6: 23–28.

Nelson, Craig. 2011. "'The Energy of a Bright Tomorrow': The Rise of Nuclear Power in Japan." *Origins* 4 (9).

Noji, Eric K. 1997. *The Public Health Consequences of Disasters.* Oxford, UK: Oxford University Press.

Norris, Fran H., Matthew J. Friedman, and Patricia J. Watson. 2002. "60,000 Disaster Victims Speak: Part II. Summary and Implications of the Disaster Mental Health Research." *Psychiatry: Interpersonal and Biological Processes* 65 (3): 240–260.

———, Matthew J. Friedman, Patricia J. Watson, Christopher M. Byrne, Eolia Diaz, and Krzysztof Kaniasty. 2002. "60,000 Disaster Victims Speak: Part I. An Empirical Review of the Empirical Literature, 1981–2001." *Psychiatry: Interpersonal and Biological Processes* 65 (3): 207–239.

———, Susan P. Stevens, Betty Pfefferbaum, Karen F. Wyche, and Rose L. Pfefferbaum. 2008. "Community Resilience as a Metaphor, Theory, Set of Capacities, and Strategy for Disaster Readiness." *American Journal of Community Psychology* 41 (1–2): 127–150.

Office of the Inspector General. 2010. *Investigative Report: Island Oil Company et Al.* Washington, DC: U.S. Department of the Interior.

O'Neill, Karen M. 2006. *Rivers by Design: State Power and the Origins of US Flood Control.* Durham, NC: Duke University Press.

Onishi, Norimitsu, and James Glanz. 2011. "Japanese Rules for Nuclear Plants Relied on Old Science." *New York Times,* March 26.

Palm, Risa I. 1981. "Public Response to Earthquake Hazard Information." *Annals of the Association of American Geographers* 71 (3): 389–399.

Park, JiYoung, Joongkoo Cho, and Adam Rose. 2011. "Modeling a Major Source of Economic Resilience to Disasters: Recapturing Lost Production." *Natural Hazards* 58 (1): 163–182.

Paté-Cornell, M. Elisabeth. 1993. "Learning from the Piper Alpha Accident: A Postmortem Analysis of Technical and Organizational Factors." *Risk Analysis* 13 (2): 215–232.

———, and Paul S. Fischbeck. 1990. *Safety of the Thermal Protection System of the STS Orbiter: Quantitative Analysis and Organizational Factors. Phase 1: The Probabilistic Risk Analysis Model and Preliminary Observations.* Report to the National Aeronautics and Space Administration. Stanford University, Stanford, CA.

———, and Paul S. Fischbeck. 1993. "Probabilistic Risk Analysis and Risk-Based Priority Scale for the Tiles of the Space Shuttle." *Reliability Engineering and System Safety* 40 (3): 221–238.

Patton, Ann. 1994. *From Rooftop to River: Tulsa's Approach to Floodplain and Stormwater Management.* City of Tulsa, OK.

Peacock, Walter G. 2010. *Advancing the Resilience of Coastal Localities: Developing, Implementing and Sustaining the Use of Coastal Resilience Indicators: A Final Report.* Hazard Reduction and Recovery Center, Texas A&M University, College Station.

———, and Rahmawati Husein. 2011. *The Adoption and Implementation of Hazard Mitigation Policies and Strategies by Coastal Jurisdictions in Texas: The Planning Survey Results.* Hazard Reduction and Recovery Center, Texas A&M University, College Station.

———, Betty Hearn Morrow, and Hugh Gladwin. 1997. *Hurricane Andrew: Ethnicity, Gender and the Sociology of Disasters.* New York: Routledge.

Peek, Lori. 2012. "They Call It 'Katrina Fatigue': Displaced Families and Discrimination in Colorado." In *Displaced: Life in the Katrina Diaspora*, edited by Lynn Weber and Lori Peek, 31–46. Austin: University of Texas Press.

Pelling, Mark. 2003a. *Natural Disaster and Development in a Globalizing World.* London: Routledge.

———. 2003b. *The Vulnerability of Cities: Natural Disasters and Social Resilience.* London: Earthscan.

Perrings, Charles. 2006. "Resilience and Sustainable Development." *Environment and Development Economics* 11 (4): 417–427.

Perrow, Charles. 1984. *Normal Accidents: Living with High-Risk Technologies.* New York: Basic Books.

———. 1991. "A Society of Organizations." *Theory and Society* 20 (6): 725–762.

———. 2007. *The Next Catastrophe: Reducing Our Vulnerabilities to Natural, Industrial, and Terrorist Disaster.* Princeton, NJ: Princeton University Press.

———. 2010. "The Meltdown Was Not an Accident." In *Markets on Trial: The Economic Sociology of the U.S. Financial Crisis: Part A (Research in the Sociology of Organizations)*, edited by Michael Lounsbury and Paul M. Hirsch, 309–330. Bingley, UK: Emerald Group.

Petroski, Henry. 1985. *To Engineer Is Human: The Role of Failure in Successful Design.* New York: St. Martin's Press.

Pfefferbaum, Rose L., Betty Pfefferbaum, and Richard L. Van Horn. 2011. *Communities Advancing Resilience Toolkit (CART): The CART Integrated System.* Terrorism and Disaster Center, University of Oklahoma Health Sciences Center, Oklahoma City.

Pfohl, Stephen J. 1977. "The 'Discovery' of Child Abuse." *Social Problems* 24: 310–323.

Phillips, Brenda, Deborah S.K. Thomas, Alice Fothergill, and Lynn Blinn-Pike. 2010. *Social Vulnerability to Disasters.* Boca Raton, FL: CRC Press.

Phimister, James R., Vicki M. Bier, and Howard C. Kunreuther (eds.). 2004. *Accident Precursor Analysis and Management: Reducing Technological Risk Through Diligence.* Washington, DC: National Academies Press.

Pidgeon, Nick, Roger E. Kasperson, and Paul Slovic. 2003. *The Social Amplification of Risk.* London: Cambridge University Press.

Pielke, Roger A., Jr., Joel Gratz, Christopher W. Landsea, Douglas Collins, Mark A. Saunders, and Rade Musulin. 2008. "Normalized Hurricane Damage in the United States: 1900–2005." *Natural Hazards Review* 9 (1): 29–42.

———, and Christopher W. Landsea. 1998. "Normalized Hurricane Damages in the United States: 1925-95." *Weather and Forecasting* 13 (3): 621–631.

Pinter, Nicholas. 2005. "One Step Forward, Two Steps Back on US Floodplains." *Science* 308 (5719): 207–208.

Platt, Anthony M. 1969. *The Child Savers.* Chicago: University of Chicago Press.

Platt, Rutherford H. 2008. "Learning from Disasters: The Synergy of Law and Geography." *Environmental Law Institute* 38 (3): 10150.

Plodinec, J. 2009. "Definitions of Resilience: An Analysis." Oak Ridge, TN: Community and Regional Resilience Institute (CARRI).

Polodny, Joel M., and Karen L. Page. 1998. "Network Forms of Organization." *Annual Review of Sociology*: 57–76.

Portes, Alejandro. 1998. "Social Capital: Its Origins and Applications in Modern Sociology." *Annual Review of Sociology* 24: 1–24.

President's Working Group on Financial Markets. 2010. *Market Conditions for Terrorism Risk Insurance*. Washington, DC: President's Working Group on Financial Markets.

Priest, Dana, and William M. Arkin. 2011. "Top Secret America: A Washington Post Investigation." *Washington Post*, July 19–21.

Pulido, Laura. 2000. "Rethinking Environmental Racism: White Privilege and Urban Development in Southern California." *Annals of the Association of American Geographers* 90 (1): 12–40.

Putnam, Robert D. 2000. *Bowling Alone: The Collapse and Revival of American Community*. New York: Simon & Schuster.

Quarantelli, Enrico Louis. 1987. "Disaster Studies: An Analysis of the Social Historical Factors Affecting the Development of Research in the Area." *International Journal of Mass Emergencies and Disasters* 5: 285–310.

Ripley, Amanda. 2005. "Hurricane Katrina: How the Coast Guard Gets It Right." *Time* magazine, October 25.

Risk Management Solutions. 2001. *Tropical Storm Allison, June 2001: RMS Event Report*. Menlo Park, CA: Risk Management Solutions.

Ritchie, Liesel A. 2012. "Individual Stress, Collective Trauma, and Social Capital in the Wake of the Exxon Valdez Oil Spill." *Sociological Inquiry* 82 (2): 187–211.

———. Forthcoming. *Social Capital and Disaster Resilience: A Review and Synthesis of the Literature*. Natural Hazards Center, University of Colorado Boulder.

———, and Duane A. Gill. 2011. "The Role of Community Capitals in Disaster Recovery." *Public Entity Risk Institute Online Symposium: Recovery from Disasters*. Available at https://www.riskinstitute.org.

———, and Duane A. Gill. Forthcoming. "Social Capital and Community Resilience: Insights from Disaster Research." In *The Resiliency Challenge: Transforming Theory into Action,* edited by John Harrald and James Bohland. Springfield, IL: Charles C. Thomas.

———, Kathleen Tierney, and Brandi Gilbert. 2010. "Disaster Preparedness Among Community-Based Organizations in the City and County of San Francisco: Serving the Most Vulnerable." In *Community Disaster Recovery and Resiliency: Exploring Global Opportunities*, edited by DeMond S. Miller and Jason David Rivera, 3–39. Boca Raton, FL: Aurbach/CRC/Taylor and Francis.

Rosa, Eugene A., and Lee Clarke. 2012. "A Collective Hunch? Risk as the Real and the Elusive." *Journal of Environmental Studies and Sciences* 2 (1): 39–52.

———, and William R. Freudenburg. 1993. "The Historical Development of Public Reactions to Nuclear Power: Implications for Nuclear Waste Policy." In *Public Reactions to Nuclear Waste*, edited by Riley E. Dunlap, Michael E. Kraft, and Eugene A. Rosa, 32–63. Durham, NC: Duke University Press.

Rose, Adam. 2009. *Economic Resilience to Disasters*. Community and Regional Resilience Institute. Oak Ridge, TN: Oak Ridge National Laboratory.

Rose, Vicki M. 1977. "Rape as a Social Problem: A By-product of the Feminist Movement." *Social Problems* 25: 75–89.

Rotberg, Robert I. 2003a. *State Failure and State Weakness in a Time of Terror*. Washington, DC: Brookings Institution Press.

——— (ed.). 2003b. *When States Fail: Causes and Consequences*. Princeton, NJ: Princeton University Press.

Rubin, Claire B. 2009. "Long Term Recovery from Disasters—The Neglected Component of Emergency Management." *Journal of Homeland Security and Emergency Management* 6 (46).

————, Martin D. Saperstein, and Daniel G. Barbee. 1985. *Community Recovery from a Major Natural Disaster*. Natural Hazards Center, University of Colorado Boulder.

Rudolf, John, Ben Hallman, Chris Kirkham, Saki Knafo, and Matt Sledge. 2012. "Hurricane Sandy Damage Amplified by Breakneck Development of Coast." *Huffington Post*, November 11.

Rutter, Michael. 1987. "Psychosocial Resilience and Protective Mechanisms." *American Journal of Orthopsychiatry* 57 (3): 316–331.

Sallenger, Asbury H., Jr., Kara S. Doran, and Peter A. Howd. 2012. "Hotspot of Accelerated Sea-Level Rise on the Atlantic Coast of North America." *Nature Climate Change* 2 (12): 884–888.

Savage, Charles. 2008. "Sex, Drug Use and Graft Cited in Interior Department." *New York Times*, September 10.

Schulman, Paul R. 1993. "The Negotiated Order of Organizational Reliability." *Administration and Society* 25 (3): 353–372.

Schwartz, Frank. 2002. "Civil Society in Japan Reconsidered." *Japanese Journal of Political Science* 3 (2): 195–215.

Schweinberger, Michael, Miruna Petrescu-Prahova, and Duy Quang Vu. 2012. "Disaster Response on September 11, 2001 Through the Lens of Statistical Network Analysis." Working Paper 116. Center for Statistics and the Social Sciences, University of Washington, Seattle.

Scott, W. Richard. 2001. *Institutions and Organizations*. Thousand Oaks, CA: Sage.

Seed, R. B., R. G. Bea, A. Athanasopoulos-Zekkos, G. P. Boutwell, J. D. Bray, C. Cheung, D. Cobos-Roa, L. Ehrensing, L. F. Harder Jr., and J. M. Pestana. 2008. "New Orleans and Hurricane Katrina. II: The Central Region and the Lower Ninth Ward." *Journal of Geotechnical and Geoenvironmental Engineering* 134 (5): 718–739.

Shrivastava, Paul. 1987. *Bhopal: Anatomy of a Crisis*. Cambridge, MA: Ballinger.

Slovic, Paul. 1999. "Trust, Emotion, Sex, Politics, and Science: Surveying the Risk-Assessment Battlefield." *Risk Analysis* 19 (4): 689–701.

————. 2010. *The Feeling of Risk: New Perspectives on Risk Perception*. London: Earthscan.

————, Melissa L. Finucane, Ellen Peters, and Donald G. MacGregor. 2004. "Risk as Analysis and Risk as Feelings: Some Thoughts About Affect, Reason, Risk, and Rationality." *Risk Analysis* 24 (2): 311–322.

————, Baruch Fischhoff, and Sarah Lichtenstein. 1981. "Fact and Fears: Societal Perception of Risk." In *Advances in Consumer Research*, edited by Kent B. Monroe, 497–502. Ann Arbor, MI: Association for Consumer Research.

————, Ellen Peters, Melissa L. Finucane, and Donald G. MacGregor. 2005. "Affect, Risk, and Decision Making." *Health Psychology* 24: 35–40.

Smelser, Neil J. 1965. *Theory of Collective Behavior*. New York: Free Press.

Smith, Gavin. 2011. *Planning for Recovery: A Review of the U.S. Disaster Assistance Framework*. Washington, DC: Island Press.

————, and Dennis Wenger. 2006. "Sustainable Disaster Recovery: Operationalizing an Existing Agenda." In *Handbook of Disaster Research*, edited by Havidán Rodríguez, Enrico L. Quarantelli, and Russell Dynes, 234–257. New York: Springer.

Solnit, Rebecca. 2009. *A Paradise Built in Hell: The Extraordinary Communities That Arise in Disaster*. London: Penguin Books.

Spector, Malcolm, and John Kitsuse. 1973. "Social Problems: A Reformulation." *Social Problems* 21: 145–158.

Stallings, Robert A. 1995. *Promoting Risk: Constructing the Earthquake Threat*. Hawthorne, NY: Aldine de Gruyter.

Starr, Chauncey. 1969. "Social Benefit Versus Technological Risk. What Is Our Society Willing to Pay for Safety?" *Science* 165: 1232–1238.

Stein, Ross S., Shinji Toda, Tom Parsons, and Elliot Grunewald. 2006. "A New Probabilistic Seismic Hazard Assessment for Greater Tokyo." *Philosophical Transactions of the Royal Society* 364: 1965–1988.

Stone, Clarence N. 1980. "Systemic Power in Community Decision Making: A Restatement of Stratification Theory." *American Political Science Review* (74): 978–990.

Subcommittee on Disaster Reduction. 2005. *Grand Challenges for Disaster Reduction.* Washington, DC: Office of Science and Technology Policy.

Susman, Paul, Phil O'Keefe, and Benjamin Wisner. 1983. "Global Disasters, A Radical Interpretation." In *Interpretations of Calamity: From the Viewpoint of Human Ecology*, edited by Kenneth Hewitt, 263–283. New York: Unwin Hyman.

Sutcliffe, Kathleen M., and Timothy J. Vogus. 2003. "Organizing for Resilience." In *Positive Organizational Scholarship*, edited by Kim Cameron, Jane E. Dutton, and Robert E. Quinn, 94–110. San Francisco: Berrett-Koehler.

Swidler, Ann. 1986. "Culture in Action: Symbols and Strategies." *American Sociological Review* 51: 273–286.

Tabuchi, Hiroko. 2011. "Japan Courts Money in Reactors." *New York Times/Reuters*, October 10.

Taleb, Nassim Nicholas. 2007. *The Black Swan: The Impact of the Highly Improbable.* London: Penguin.

Tasca, Leo. 1989. "The Social Construction of Human Error." Doctoral dissertation, State University of New York at Stony Brook.

Thomas, William I., and Dorothy S. Thomas. 1928. *The Child in America: Behavioral Problems and Programs.* New York: Knopf.

Tierney, Kathleen. 1997. "Impacts of Recent Disasters on Businesses: The 1993 Midwest Floods and the 1994 Northridge Earthquake." In *Economic Consequences of Earthquakes: Preparing for the Unexpected: Perspectives on Mitigating the Impact of Earthquakes on the Economy*, edited by Barclay Jones, 189–222. Report No. NCEER-SP-0001. National Center for Earthquake Engineering Research, State University of New York at Buffalo.

———. 2003. "Disaster Beliefs and Institutional Interests: Recycling Disaster Myths in the Aftermath of 9-11." In *Terrorism and Disaster: New Threats, New Ideas. Research in Social Problems and Public Policy.* Vol. 11, edited by Lee Clarke, 33–51. Amsterdam: Elsevier Science.

———. 2005. "Social Inequality, Hazards, and Disasters." In *On Risk and Disaster: Lessons from Hurricane Katrina*, edited by Ronald J. Daniels, Donald F. Kettl, and Howard C. Kunreuther, 109–128. Philadelphia: University of Pennsylvania Press.

———. 2006. "Recent Developments in U.S. Homeland Security Policies and Their Implications for the Management of Extreme Events." In *Handbook of Disaster Research*, edited by Havidán Rodríguez, Enrico L. Quarantelli, and Russell R. Dynes, 405–412. New York: Springer.

———. 2007. "From the Margins to the Mainstream? Disaster Research at the Crossroads." *Annual Review of Sociology* 33: 503–525.

———. 2010. "L'analyse des risques et leurs dimensions sociales" (Risk analysis and the social dimensions of risk). *Telescope* 16: 93–114.

———, and James D. Goltz. 1997. *Emergency Response: Lessons Learned from the Kobe Earthquake.* Disaster Research Center, University of Delaware, Newark.

————, Michael K. Lindell, and Ronald W. Perry. 2001. *Facing the Unexpected: Disaster Preparedness and Response in the United States*. Washington, DC: Joseph Henry Press.

————, and Anthony Oliver-Smith. 2012. "Social Dimensions of Disaster Recovery." *International Journal of Mass Emergencies and Disasters* 30 (2): 123–146.

————, and Joseph Trainor. 2004. "Networks and Resilience in the World Trade Center Disaster." In *MCEER: Research Progress and Accomplishments 2003-2004*, 157–172. Buffalo, NY: Multidisciplinary Center for Earthquake Engineering Research.

Times-Picayune. 2002. "Washing Away: Special Report from the Times Picayune." June 22–27.

Topper, Curtis M., and Kathleen M. Carley. 1999. "A Structural Perspective on the Emergence of Network Organizations." *Journal of Mathematical Sociology* 24 (1): 67–96.

Townsend, Anthony M., and Mitchell L. Moss. 2005. *Telecommunications Infrastructure in Disasters: Preparing Cities for Crisis Communications*. Center for Catastrophe Preparedness and Response, New York University, New York City.

Tullock, Gordon. 1967. "The Welfare Costs of Tariffs, Monopolies and Theft." *Western Economic Journal* 5: 224–232.

Turner, Bryan S. 1994. *Orientalism, Postmodernism and Globalism*. London: Routledge.

Turner, Ralph, and Lewis M. Killian. 1987. *Collective Behavior*. 3rd ed. Englewood Cliffs, NJ: Prentice-Hall.

Tversky, Amos, and Daniel Kahneman. 1974. "Judgment Under Uncertainty: Heuristics and Biases." *Science* 185 (4157): 1124–1131.

United Nations. 2003. *The Challenge of Slums: Global Report on Human Settlements*. London: Earthscan.

————. 2005. *The Hyogo Framework for Action*. New York: United Nations International Strategy for Disaster Reduction.

————. 2006. *World Urbanization Prospects: The 2005 Revision*. Working Paper No. ESA/P/WP/200. New York: United Nations, Department of Economic and Social Affairs, Population Division.

————. 2008. *World Urbanization Prospects: The 2007 Revision*. New York: United Nations.

————. 2010. *Protecting Development Gains: Reducing Disaster Vulnerability and Building Resilience in Asia and the Pacific*. New York: United Nations International Strategy for Disaster Reduction.

————. 2011. *Global Assessment Report on Disaster Risk Reduction 2011*. New York: United Nations International Strategy for Disaster Reduction.

URS Corporation. 2009. *Delta Risk Management Strategy: Executive Summary, Phase 1*. Sacramento: California Department of Water Resources.

————. 2011. *Delta Risk Management Strategy: Final Phase 2 Report*. Sacramento: California Department of Water Resources.

U.S. Fire Administration. 1988. *Interstate Bank Building Fire, Los Angeles, CA*. Washington, DC: Department of Homeland Security.

U.S. Indian Ocean Tsunami Warning System Program. 2007. *How Resilient Is Your Coastal Community? A Guide for Evaluating Coastal Community Resilience to Tsunamis and Other Coastal Hazards*. U.S. Agency for International Development and partners, Bangkok, Thailand.

Varley, Ann. 1994. *Disasters, Development and Environment*. New York: Wiley.

Vaughan, Diane. 1990. "Autonomy, Interdependence, and Social Control: NASA and the Space Shuttle Challenger." *Administrative Science Quarterly* 35: 225–257.

———. 1996. *The Challenger Launch Decision: Risky Technology, Culture, and Deviance at NASA*. Chicago: University of Chicago Press.

———. 2006. "Changing NASA: The Challenge of Organizational System Failures." In *Critical Issues in the History of Spaceflight*, edited by Steven J. Dick and Roger D. Launius, 349–375. Washington, DC: Smithsonian National Air and Space Museum.

Visano, Brenda Spotton. 2012. *The Role of Financial Panics in Early—and Not so Early—Theories of Financial Crises*. Presented at the meeting of the History of Economics Society, St. Catharines, Ontario, June 25.

Wachtendorf, Tricia. 2004. "Improvising 9/11: Organizational Improvisation in the World Trade Center Disaster." Doctoral dissertation, Department of Sociology, University of Delaware.

———, and James M. Kendra, 2006. "Improvising Disaster in the City of Jazz: Organizational Response to Hurricane Katrina." Available at Social Science Research Council. "Understanding Katrina: Perspectives from the Social Sciences." http://understandingkatrina.ssrc.org/.

Wacquant, Loic. 2004. "Habitus." In *International Encyclopedia of Economic Sociology*, edited by Jens Beckert and Milan Zafirovski, 315–319. London: Routledge.

Wald, Matthew L. 2009. "Pilots Set Up for Fatigue, Officials Say." *New York Times*, May 13.

Walker, Brian, and David Salt. 2006. *Resilience Thinking: Sustaining Ecosystems and People in a Changing World*. Washington, DC: Island Press.

Webb, Gary R., Kathleen J. Tierney, and James M. Dahlhamer. 2000. "Businesses and Disasters: Empirical Patterns and Unanswered Questions." *Natural Hazards Review* 1 (2): 83–90.

———, Kathleen J. Tierney, and James M. Dahlhamer. 2003. "Predicting Long-Term Business Recovery from Disaster: A Comparison of the Loma Prieta Earthquake and Hurricane Andrew." *Environmental Hazards* 4 (2): 45–58.

Weick, Karl E. 1993a. "The Collapse of Sensemaking in Organizations: The Mann Gulch Disaster." *Administrative Science Quarterly* 38: 628–652.

———. 1993b. "Organizational Redesign as Improvisation." In *Organizational Change and Redesign*, edited by George P. Huber and William H. Glick, 346–379. Oxford, UK: Oxford University Press.

———. 1998. "Improvisation as a Mindset for Organizational Analysis." *Organization Science* 9 (5): 543–555.

———, Kathleen M. Sutcliffe, and David Obstfeld. 1999. "Organizing for High Reliability: Processes of Collective Mindfulness." In *Research in Organizational Behavior*. Vol. 21, edited by Robert I. Sutton and Barry M. Straw, 81–124. Greenwich, CT: JAI Press.

———, Kathleen M. Sutcliffe, and David Obstfeld. 2005. "Organizing and the Process of Sensemaking." *Organization Science* 16 (4): 409–421.

Weil, Frederick D. 2011. "Rise of Community Organizations, Citizen Engagement, and New Institutions." In *Resilience and Opportunity: Lessons from the U.S. Gulf Coast After Katrina and Rita*, edited by Amy Liu, Roland V. Anglin, Richard M. Mizelle, and Allison Plyer, 201–219. Washington, DC: Brookings Institution Press.

Wenger, Dennis E., and Thomas F. James. 1994. "The Convergence of Volunteers in a Consensus Crisis: The Case of the 1985 Mexico City Earthquake." In *Disasters, Collective Behavior, and Social Organization*, edited by Russell R. Dynes and Kathleen J. Tierney, 229–243. Newark: University of Delaware Press.

Wijkman, Anders, and Lloyd Timberlake. 1984. *Natural Disasters. Acts of God or Acts of Man?* Philadelphia: New Society.

Wildavsky, Aaron B. 1988. *Searching for Safety.* New Brunswick, NJ: Transaction Books.

Wilford, John Noble, and Matthew L. Wald. 1999. "A Flash, and an Uncontrolled Chain Reaction." *New York Times,* October 1.

Willis, Henry H., Andrew R. Morral, Terrence K. Kelly, and Jamison Jo Medby. 2005. *Estimating Terrorism Risk.* Arlington, VA: Rand Corporation.

Wisner, Benjamin, Piers Blaikie, Terry Cannon, and Ian Davis. 2004. *At Risk: Natural Hazards, People's Vulnerability and Disasters.* London: Routledge.

World Bank/United Nations. 2010. *Natural Hazards, Unnatural Disasters: The Economics of Effective Prevention.* Washington, DC: International Bank for Reconstruction and Development/World Bank.

Index

Key concepts in risk and resilience are highlighted in boldface and defined on highlighted pages.

and doxa to study, 54–56; cultural assumptions on nature, growth, and progress influence on, 56–57; engineering as hypothesis thesis, 60–67; examining the role of culture and ideas in, 50–56; financial engineering and alchemy of risk, 67–80; frames and framing analysis to understand, 53–54, 56; justifying JARring actions, 57–59; review of the, 228–29; social constructionism theoretical perspective on, 50–53

cultural hegemony, 241–42

culture: constant change and shifts experienced by, 53–54; influence on socially constructed perspectives by, 47–48; power as the ability of dominant groups to shape, 241; shared beliefs, norms, and social realities elements of, 47; social production of risk and, 46–49; as a "tool kit" for behavior, 47

"culture of disaster," 234

Cutter, Susan L., 166, 167, 171, 180

Damasio's somatic marker theory, 22–23

Davis, Mike, 153

day-care facilities child abuse accusations (1980s and 1990s), 52

decision making: concentration of economic and political power of actors making, 90–94; continuity heuristic influence on, 74–75; Damasio's somatic marker theory on, 22–23; "garbage can" model of organizational, 122; by Los Angeles landlords to oppose retrofitting buildings, 38; for Pombaline architecture after Lisbon earthquake (1755) to reduce risks, 36–37; risk buildup as consequence of diverse, 147. *See also* risk reduction

Decision Research (Eugene, Oregon), 20

"deep capture": definition of, 100; within the financial sector, 100–101

Deepwater Horizon oil platform disaster (2010): BP's failure to learn from

Texas City refinery explosion prior to, 118–20, 121; deep-water drilling technology helping to create the, 60; efforts to reduce regulatory capture following, 123; examining the disaster of, 1, 3, 4; following previous BP accidents, 46, 118–20, 121, 229, 244; Grand Bayou recovery from, 191–92, 195; legislative failure to prevent, 244; myopia bias explaining the public perception of risk of the, 21; National Academy of Engineering report on the, 113; National Commission on the BP Deepwater Horizon Oil Spill and Offshore Drilling investigation into, 97; production pressures role in the, 113; regulatory capture contributing to the, 95; Vietnamese community losses following, 223. *See also* BP Corporation; environmental disasters; oil industry accidents

Democracy Now!, 191

development: disaster resilience discourse tied to sustainable, 165–66; disasters resulting from unsustainable, 151; hegemonic power shaping policies for, 241; increasing exposures due to building booms and, 138–40; *Koontz* decision on, 149; *Lucas* decision on, 148; moving toward sustainability resilience as part of, 237–40; patterns of social inequality combining with processes that shape, 232–33; United Nations "Agenda 21" resolution on sustainable, 149–50. *See also* growth machine politics; urbanization

Dillon, Robin, 120–21

Dingwall, Robert, 34

"disaster archipelago," 39

disaster mortality rates: Chicago heat wave (1995), 187–89; comparing losses of Haiti earthquake to Hurricane Katrina, 150–51; environmental justice research on Hurricane Katrina, 145–46; Indian Ocean earthquake and tsunamis (2004)

Francisco earthquake (1906), 16, 126; Sichuan earthquake (2008), 1, 37, 155, 157; Tangshan earthquake (1976), 37; Tohoku earthquake and tsunami (2011), 2, 3, 4, 75, 77, 169, 178, 230. *See also* hazards
eclipsing practice, 76
"ecology of support," 187–89
economic capital, 184
economic forces: Beck's risk society thesis on, 32–38; community risk production due to politics and, 140–48; concentration of economic and political power of actors making decisions, 90–94; efforts to control risk-generating, 243–48; JARring action undertaken in the name of, 57–58; power to create risks with impunity, 243; "pressure and release" model on risk built up by, 39–41; safety–productivity tension, 231–32; tension between productivity and safety, 231–32; vulnerability of levees due to political economy and, 38, 129–31, 196, 232. *See also* hegemonic power
Eden, Lynn, 79, 80
electrical power grid accidents, 99
Elliot, Anthony, 34
Emergency Operations Center (EOC) [New York City], 209–10, 211, 212
Emergency Planning and Community Right-to-Know Act, 244
emergent collective action, 199–203
emergent groups: definition of and functions of, **201**; following the 9/11 attacks, 204–5; Hurricane Katrina, 203; similarities between EMONs and, 204
emergent multiorganizational networks (EMONs): definition of, **204**; how resilience is enhanced by, 235; research on disaster resilience and, 204–7; social capital role in, 207–8
Enarson, Elaine, 141
"engineered" structures, 174–77
engineering as hypothesis thesis: on experience that increases faith in

technology, 61; Henry Petroski on his, 60–61; problems and implications of, 61–67
environmental disasters: *Exxon Valdez* spill (1989), 1–2, 3, 4, 60, 113–14, 123, 192, 195, 243–44; rapid urbanization and depletion of natural resources and risk of, 153–55; United Nations and World Bank programs trying to reverse damage of, 234. *See also Deepwater Horizon* oil platform disaster (2010)
environmental justice and injustice, 145–46
environmental refugees, 3
environmental resources: communities high in natural capital assets, 184–85; rapid urbanization and depletion of, 153–55; resilience of a community linked to condition of, 165; as source of inherent resilience, 174. *See also* nature
environmental risks: critique of Beck's risk society thesis on, 36–38; Pombaline architecture after Lisbon earthquake (1755) to reduce, 36–37; rapid urbanization and depletion of natural resources increasing, 153–55; resilience as theme in ecological and social-ecological systems research, 164. *See also* built environment hazards
Environment (journal), 20
epidemic disasters: Black Death, 35; HIV/AIDS, 35; influenza pandemic (1918 and 1919), 35
Erikson, Kai, 194
Escaleras, Monica, 157
Everything in Its Path: Destruction of Community in the Buffalo Creek Flood (Erikson), 194
e-waste problem, 40
exposures: definition of, 138; environmental justice research on social inequalities and, 145–48; increasing disaster losses due to building booms and development, 138–40; patterns of

98–100; on U.S. society as "society of
organizations," 42
Petronas Towers (Kuala Lumpur), 61
Petroski, Henry, 60–61, 66
Philippine archipelago region, 154–55, 234
Phoenix case study: comparing social
inequalities and extreme heat vulnerability in, 142–48, 233; risk buildup
as consequence of diverse decisions
in, 147; "urban heat islands" within,
143
physical capital, 184
Piano, Renzo, 62
Pielke, Roger, 88, 133
Pinter, Nicholas, 131
Piper Alpha offshore drilling platform
fire (1988), 112–13
Planet of Slums (Davis), 153
Platt, Rutherford, 149
Pliny the Elder, 37
"policy without a public," 246
political capital, 184, 185
political economy: Beck's risk society thesis on processes of, 32–38;
community risk production due to
economic and, 140–48, 231–32; concentration of economic and political
power of actors making decisions,
90–94; description of, 8–9; efforts
to control risk-generating, 243–48;
examining risk through the lens of,
9; growth machine politics, 125–48,
237–40; Los Angeles landlords opposition to retrofitting buildings, 38;
"nuclear village" and *amakudari*
("descent from heaven") feature of
Japan's, 92–93; power to create risks
with impunity, 243; "pressure and
release" model on risk built up by,
39–41; vulnerability of levees due
to economic forces and, 38, 129–31,
196, 232. *See also* hegemonic power
Pombal, Marquis de, 36
"positive asymmetry" tendency, 76
possibilistic reasoning, 76–78
postdisaster adaptation. *See* adaptive
resilience

postdisaster improvisation: adaptive
resilience and creative, 208–17; jazz
improvisation similarity to, 211–13;
during September 11 attacks, 209–
12, 214–15
postdisaster mobilization patterns,
198–99
Post-Katrina Emergency Management
Reform Act, 123
poverty: environmental justice research
on exposures and, 145–48; greater
vulnerabilities of poorer countries,
151–52; Haiti earthquake (2010)
catastrophe due to corruption, vulnerability, and, 233; Phoenix case
study on extreme heat vulnerability
and, 142–48, 233; social fields and
disparities of power and, 55; as social
vulnerability factor, 141
power. *See* hegemonic power
Pre-disaster Mitigation Program
(FEMA), 165
predisaster planning, 208–9
preindustrial natural disasters: Beck's
risk society thesis on late modernity
vs., 32–38; religious debate over Lisbon earthquake (1755), 36–37
Presbyterian Church (USA), 190
"pressure and release" model, 39–41
Prince, Eric, 67
probabilistic risk analysis (PRA), 77, 78
probabilistic thinking, 76–77
production pressures: Colgan Air flight
crash (2009) role of, 114–15; *Deepwater Horizon* oil platform disaster
(2010) role of, 113; definition of and
manifestation of, 111; *Exxon Valdez*
oil spill role of, 113–14, 243–44; *Piper
Alpha* offshore drilling platform fire
(1988) due to, 112–13; risk expansion
through, 112–16; tension between
costs of safety protocols and, 231–32
Project Impact (FEMA), 165
Project Impact Program (FEMA), 193
property rights: balancing sustainable
development with, 237–40; disaster
vulnerability and, 148–50; *Koontz*

CPSIA information can be obtained
at www.ICGtesting.com
Printed in the USA
JSHW022153200323
39178JS00001B/1